Schools, Conflict, and Change

Schools, Conflict, and Change

MIKE M. MILSTEIN, EDITOR
Professor
Faculty of Educational Studies
Department of Educational Administration
State University of New York at Buffalo

Teachers College, Columbia University
New York and London 1980

To Martin and Dorothy

Library of Congress Cataloging in Publication Data
Main entry under title:

Schools, conflict, and change.

Includes index.
1. School management and organization—United States—Addresses, essays, lectures. 2. Educational equalization—United States—Addresses, essays, lectures. I. Milstein, Mike M.
LB2805.S425   371.2   79-20327
ISBN: 0-8077-2571-4

10 9 8 7 6 5 4 3 2 1   88 87 86 85 84 83 82 81 80
Manufactured in the U.S.A.

Contents

Contributors

Jane H. Arends is Associate Director of the Center for Educational Policy and Management, College of Education, University of Oregon.

Richard I. Arends is Assistant Professor in the Division of Teacher Education, College of Education, University of Oregon.

George W. Bailey is Superintendent of Schools in School District No. 12, Adams County, Northglenn, Colorado.

Marc Bassin is Special Management Consultant from the Economic Development Council of New York to the Chancellor and Executive Director, Division of High Schools, New York City Board of Education.

Paul Berman is a Social Scientist, Rand Corporation, Santa Monica, California.

Charles M. Bernardo is Superintendent for the Montgomery County Public Schools, Rockville, Maryland.

C. Gordon Bishop is Superintendent for the Lindsay Unified School District, Lindsay, California.

Arthur Blumberg is Professor of Education and Chairperson in the Area of Educational Administration and Supervision, School of Education, Syracuse University.

Bunyan I. Bryant, Jr., is Professor in the School of Natural Resources and the Program in Urban and Regional Planning, University of Michigan.

James A. Conway is Associate Professor of the Faculty of Educational Studies, Department of Educational Administration, at the State University of New York at Buffalo.

Mark A. Chesler is Associate Professor in the Department of Sociology at the University of Michigan.

William T. Crocoll is District Superintendent for the Board of Cooperative Educational Services—Erie #2, Eden, New York.

James E. Crowfoot is Associate Professor in the School of Natural Resources and the Program in Urban and Regional Planning, University of Michigan.

C. Brooklyn Derr is Associate Professor of Management in the Department of Management, College of Business, University of Utah.

Norman Drachler is a former Superintendent of the Detroit Public Schools, Detroit, Michigan.

Michael Fullan is Chairperson in the Department of Sociology at the Ontario Institute for Studies in Education.

Thomas Gross is Program Director for the High School Self-Renewal Program, Economic Development Council of New York.

Ann Lieberman is Associate Professor of Education at Teachers College, Columbia University.

Charles S. Lusthaus is Associate Professor of Education and Director of the Division of Educational Leadership, McGill University, Montreal, Quebec.

Evelyn W. Lusthaus is Assistant Professor of Education at McGill University, Montreal, Quebec.

Milbrey Wallin McLaughlin is a Social Scientist, Rand Corporation, Santa Monica, California.

Matthew B. Miles is a Senior Research Associate at the Center for Policy Research in New York.

Mike M. Milstein is Professor of the Faculty of Educational Studies, Department of Educational Administration, at the State University of New York at Buffalo.

Robert G. Owens is Professor in the Department of School Administration, School of Education, Indiana University.

Richard A. Schmuck is Co-Director of the Program on Strategies of Organizational Change, Center for Educational Policy and Management, and Professor of Educational Psychology at the University of Oregon.

Terry Ann Schwartz is Assistant Professor of Education in the Bureau of Educational Research, University of Virginia in Charlottesville, Virginia.

Kenneth A. Tye is Program Officer in the Institute for Development of Educational Activities, an affiliate of the Charles F. Kettering Foundation, Los Angeles.

Foreword

AMERICAN EDUCATION IS UNDERGOING rapid and basic changes in the next several decades. The transformation from growth to steady state and decline is well known. This volume focuses on one of the manifestations of this transformation that is rarely systematically explored—the growth of conflict. The authors discuss the essence of educational change in an era of new circumstances.

The "golden era" of low conflict for the school administrator and educational professional was spawned during the turn of the 20th century. There was a nationwide social movement pushing centralization, bureaucratization, expertise, professionalism, and leadership by the administrative chief—the local superintendent. The idealogy spread that the school board member was a trustee, not a representative. Conflict and popular expression were to be minimized behind an image of factitious expertise and trusteeship. For example, the Baltimore school board met in a room up to the 1960s that could seat no more than 25 people.

Milstein traces the gradual eroding of this low conflict system, and several authors portray the current scene. Indeed, conditions have changed so radically that we are witnessing a period when nobody is in charge of the school system because of the fractionated and conflicting forces surrounding school policy. The past twenty years have brought dramatic increases in the influence of federal and state agencies, courts, private interstate organizations, foundations, businesses, local citizen groups, professional interest groups (e.g., counselors, categorical program administrators), teacher unions, parents, and midlevel administrators. The local superintendent must juggle diverse and conflicting factions across different issues. Coalitions are more difficult to form as declining enrollment erodes slack resources to pay off numerous conflicting groups.

Milstein and his contributors explore these elements of conflict and point out the variations in form and intensity depending on state and local environments. But they move from this to an examination of how to change schools. In the past many school reforms disappeared, but those that left a residue were structural organizational changes that could create a constituency and be easily monitored. Change was primarily through a tremendous growth in *added specialized functions* such as vocational education, driver education, nutrition, remedial reading, and so on. But constricting fiscal support, declining enrollment, and the conflicting forces outlined above imply new strategies will be necessary to adapt schools to the 1980s and beyond. The authors of this volume explore several strategies that do not entail huge costs, including organization development (OD). The writers recognize that past OD efforts have often been micro-interventions that were oblivious to the macro-political changes earlier parts of the volume elucidate. They suggest specific linkages between the micro- and macro-strategies for change.

This volume does not suggest that school leadership is hopeless. It demonstrates, however, that superintendents and managers cannot control their agendas or structure many decision outcomes as they have in the past. They will not have the money to satisfy many conflicting claimants. There will be younger recruits or little staff added. Consequently, the change perspective presented in this book is clearly timely and might be effective. There are several strategies presented for the reader to choose from.

My overall reaction to the book is that preparation for educational leadership needs to be revamped to include new skills. If conflict is common and change difficult, some of the skills required are bargaining, negotiating, compromising, coalition building, and some of the organization development approaches suggested by the authors. Rarely do universities develop these skills in their administrator training programs. Moreover, the public must be led to understand the difficult and conflicting context that schools must contend with. An increase in public loyalty to the concept of a public school will be necessary for the institution to do more than survive.

Michael Kirst
Professor of Education, Stanford University
President, California State Board of Education

Introduction

WHERE HAVE THE GOOD DAYS GONE? The days when school administrators controlled education; when being a principal or a superintendent was viewed with pride by the incumbent and with high status by others; when parents and students passively accepted whatever education was put before them; when teachers eagerly volunteered to work on programmatic needs; when resources required to maintain the educational sector could be counted on and grew at a steady pace.

Somehow the 1950s and the early 1960s are perceived as the good old days by today's lamenters. Partially this is because the fifties was when most of these critics were coming of age. Partially it relates also to the national yearning of the fifties to return to "normalcy" after the upheavals of the depression years and World War II, a yearning which is not greatly different from today's desire to find a place of quiet after the turbulence of the sixties.

Well, the good old days are gone, if indeed they ever really existed. But, upon closer examination, the years of normalcy can be viewed as the seedbed of today's conflictual environment in American society and, consequently, in public education. Three particular germination points can be readily identified. First, the historic Supreme Court decision in *Brown* v. *Board of Education of Topeka* can be viewed as the genesis of much of today's loud debate over school desegregation. Second, the accomplishment of the Soviet Union in launching Sputnik I on October 4, 1957 had much to do with the debate that has raged ever since about the quality of American public education. Third, the realization in the early 1960s that many of our youth were educationally deprived, particularly minority students in urban schools, led to the subsequent outpouring of federal, state, and local programs geared to remediation and equalization of educational opportunities. In short, today's issues can be traced backward to societal phenomena that occurred up to and beyond a quarter of a century ago.

Given such historical antecedents the conflictual interactions that presently mark public education should not be at all surprising. We are living through a time of major reassessments in education—reassessments of who our clients are and what our purposes are; of what our instructional methodologies shall be and who will decide what they will be; of how services shall be delivered; and of what society will be willing to accept as appropriate and sufficient "outcomes."

As these debates rage the malaise within the public schools seems to be intensifying. Discussions with school board members, administrators, and teachers leave me with the impression that these people are trying harder than ever before but often are finding their efforts unrewarding and unproductive. They complain about the increasing demand for technological inputs such as computers, highly sophisticated management planning systems, and instructional machinery that are making interactions less human and more mechanistic. In addition, there is a sense that the ground rules changed *after* these participants had agreed to play the game. The new rules,which open the system to more participants being involved in more decisional areas, from policy development to program implementation and evaluation, often lead to greater stress. Consequently, intrinsic rewards are harder to find and extrinsic rewards come less frequently and typically only after bitter squabbling among the players. There is a sense that the sands are continuing to shift, and this leaves everyone involved highly doubtful that the future will be any easier to manage than the present.

One thing seems fairly certain: Yesterday's responses—avoidance, confounding the opposition, minimal implementation, and camouflaged sameness—are becoming easily identifiable and less tolerated. Teachers, parents, students, legislative bodies, executive agencies, and the media have all become more knowledgeable and more demanding as the gap between societal expectations and the schools' responses has widened. In other words, efforts to maintain the status quo simply will no longer suffice.

If the amazing resiliency of our country's schools over time is any indicator, it is possible that we can still find our way out of our difficulties. America's history is marked by epochal societal shifts—from colonial status to nationhood; from an agrarian economy to the world's foremost industrial complex; from slavery to freedom; from relative global isolation to leadership of the free world. Through these seismic shifts the schools somehow have managed to keep apace, or at least they have not fallen so far behind that they have been scrapped in favor of a "better" system. Thus the issue is not whether the schools will survive, but rather, in surviving, how long it will take to reestablish a semblance of balance, how difficult it will be, and what strategies will have to be designed or modified to accomplish the task.

This book is based upon the belief that the time is right for exploring these issues. The time is right, partially because society will no longer tolerate yesterday's responses, but also because we are beginning to develop a critical mass of knowledge about change in schools that can be used to design a base for more effectively responding to demands for changes in our schools.

We cannot afford to be so naive as to assume that a packaged approach will be appropriate for all settings. Idiosyncracies of local communities must be taken into account. Still, the flurry of change programs initiated in schools over the past several decades has taught us some things about what works and what doesn't work. We can identify trends or commonalities that can be anticipated across diverse school settings.

The intent of the book is to heighten the awareness of the reader, both about the conditions under which would-be change agents must function and the approaches or strategies that might be utilized in change programs under conflictual conditions. More specifically the book has three objectives. First, it attempts to provide a snapshot of the situation: how we got to the present, what our major responses to the issues have been, and what impact these responses are having. Second, it is intended to widen and deepen the dialogue: educators and other interested parties will need to devote more time to exploring their situations as a first step to improving them. Third, and on a hopeful note, it will provide useful concepts that can assist those who make a commitment to change schools in these difficult times.

To facilitate these objectives the book is divided into four parts. Part One provides a present-tense snapshot and includes several alternative interpretations of the possibilities for movement, given the conflictual environment surrounding education. Part Two presents a summary of efforts affecting schools from the outside change agent's point of view. Included are perspectives of overall, nationwide learnings and of specific strategies and their impact. Part Three explores the same area, but this time from the perspective of the practitioner. School superintendents are here given a rare opportunity to present their side of the picture, to identify what they think has led to our present situation. Finally, Part Four presents some emerging change strategies that might have implications for educational leaders who are ready to take the risks required to move their schools.

The book had its initial impetus as a result of a symposium I chaired on conflict and change in education at the American Educational Research Association meeting in 1977. Since then it has benefited from critiques and encouragement by a number of people, including many of those who ultimately agreed to make a contribution to the book and others such as Chris Argyris, Per Dalin, John Goodlad, Dale Mann, Barry Oshry, and George Peabody. Mary Allison and Marianthi Lazos at Teachers College Press have been most supportive throughout the entire venture; Don Raw has provided much needed assistance in organizing the work; and Sue Gale and Ann Del Bel went beyond the call of duty in seeing that communications to all involved parties were clear and consistent. For all this support I am truly grateful.

Mike M. Milstein
Buffalo, New York

PART ONE

The Setting and the Probabilities

ESTIMATING WHERE WE ARE and how we got here as regards conflicts in schools is a prerequisite to understanding the potential for changing or improving them. Schools, in form and substance, are the products of a complex web of societal interactions and can only be understood within that context. That is, major forces that buffet society inevitably shape the purposes and interactions that dominate our schools.

No doubt the same thing can be said about any institution, but it becomes ever-more relevant to stress this regarding schools today because the traditional protective coatings that have insulated them are being stripped away. In the past leaders of schools have been successful in convincing local communities and governmental policy makers that schools should enjoy a special status because they deal with our nation's youth. As a result school governance has been viewed as nonpolitical, or above the partisanship and open debate that typifies other governmental jurisdictions. Similarly, they successfully argued that resources must be guaranteed if schools are to provide at least a minimum of education for our youth. They were also effective in arguing that educational decision making should be dominated by teachers and administrators because these professionals alone possess the skills and knowledge required to make such decisions.

These long-standing protective coatings have clearly been torn away. School politics have become open and competitive as opposed to closed and controlled. Resource acquisition for schools has become a high-risk venture, one in which there is relatively little special status leverage and in which the resource base itself is declining relative to need. The slow and sometimes inadequate response of educators in meeting escalating demands of society (e.g., for desegregation, compensatory education, and mainstreaming) has, similarly, stripped the professionals of their former special status as the arbitrators of programmatic preferences.

Because an understanding of these rapidly shifting conditions is so vital, Part One is devoted to an estimation of the forces that are at play and the potential impact these forces have on educational change. To begin, Milstein, Lusthaus, and Lusthaus, after an initial definition of conflict, provide a framework for understanding and responding to the major sources of conflict in education. They identify goal incompatibility, shared resources, and interdependence of activities as primary contributors to conflict. They examine the school's responses to these conflict sources and the potential for effectively changing schools. They also present a conceptual map of the various approaches that might be taken to changing schools.

The remaining two contributions to this part explore, from alternative points of view, the schools' willingness and ability to respond to the growing demands for change. Blumberg takes the position that schools, "by virtue of their sense of being, value system, structure and technology, and their reaction to conflict, generically tend to resist change." On the basis of his broad experience with school change efforts, Blumberg concludes that it is the unique school setting that is able to overcome these deeply rooted elements, and, when this occurs, it is directly associated with exceptional leadership inputs.

Chesler, Crowfoot, and Bryant focus on the conflict element noted by Blumberg and argue that conflict should be viewed as creating the potential for changing schools. That is, *escalation* of conflict may have to occur if we hope to have an impact on educational purposes and processes (e.g., note the conflicts associated with school district desegregation and community control of schools). Chesler, Crowfoot, and Bryant take a particular value position, arguing that movement is not likely as long as there is the present enormous gap in resources possessed between the participants, particularly as related to educational administrators who have access to policy makers, budgets, and authoritative command as opposed to students and parents who have no such access. Further, they argue that educational administrators cannot truly represent these dispossessed groups: administrators are employed to maintain the institution's rules and value preferences, not to change them! Their conclusion is that to argue otherwise is manipulative at best and self-deluding at worst.

CHAPTER 1

Conflict in Education

MIKE M. MILSTEIN
CHARLES S. LUSTHAUS
EVELYN W. LUSTHAUS

As POWERFUL AND DIVERSE GROUPS aggressively pursue their preferences, conflict has inevitably reached staggering dimensions in our
nation's schools. Parents have organized into community interest
groups to influence school board policy, teacher and administrator
unions have linked with national associations to improve their influence on all aspects of educational governance, and federal and state
policy makers and executive agencies have imposed legislation and
rulings on school district functioning.

One spillover of this development is that designing and implementing
change strategies in educational settings is becoming an increasingly
complex and hazardous business. Critical questions are being raised
about the feasibility of effecting change in schools. Have adversarial
conditions made planned change efforts unworkable? Are strategies
that were designed and implemented in the past effective today? Do
traditional assumptions need to be reviewed before we can design effective intervention strategies? To provide a context for dealing with
such questions, this chapter will explore the nature of conflict in education and the implications for those who seek to reform educational
institutions.

A PERSPECTIVE ON CONFLICT

As is the case with many social science concepts, there is a reign of
confusion over the multiple meanings that researchers have employed
when referring to conflict. The concept is part of most of the social

science disciplines, but each conceptualizes the term within its own framework and even within disciplines various interpretations are given.

Essentially, conflict is a situation that evolves when individuals, groups, or organizations believe that their interests are incompatible. Or, even more simply, "conflict refers to a social condition in which two or more persons or groups cannot [or at least *perceive* that they cannot] have the same thing at the same time" (Schmuck et al., 1977, p. 191).

There are three conditions in which conflicts are likely to arise (Schmidt and Kochan, 1972). First, conflict arises *when goals of individuals or groups are incompatible, or at least are perceived to be incompatible* (e.g., equal educational opportunity versus special enrichment programs for the gifted). Second, *when those involved share resources* (e.g., funds, space, or supplies) there could be concern of encroachment upon one individual or group's fair share of these resources by another individual or group. Third, *when activities of individuals or groups are interdependent,* such as when a number of departments in a single school have legitimate input into the curriculum, there could be perceptions of interference into the authority realm of one group by another. Any one of these conditions or a combination of them could lead to behavior that results in one group being blocked while another group advances.

HOW THESE CONDITIONS APPLY TO EDUCATION

These conditions can be used as a basis upon which to clarify our understanding of conflicts in education. By analyzing the problems involved with incompatible goals, resource sharing, and interdependent activities as a means of differentiating and categorizing phenomena, we can explore the escalation of conflicts over the past several decades.

Incompatible Goals　Schools are organizations in flux. Today's transitional phase seems to be leading toward a drastic shift in purposes. Purposes are being redefined in a variety of arenas: by policymaking bodies at several levels of government, by state and federal courts, and by a variety of groups in communities that insist upon special consideration of their particular needs. It is not uncommon, for example, to find a local high school filled to capacity with parents, teachers, and others in heated debate with each other, as well as with school boards and administrators, about what is and/or is not being done in schools. Rightly or wrongly, education is becoming everybody's business. Educators, government policy makers, and the public are debating and redebating the goals of schools. Goals are rooted in values, but value systems, even within individual communities, are extremely diverse. Thus, throughout this era, we have had increased communication between groups that hold different goals that are derived from divergent values. Conflict is an inevitable outcome of this situation.

The goals debate in education can be profitably viewed from two different perspectives. The first is that *schools exist to meet societal demands*. In this view educational goals relate to beliefs that the types of activities students encounter should reflect societal demands. Thus in the early 1960s schools tried to respond to the demand for more emphasis on the hard sciences and for more options, such as comprehensive high schools and educational parks. This changed in the mid-1960s to demands for more humane schools, schools without failure, and more individualized instruction. More recently the goals debate has focused upon such issues as competency-based education and back to the basics.

The second approach is to view schools as either *promoting maintenance or change of the social order*. As maintainers schools have had a historical role of socializing students into dominant cultural norms. For example, schools have been expected to inculcate the young about the sanctity of society's governmental precepts and structures, foster a belief in free enterprise and the continuance of the nuclear family, and encourage respect for law and order. However, there has also been a competing demand, which has increased rapidly over the past twenty-five years, for the schools to be in the vanguard of social change. (Most frequently these demands come from forces outside of the local setting.) There have been demands that the schools play pioneering roles in such areas as racial integration, bringing the mentally and physically handicapped back into the mainstream, and equalizing lifelong opportunities.

Resource Sharing   Economically, the sixties was a time of expansion and growth. Even when local revenues were becoming scarce, it appeared that state and federal funds would always be available to help school systems meet their programmatic needs. Although many groups competed for a share of the pie, the pie seemed big, so there was enough for all. However, toward the end of the sixties this was no longer the case; growth came to a crashing halt and funding sources began to dry up as the economy stalled.

The primary resource-sharing issue is how to allocate and reallocate available economic resources. More conflict will ensue as groups vie for these scarce resources at all levels, from national groups fighting for a percentage of the federal budget, to groups within the same school fighting over the allocation of funds for different aspects of the curriculum.

Economic resources are not the only resource over which conflict is occurring. Control and power (playing a role in decision making, status, or other influencing mechanisms) seems to loom equally high in the resource battle. Slogans such as Teacher Power, Community Power, and Student Power frequently make headlines and illustrate the conflict resulting from various groups attempting to influence the governance of schools. Often, the assumption of these groups is that power, like money, is a zero-sum game: in order to receive your share it must be gotten at the expense of others. Again, an inevitable component of this situation is conflict.

Interdependent Activities   A major basis for conflict in education has been the constant push for interdependent activities among many extremely divergent groups and individuals. Traditional divisions of tasks among federal, state, and local governments have been shattered. Federalism today means shared jurisdictional responsibilities as often as it does clear division of tasks in education. Local school authorities spend much of their time responding to state and federal demands. This is particularly difficult to do when these demands run counter to those of the local community. At the local level representatives from an increasing number of roles, including parents, teachers, administrators, and students, are participating in formal governance structures such as school boards, advisory committees, and long-range planning committees. The outcome is frequent and loud debate. Within school structures themselves, the heterogeneity of students with diverse educational needs has led to the employment of an increasing number of specialists and has made integration of roles more difficult. Finally, changes in curriculum and organizational structure, including team teaching and open space schools, have produced a greater need for interaction and interdependence.

These demands for interdependence are relatively new. Weick (1976) has characterized schools as loosely coupled systems, postulating that different levels of a school organization have very little influence on other levels. Without strong precedents for interrelating it should not be surprising that the necessity of closely relating is a major condition fostering conflicts in schools.

THE IMPACT OF CONFLICT ON EDUCATION

The outcomes of these stresses may not all be apparent, but one thing seems certain: there is *less joy for all involved in the educational process*. In most communities one hears wistful calls for a return to normalcy, which is vaguely associated with the years that preceded the turbulent 1960s. These calls come from representatives of all groups involved—administrators, teachers, and school boards as well as community leaders and, in particular, parents. Most participants feel that the educational process is more complex, more hazardous, and less fulfilling than in former times.

They have responded in various ways: communities with the power to vote on fiscal issues are reducing their support for schools; administrators are focusing upon job security and salary differentials; teachers are leaving en masse from school at precisely the time stated within contract agreements; and so on. In many cases, educators have reacted by becoming more resistant to change efforts, withdrawing into defensive stands, and, ultimately, becoming incapable of responding creatively to conflict situations. In looking at issues in the politics of education, Milstein (1978, p. 175) posited several questions that touch on the reactions and responses of educators to adversary conditions:

1. Studies of change in education tend to conclude that educators resist change efforts, at least in part because they are not convinced that making adaptations in structure, process, technology, or pedagogical methods will have any major impact on educational outcomes. Does this sense of equifinality truly exist? If so, does this mind-set give educators pause when they are dealing with adversarial situations? That is, do educators assume that what is actually going on in the world is really peripheral to their tasks and thus should be ignored? Are educators incapable, therefore, of responding to changing social conditions?
2. Have we moved so far away from the fabled little red schoolhouse that we have devised an organizationally based, built-in incapacity to respond to conflict situations? We are now an army of specialists, but is anyone in charge? Is there a sense of proprietorship on the part of the professionals, or has specialization made it impossible for them to have a sense of overall purpose?
3. Does the rising tempo of criticism from society cause educators to react ever-more defensively? Are they, in effect, becoming locked into their present incapacities because of their defensiveness? Do they think that if they take the criticism seriously they might reach the undesirable conclusion that what they are presently doing is not adequate?''

Teachers have taken collective stances in response to conflict, making increased demands for extrinsic rewards as they try to protect themselves. However, it is less and less feasible for school districts to meet demands for increasing pay levels. Consequently, teachers, disillusioned and frustrated with their inability to influence the system, focus much of their anger upon their schools' administrators. Administrators find themselves being made scapegoats of teachers who see them as the source of all their frustrations or, worse yet, superfluous to the entire educational endeavor; they are thus lonelier than ever before in their jobs.

One wonders whether school boards and superintendents can realistically lead schools under these conditions. Is it feasible for educational managers and teachers to move toward fulfilling experiences or will the unresolved conflicts in schools continue to intensify? Change, however difficult it may be, must be viewed as vital if conditions are to be improved.

THE POTENTIAL FOR CHANGE

What does all of this imply as far as our ability to effect change in schools? In a sense we are witnessing a not-so-funny irony. In the past, when conditions were less conflictual, the potential to lead and to change schools may have been greater than is presently the case, but it is now that there are increasing demands for change. The potential to use cooperative models for change was greater when communities supported fiscal measures, parents and students were less critical of school programs, and teachers were not yet caught up with unionism. Under these former conditions the field was fertile for instituting planned change programs that assumed good will and trust as a base upon which to build. However, with such secure conditions the impetus for change was less apparent and educational leaders, for the most part, sought to maintain the status quo rather than rock the boat.

Now, as a result of the escalation of conflict in schools, and between schools and communities, educational leaders are concluding that something must be done but are less confident than ever before of *how* to do that something. Thus the irony: in the past while the potential for movement seemed high, interest in change was minimal. Now the interest in change is growing, at least on the part of segments of communities and many school boards and administrators, but the potential of devising effective responses to change has been lessened. More and more we find school districts turning to outside resource persons to help them devise adequate change strategies to meet the more difficult conditions they are confronting.

The implications for those involved in the governance of schools are significant. Is the belated recognition of need too late? Do we have too little knowledge and skill to respond? Do those who are calling for help realize that they may be unleashing forces that can drastically change their own roles, to say nothing of the impact it could have on the substance and form of education in their communities? Or do they believe that just one more show of concern will be sufficient and that those involved will be content and become more pacific because an "effort" has been made? Assuming that we have potent tools and those calling for planned change efforts are sincere and willing to risk the fallout, will others who will have to participate in the change effort trust those who are calling for it? If not, they will likely subvert any attempts to modify conditions.

Responses to these questions depend, in part at least, upon one's perspective on conflict as facilitating or hindering the change process. The dominant perspective is that the effective administrator is one who overcomes conflict situations, or at least reduces them to a minimum. Robbins (1976) has argued that, on the contrary, conflict is a necessary ingredient for moving organizations. While some conflicts may be dysfunctional, others may well enable leaders to insitutionalize necessary change. In fact, he argues, effective administrators sometimes promote conflicts where none exist so they can stimulate debate and, hopefully, move their organizations' members to consider modifying purposes or practices.

The place of conflict in change is a live issue and one that will be addressed from contrasting perspectives in the two chapters that follow by Blumberg and by Chesler, Crowfoot and Bryant. For now, we ask that the reader consider his or her own point of view on this question. Ultimately, he or she will have to make decisions regarding change under conditions of conflict and these decisions will be significantly affected by his or her perspective concerning conflict.

STRATEGIES FOR MANAGING CONFLICT

Let us assume that the leader of an educational organization is interested in confronting conflicts and bringing about necessary changes. Does she or he have any alternatives to sitting back and watching the inevitable hardening of the organization's arteries? Does she or he have access to strategies that can lead to the alteration of an unsatisfactory status quo? Are there ways of bringing adversaries together to interact in ways that can lead to ends that are at least satisfactory to all parties involved?

What that leader requires is knowledge of the strategies that are available to be called upon. She or he also needs to know which of these require modifications before they can be applied and what new strategies are being developed but may not yet be fully tested.

In this book we will explore some of the best change strategies that are being applied in school-based change programs as well as strategies that seem to be evolving into potent responses that might help to bring about changing conditions in educational settings. As a beginning, in this chapter we will offer a brief sketch of the several forms that change efforts might take. The purpose is not to be evaluative or judgmental, but to lay out a map so the reader can place the strategies discussed into an overall context.

Administrators have attempted and continue to develop a variety of responses to conflict. In general these approaches include consensus building, competition, structural modifications, avoidance, or a mixture of these approaches.

Consensus Building
The prevalent mode of interaction in education is face to face. Accordingly, the first and probably the primary conflict resolution strategy used by educational administrators usually involves establishing a climate conducive to building consensus between parties. This conflict management approach provides a potential base upon which information and opinions can be exchanged and mutual understanding can be fostered. Increasingly, a third, and often external, party is being used in this approach, who gathers and feeds back data regarding conflict and teaches a variety of skills such as joint goal setting and communications.

Competition
Individuals and groups within our society are turning more and more to competitive approaches to resolve educational disputes. These approaches are based upon win/lose postures on the part of opposing parties. Essentially it is a game of "power, power, who has the power?" In this sense power refers either to reliance on external authority such as the courts and legislatures or to more internal expressions of power such as strikes and protests. Consequently, parties to a conflict that are not in the seat of authority will tend to be those that initiate and pursue these strategies. Administrators and school boards, as the legitimate authorities, typically attempt to block these kinds of efforts.

In our experience competitive approaches to conflict management frequently intensify issues and polarize the participants, at least for a period of time. However, in retrospect many of the school-based changes that have occurred during the past twenty-five years have resulted from application of the competitive approach. Advocates employing this approach have often utilized our legal system, for example, as a means of attaining racial integration and mainstreaming. At other times they have gone outside the legal system to gain their ends—for example, as have citizens who have organized school boycotts and teachers who have withheld their services.

Structural Modifications In response to conflict, school boards, superintendents, and principals frequently attempt to manage the relationship between and among the various participants in the process by modifying structures. One such structural response is the expanded use of committees. Teacher unions are being included on committees that explore policy alternatives. Parent advisory committees are being formed for similar reasons. Another structural response, the decentralization of large school systems, has occurred in part for reasons of efficiency and economy, but also because of the need to be more responsive. At the school level more experimentation is going on with alternative educational approaches, such as the voucher system and schools-within-schools.

Avoidance Sometimes conflict that arises in educational settings is virtually ignored. When a conflict arises the parties tacitly agree to let it alone, do nothing, or play down the differences. Most frequently this approach is employed at the authoritative level, for it is at this level where the perception is that there is more to be gained by leaving things as they are and more to be lost by confronting the situation. In essence, the response is to avoid reacting to the initial overt blocking behavior.

Sometimes the conflict does go away, being burned out or mediated at another level, but more often than not it lingers on, intensifies, grows in scope, and must eventually be confronted.

A Mixture of Approaches As conflicts become more and more complex, our ways of dealing with them are also tending to become more inclusive. Conflict managers are becoming adept at designing and redesigning approaches that cut across the several approaches of consensus building, competition, structural modifications, and avoidance. For example, in many instances structural modifications will probably be more effective when combined with consensus building. Competition may have to be injected into a happy but nonproductive situation before consensus building or structural modifications can be attempted. Sometimes participants may become exhausted by the process and temporary avoidance might be the best course of action.

The key is to know when to employ which approach or combination of approaches. Ultimately, experience in conflict situations will be the best guide upon which to base responses to conflict. However, this is a high-cost approach to the training of effective conflict managers. There is less room for mistakes than ever before and many a neophyte in the game has been irreparably scarred in the process.

To improve chances for survival and, hopefully, for effectiveness, the would-be conflict manager can benefit from a review of what is happening around the country; what conflict situations are being incurred; what strategies are being formulated in response to these conflicts; what is the result of the efforts; and what possibilities exist for improving our responsiveness and our chances of effectively reforming schools.

REFERENCES

Milstein, M. M. Analyzing the impact of adversarial relations on the management of educational systems. In E. K. Mosher & J. L. Wagoner, Jr. (Eds.), *The changing politics of education: prospects for the 1980's*. Berkeley, Calif.: McCutchan, 1978, pp. 171–176.

Robbins, S. P. *The administrative process*. Englewood Cliffs, N.J.: Prentice-Hall, 1976.

Schmidt, S. M., & Kochan, T. A. Conflict: toward conceptual clarity. *Administrative Science Quarterly*, 1972, *17*, 359–370.

Schmuck, R. A., Runkel, P. J., Arends, J. H., and Arends, R. I. *The second handbook of organization development in schools*. Palo Alto, Calif.: Mayfield Publishing, 1977.

Weick, K. Educational organizations as loosely coupled systems. *Administrative Science Quarterly*, 1976, *12*(1), 1–19.

CHAPTER 2

School Organizations: A Case of Generic Resistance to Change

ARTHUR BLUMBERG

THE PAST TWENTY YEARS have witnessed a tremendous effort to change and improve the character of public education. In dollars, these efforts may be measured in the billions. Concerning time, the days and hours committed to programs of change may be considered in terms that are astronomical if they are calculable at all.

Despite this huge outpouring of human and financial energy, it is hard for a person who even occasionally visits schools to escape the gnawing feeling that things are pretty much the same as they always have been. This is not to say that conditions and what transpires in the schools are bad. Nor is it to say that there are not some schools that have not changed radically and in a productive manner. It is simply to suggest that the system seems to have remained relatively stable in the face of tremendous effort to make it different. For the most part, for example, it would appear that relationships between teachers and administrators have not changed and neither have those between and among teachers nor between teachers and students. Approaches to problem solving seem not to have varied and the curriculum, though new programs have been introduced, seems to result in learning achievement that is about the same as it always has been, if, indeed, it

This paper is adapted from one that was originally presented at the International Conference on Social Change and Organization Development, Dobrovnic, Yugoslavia, February 28–29, 1977.

has not declined (witness the recent concern over lowering SAT scores).

The intent of this chapter is not to criticize the schools for not having changed in any essential manner. Indeed, a case can probably be made to support the position that there was and is no need to try and change the schools and that problems that have been encountered in them could best be dealt with by staying with tried and true fundamentals and enforcing stricter disciplinary measures. Nor is it the intent to suggest that there have been no examples of imaginative or productive educational change or that there are no outstanding teachers and administrators who have made significant changes in their school organizations. Rather, the purpose is to take the position that schools are an example of organizations that, by virtue of their sense of being, value system, structure and technology, and their reaction to conflict, generically tend to resist change.

Schools, of course, bear many similarities to other types of organizations. However, it is the contention here that there are aspects of school life that are strikingly idiosyncratic to schools as social systems. Further, it is contended that their effect is to set in motion forces that counter efforts to induce change. It is not necessarily true that these forces activate a conscious conspiracy to resist change, though that, at times, may be the case. More importantly, the working hypothesis here is that the cumulative effect of the way these organizational factors operate is to create a condition in which ultimately "the more things change, the more they remain the same" (Sarason, 1971, p. 2). It is as if schools as systems have an implicit goal to maintain things the way they are.

THE SCHOOLS' SENSE OF THEIR INSTITUTIONAL BEING

It is probably true that aside from institutions of government, few systems have come under more attack from a wide spectrum of groups than have the schools. For example, conservatives complain that there is not enough emphasis on the basics; liberals criticize the schools because they do not offer sufficient learning alternatives; newspaper editorials focus on too much permissiveness. Blacks attack the schools because they don't take into consideration the needs of black children, and public advocacy groups take the schools to task for not adequately paying attention to the needs of handicapped youngsters.

For our purposes, the substance of these attacks is less important than their effect. One crucial effect that is observable is the creation of a sort of siege mentality in the schools. It's as though school personnel find it necessary to be on their guard, continually. There seems to be a spillover effect of distrust that is directed at strangers, at people who are not directly involved on a daily basis in trying to do the job of schooling, whatever that job may be. Perhaps a more important result, though, of these criticisms and attacks is that, legitimate or not, they call into question both in the minds of the public and of professional educators the very institutional being of the schools. Laing (1969) suggests this condition is one that is related to the relative ontological insecurity of a system.

Laing, a psychiatrist, focuses his concerns on problems of individuals, not organizations. It seems, though, that the concept of ontological insecurity may well be transferred from the analysis of an individual to that of an organization. Speaking of individuals, Laing (p. 44) suggests:

> We can say that in the individual whose own being is secure in this primary experiential sense, relatedness with others is potentially gratifying: whereas the ontologically insecure person is preoccupied with preserving rather than gratifying himself: the ordinary circumstances of living threaten his *low threshold* of security.
>
> If a position of primary ontological security has been reached, the ordinary circumstances of life do not afford a perpetual threat to one's own existence. If such a basis for living has not been reached, the ordinary circumstances of life constitute a continual and deadly threat.

Laing uses the concept of ontological insecurity to account for individual psychoses. By my transfer of the concept to the schools I am not suggesting that they are psychotic or that there are such things as psychotic organizations. What I *am* suggesting, however, is that the behavior of schools as organizations frequently communicates a strong sense of insecurity as to what it is they are all about. This does not necessarily mean that individual teachers or administrators are not ontologically secure. But the whole is different from the mere sum of its parts, and it is the whole with which this chapter is concerned.

There is a point in Laing's comment that is key to this analysis. It is the suggestion that a condition of ontological security promotes a situation in which relatedness with others is potentially gratifying. Contrariwise, a condition of ontological insecurity creates conditions where the organism's thrust is on preservation, on scanning the environment for potential threats even if the environment is filled largely with the ordinary circumstances of living. As one or the other of these conditions gets translated into interpersonal or group situations, the behavior that becomes evident takes on the character of a psychological movement *toward* or a movement *against* or *away* from people (Horney, 1945). It is not difficult to sense when people perceive a circumstance to be potentially gratifying and engage with each other or, the obverse, when they perceive a threat and exhibit avoidance behavior. A summary of personal experience relative to the schools, however, may clarify my point.

Like many of my colleagues, I have held untold numbers of conversations and work sessions with individual administrators and teachers outside the immediate context of the school as an organization. By and large, these situations have been pleasant and productive. It was as though people involved wanted to relate, work, learn, or change. On the other hand, there have been many occasions where I have attempted to deal with the school as an organization, but my experiences were much different. I was confronted with lethargy, defensiveness, and an attitude that might be best expressed as ho hum. The startling thing was that in a number of these cases, individual and organizational, some of the same people were involved.

Why the difference between the individual and the organization? I can only speculate, of course, but as I rethink these circumstances I can't avoid the recurrent and underlying theme of security of being as an individual as opposed to insecurity of being as an institution. As I say this I also realize that there may be a myriad of other factors that enter the picture—factors that may be related to my own lack of skill, or at times, my inability to communicate adequately. Or, the factors may be those that attach to the system's previous experience with people from the outside. Nevertheless, over and over again I get the feeling that many school systems and faculties, by their behavior, communicate that they are unsure of their essential institutional being and react accordingly.

I don't make these points to administer a spanking to the schools with the admonition to them to behave and "be secure." On the contrary, I raise them to suggest that one cannot fully understand the "no change" phenomenon in the schools without also accepting the possibility that school-oriented change agents are dealing with ontologically insecure organizations.

ORGANIZATIONAL VALUE SYSTEM

Schools, like other organizations, are permeated by a value structure. Some of the values are explicit and committed to writing; the valuing of each child's individuality, for example. I hold the position, however, that the values that most strongly influence a system and the people who participate in it are the ones that are implicit in the behavior of those people. They can be learned by the outsider through a variety of means. In this case the data that is relatively easy to come by is that which derives from teachers as they talk about what concerns are uppermost in the minds of administrators and supervisors. Over and over again the theme that gets repeated is, "Are things going smoothly?" The implicit and pervading value, then, is keeping the peace. Concurrent with the value of peace keeping is that of loyalty. It is very important in the schools for principals to be loyal to their central office administrators and for teachers to be loyal to their principals—at least publicly.

The implications for programs of change of a value system that places a high priority on peacefulness and loyalty are clear. The process of creating change that makes a difference is not necessarily a peaceful business, and it may also create the impression on one's organizational seniors that the enactors of change are not quite as loyal as they might be. If not, why would they be involved in disrupting the peace when they know that the system values peacefulness so highly?

The systemic values of the need to maintain peace and display loyalty are reinforced in the schools, from my view, by another part of the value system that is concerned with the types of changes that are supported and encouraged. Those changes are of the nature of being additive or subtractive. They usually take the form of creating an add-on feature, a newly developed technique for teaching reading, for example, or the removal of some constraining administrative procedure. The changes that receive little support or encouragement are those that require reconceptualizing and restructuring some part of the system—the curriculum or the manner in which school is organized, for example.

Watzlawick, Weakland, and Fisch (1974) think of these two types of changes as being either of the first or the second order. First order changes involve essentially the rearrangement or substitution of parts of a system without disturbing the structure of a system. When first order changes are the basis of new programs the results may, indeed, achieve some illusions of basic change. What is left untouched, however, is the framework through which people conceptualize their tasks and their relationships with others. There is change—but things remain the same.

A second order change involves interventions in the system that enable the people in it to transcend their present frame of reference relative to the problems they are confronting. The issue is to create conditions that foster a reformulation of problems so that they may be viewed in new and creative ways. When second order changes are successfully induced into a system, the system itself becomes different in contradistinction to the results of first order change.

All this, of course, is not to suggest that first order change is bad and second order change is good. To the contrary, no value is placed on either. The issue is, however, that schools *do* seem to place a value on them. What does indeed get communicated is that first order change is good by definition. It is not apt to disrupt things. In Sarason's (1971) terms it does nothing to disturb the "regularities" by which schools operate. Second order change, on the other hand, tends to be viewed with reserve, for it contains the potential for disruption of the regularities.

There are many cases that are illustrative of the point. They may be found in individual classrooms, in school buildings, or in a total school system. For example, an elementary school teacher had decided to restructure her classroom by changing it from a traditional teacher-to-student interaction pattern to one where the locus of interaction would be among the students. The result was highly satisfactory to the teacher. The students seemed very much involved. There was much discussion among them and a lot of "doing." There was also more noise in the classroom than there had been formerly. The principal of the school took a dim view of this change. He saw it as disruptive to the peaceful scene for which the school had been noted and he made his views known to the teacher. The classroom was restructured to its original form.

A high school principal wanted to change the decision-making process in the school from one that was unilateral in structure to one that heavily involved the faculty. The plan was put into effect but it failed. The explicit message from the teachers was "you get paid to administer, we get paid to teach"—this despite the move toward teacher unionism with its concern for more power and control for teachers.

A consultant was asked by a school superintendent to help construct a new evaluation instrument for teachers in the district. Upon discussion it developed that the root problem was not the instrument in current use, though it did need some improvement, but the whole pattern and quality of communications that existed between teachers, supervisors, and administrators. Merely to construct a new instrument without concurrently changing the communication structure and climate of the system would result in no change of any substance. The proposal was made that the two problems be worked on simultaneously. It was rejected as containing the seeds for disruption.

These brief examples, and they could be repeated endlessly, are not offered by way of criticism. Rather, they are given as data to help explain and understand the stability, some would call it the inertia, of schools as organizations. They suggest that caution, indeed, becomes the better part of valor in the schools. Life for all is simply easier if efforts to change do not disturb the regularities of the system and do not interfere with smoothness of operation. To some extent, of course, this is true of any social system. Reconceptualization of problems and restructuring of settings are not easy processes and they do disrupt things. The issue, though, goes beyond the idea that second order change, for example, is not easy to accomplish. What is involved, as I see it, is the central and powerful normative value-thrust of the schools—to maintain what presently exists in smooth running order.

ORGANIZATIONAL STRUCTURE OF THE SCHOOLS

An unrecognized problem which, in my judgment, has hampered the efforts of researchers to understand the organizational behavior of the schools has been that they have been conceived of, for the most part, as possessing structural patterns that are only slightly different from those one might find in an industrial organization. One of the results of this has been that when research has been conducted on school organizations the measuring instruments tend to be modifications of instruments that are used in industrial or governmental bureaucracy. Large numbers of studies have been conducted that have made use of adaptations of Likert's (1967) profile of an organization instrument, for example, and many of them have, indeed, resulted in statistically significant findings. But it seems to me that what is not yet available, in thorough form, is a theoretical framework for understanding schools as organizations that will shed a clear light on the differences between them and other organizational types. It is not that similarities do not exist. The problem is that significant differences also exist and these differences contribute, I think, in a major way to the systemic resistance to change that has been observed.

In a fascinating paper, Weick (1976) has offered a conceptual direction that could lead to a much deeper level of understanding of the nature of school organization structures and resulting behavior. His proposal is that contrary to prevailing notions of organizations being structured through dense, tight linkages, it may be more appropriate, particularly in the case of educational organizations, to conceive of them as "loosely coupled systems." Weick's central explanation of loose coupling is that "coupled events are responsive, *but* that each event also preserves its own identity and some evidence of its physical or logical separateness" (p. 3). The picture, then, is one of noninterdependence on a system-wide level. This does seem to be the case in the schools. What occurs between a teacher and a principal relative to the teacher's work, or what occurs between a teacher and his or her students is not necessarily relevant to what occurs elsewhere in the school, for example.

The relationship between a loosely coupled, noninterdependent organization and the notion of systemic resistance to change seems potentially to be clear. As long as what teacher A is doing affects teacher B only minimally, if at all, there is little motivation for A and B to be concerned about their work relationships or changing the character of those relationships. Further, given that the coupling between A and B and the principal is also loose, the common ground that might relate them in a combined effort is shaky. Weick (p. 4) approaches this problem in his discussion of the relationship between intentions and action:

> There is a developing position in psychology which argues that intentions are a poor guide for action, intentions often follow rather than precede action, and that intentions and action are loosely coupled. Unfortunately, organizations continue to think that planning is a good thing, they spend much time on planning, and actions are assessed in terms of their fit with plans. Given a potential loose coupling between the intentions and actions of organization members, it should come as no surprise that administrators are baffled and angered when things never happen the way they're supposed to.

The comment above is, perhaps, another way of saying that "the road to hell is paved with good intentions." For our purposes, the suggestion is strong that the very nature of schools as organizations inhibits the induction of change into them as organizations. And it does this in a way that, as Weick noted, administrators (and others, it might be added) find baffling.

In a paper that was written prior to Weick's, thus without the benefit of his overarching concept of schools as loosely coupled systems, Blumberg and Schmuck (1972) spoke more specifically about some school structural characteristics that seem systematically to create barriers to organizational development training and organizational change. Their analysis flows naturally from the loosely coupled notion. It included a concern with the individuated nature of the teacher's role, the dyadic nature of the principal's role, and the lack of formal organizational complexity in the schools. A summary of their analysis follows.

Individuated Nature of Teacher's Role
In Woodward's terms (1958), teaching is a single unit or small batch type of technology. For most intents and purposes, the teachers have responsibility for managing the total work environment within the classroom. Further, the teacher's role in the school tends to be organizationally nonintegrative. Teachers can do what is expected of them, for the most part, without ever communicating with one another. This lack of integrativeness of teacher roles would seem to be quite influential in the

development of school norms that might best be described as collaborative. That is, the norms of a school staff are not necessarily against collaboration and integration. They simply tend not to be at all salient in most schools.

The primary orientation of a teacher to a school, then, is one of individuation and not in the direction of what might be called organizational membership. The school for a teacher is the organization in which one does the work of a teacher. Except in a disjointed fashion, it is not the social organism that provides the goals, the relationships, and the setting within which a teacher channels efforts to produce something in consort with others. Because there often is little concern on the part of teachers with the school as an organization, the idea of devoting energy to improving the organization seems vague and irrelevant.

TEACHING AS AN IDIOSYNCRATIC ACT. A corollary of the phenomenon of the individuated role structure of the teacher is the idea that the act of teaching is idiosyncratic. Each teacher adapts his or her own personality and values to the demands of the classroom and develops a unique behavioral repertoire to cope with the problems of the teaching/learning process and classroom management. The process by which teaching and other interpersonal behaviors are learned is one of long-term socialization. It starts with early family learning, proceeds through school as youngsters, consciously or unconsciously, select teaching models for themselves, and then into college where other models are presented as well as opportunities to test out different ways of behaving.

The point is that after a person has been engaged as a teacher for a period of time, it is not unreasonable to suspect that that person develops a strong ego-stake in the way she or he organizes and conducts a learning experience. This circumstance becomes reinforced when the teacher is granted tenure with its implicit stamp of competency. Change programs in the schools are aimed ultimately at improving the education of youngsters which means, in effect, changing what occurs in the classroom. The conflict is obvious. On the one hand, teachers are told by the system that they are doing a good job. They have been granted tenure. What they do and the way they do it is important to them. On the other hand, a program of organizational or curricular change implies that "someone" thinks they are doing not as good a job as they might. To ask a teacher to change, particularly to adopt a new concept of teaching, almost automatically triggers resistance. In his discussion of one of the reasons for what is acknowledged to be the failure of the "new math" curriculum to take hold and be productive, Sarason (1971, p. 41) summed it up in this way:

All were agreed that teachers would for a time become pupils again and learn the new math. No one formulated the problem as one requiring teachers to *unlearn* and *learn*—to give up highly over-learned ways of thinking at the same time that they were required to learn new procedures and new ways of conceptualizing. To state the problem in this way would require, at the very least, the acute awareness that one must make explicit and examine the degree to which one's theory of change takes account of the important social and psychological dimensions that characterize the setting. Such awareness was clearly not present.

Sarason states the problem neatly. His comments suggest pointedly that systemic variables related to the work of teachers are such that they mitigate against programs of change. The implications are clear that unless these variables are acknowledged and dealt with things in the schools will, indeed, remain the same.

Dyadic Nature of Principal's Role
The single unit or small batch technology that encourages individuated teacher's roles also has influence on administrative behavior. The principal is confronted with the nonintegrative norms of the staff, and her or his behavior often reinforces these norms. As in the case of the teachers, the principal's view of his school tends to be oriented toward interpersonal relations and not toward the organization as a whole. Thus, the principal's concerns for change and development move her or him in the direction of improving communications with individuals and not with organizational norms and group problem solving.

On a behavioral level, what seems to happen is that principals spend a good bit of their time trying to build good relationships with individual teachers and not with groups of teachers. The norms of school staffs legitimize and sanction this way of working; it is not the doing of the principal alone. Further, the principal's socialization into that role began when the principal was still a teacher. What is learned in that situation tends to be repeated when a teacher becomes a principal. In this way, the organizational pattern of dyadic relationships with individual teachers on the part of the principal is circular and reinforced.

Lack of Formal Organizational Complexity
Schools, particularly elementary schools, are hierarchically very flat. Elementary schools tend to have one-step hierarchies (teacher-principal). Secondary schools typically are more complex, having hierarchies of three steps (teacher-department head-assistant principal-principal). Even in secondary schools, however, the formal authority hierarchy is fairly simple because department heads usually have little power and assis-

tant principals function as staff officers with specialized duties and not as next in line to the principal in decision making.

The flat organizational hierarchy reinforces and lends reality to the staff's perception that the school is an individuated and dyadic organization. Teachers have relatively easy access to the principal and feel little need to coordinate their efforts with one another. There is little in the way of chain of command that needs to be engaged in order to communicate up and down. Consequently, the communication networks tend to get organized into a series of separated one-to-one relationships for those who have something to talk about. In other words, teachers don't have to use extended organizational linkages to communicate and see little need for improving something that doesn't exist—a complex communication pattern.

Typically, organizational change programs are directed, initially, toward working with power and communication relationships that are up, down, and across organizational roles and functions. Yet, the nature of the teacher's role as far as the professional staff is concerned means that there are no "down" and few "across" relationships. The teachers have no adults to manage or supervise. Consequently, organizational change programs ask teachers to devote time and energy to improving functioning and relationships that have little salience for them except, perhaps, interpersonally. Put another way, teachers, when invited to participate in such a program, ask "What's in it for us?" Chances are that whatever answer is given will be minimally persuasive, especially when teachers feel positive about their teaching and enjoy good relationships with their principal.

CONFLICT AND CHANGE

Conflict is endemic to organizational life and the schools are no exception to this rule. As we indicated earlier, the very existence of schools as public institutions seeking to serve and accommodate various people appears to create fertile ground for the emergence of conflict, particularly given the turbulence of American society in recent years. Conflicts have erupted among students, between students and teachers, parents and the schools, teachers and the schools, and politicians and the schools. The issues that have been attacked have been racism, control, student rights, regimentation, curriculum—to mention but a few.

It can be argued that the conflict that has occurred and will continue to occur constitutes a source of change in school life. The counterargument, the basis of which has already been discussed, is that the opposite condition holds—that the emergence of conflict in and about the schools typically generates forces and behaviors that have the effect over the long run of maintaining things as they are. This is what I take to be the underlying and pervasive value that pervades schools as social systems—to keep things peaceful—with its accompanying hypothesis that if the school scene is a tranquil one, youngsters will learn and the schools will have fulfilled their societal function.

Here are some examples that, in my mind, lend substance to the counterargument.

Conflict over Community Control of Schools In the late

1960s and early 1970s there was a great deal of furor over community control of schools, particularly in the larger cities. Stemming from charges of racism, of what appeared to be (and quite possibly was) the inability of the schools to meet the learning and emotional needs of black and other minority group children, and of bureaucratic inefficiency and insensitivity (both quite likely the case), the resolution of the conflict in many cases was to create subdivisions of community control and, in some situations, community boards that had responsibility for a single school. The system accommodated to the desires of its constituents. But what of the long-term effects? Have things changed or haven't they? Hard data is difficult to come by, but observations and discussions of the scene suggest quite strongly that though the structure of control may have changed, that which transpires in the schools relative to teaching and learning has not. However, it is clearly true that things are more peaceful than they were. Though that fact may and should be interpreted in a positive light, it is important to note that the essential elements of the system seem to have been maintained in only slightly altered states.

Conflict over Student Rights and Participation Concur-

rent with the demands for local community control of schools and undoubtedly related to it was the conflict over the rights of students to participate in organizational decision making. This was true particularly at the college level but there was a spillover effect into the secondary schools. Again, there was accommodation. In higher education students became members of most operating committees and in the public schools participation frequently took the form of principal or superintendent-student advisory committees.

How has this change fared? Again, hard data is probably nowhere to be found. The structures to accommodate student participation and consultation are, so it seems, still in place. Committees do meet and students still attend, though at the college level there seems to be a distinct drop in student concern with larger institutional matters. In any event, one would be hard pressed to detail any substantive changes that have taken place because of the student revolt. And particularly in higher education many of those changes that did occur (pass-fail courses, open curricula, for example) now seem in the process of being dropped as the faculty moves more strongly on to the scene and things become what they once were.

One may make various interpretations of these circumstances. The interpretations offered here are twofold: (a) It is deeply important on some curious level to the huge bulk of American society for the schools not to change relative to both their basic form and substance and to the nature of the human relationships that occur in them. What is currently seen in many places as a myth—that advancement through school and college is the sure road to success and prosperity—is not necessarily seen as a myth by millions of adults who traveled that road. Thus, the maintaining of the schools as they are becomes equated with maintaining American society. (b) When conflicts erupt over the schools, their form, function, or achievement, this conflict is seen as only reinforcing the necessity not to change. To accommodate, perhaps, but to keep the system as it was. To do otherwise would be to deny the validity of a substantial part of the lives of most of us.

It is not, to repeat an earlier comment, that there exists a conscious conspiracy of individuals reacting in the manner that has been described. Rather, the situation seems to involve some generic characteristics of the system and neither the benign nor evil intent of any individual or group of individuals.

Conflict between Teachers Unions and the Management of the Schools

In the schools, much as in other work organizations, there have always been underlying conflicts between teachers (the workers) and management (the school board and administration). The relatively recent legal sanctioning in many states of the right of teachers to organize and engage in collective bargaining has acknowledged, legitimized, and made public these conflicts—and quite appropriately so.

It is undoubtedly true that the strength of teachers unions has a large impact on the way schools are managed, on the economic well-being of teachers and, in some cases, on the configuration of both local and state politics. Through strikes or the threat of strike, teachers unions have, indeed, been able to change things. They have also exacerbated the conflict so that in numerous communities today there is silent—

and, in some cases—open warfare between the teachers and the communities in which they work. This is certainly an unintended consequence of the growth of teacher unionism, but it is undeniably a current fact of life in the schools today.

One must ask, going along with the theme of this chapter, what has been the effect of the conflict between teachers and school management having thrust itself so forcibly on the public. As was noted above, there seems to be little question that the working conditions of teachers have improved. Aside from the undeniable need to better the economic condition of teachers, the underlying assumption behind the push to improve salaries and working conditions seems to be that as they improve so will the quality of education. Happier teachers will be better teachers. This assumption is open to question. One can take the position, as I do, that the implicit motivating factor operating in the drive to improve the working lot of teachers, and the conflicts that emerge in the course of this drive, is to maintain the essential school functions and processes the way they have been.

Teachers have a very strong stake in keeping the system as it is (or perhaps as they remember it). So do administrators and so does the community. At the heart of the conflicts that have occurred in the collective bargaining process, then, seems to be the question of control. Who will control the system, not to change it, I reiterate, but to keep it from changing—to maintain it, possibly, in the way our youthful fantasies tell us it was?

One example may make the point with more clarity. In a school district with which I am familiar, the district and the union have recently declared an impasse in their bargaining over the issue of class size. The district wishes to remove the contract restriction on class size, for economic reasons, and the union is adamant on maintaining class size for educational reasons. The research on class size suggests little relationship between achievement and numbers of youngsters in a class. However, it would seem to be undeniably true that a class of 35 would be harder to manage than a class of 25. In short, to lift the restriction on class size would make the teachers' job harder, relative to management, and school life for the teacher would probably not be so peaceful.

I wish to make it clear that I am not antiunion. I believe that teachers should have every right to try and better the conditions under which they work. The point that is focal, however, is that as these conflicts continue, as they will, their long-range, unspoken goal will be to maintain the stability and relatively unchanging nature of the total system.

The aim of this chapter has been to scrutinize the schools as organizations in order to inquire why, considering the tremendous human and financial efforts to change the schools, they seem not to have changed in substantial ways. The theoretical position taken has been that schools as social systems have developed a character that generically moves them in the direction of resisting change, particularly that type of change which is more than slightly additive to current ways of operation and teaching. And this appears to be the case, as well, when change efforts have erupted into open conflict. Certainly all the variables have not been considered; for example, the way rigid time schedules (the tyranny of the schedule) affect the willingness and ability of school personnel to engage in training for change.

As I have tested out the ideas in this chapter with school people, they have met with an affirmative nod of the head. This confirmation is at the same time satisfying and depressing. It is satisfying because of the reinforcement for my ideas, depressing because of the magnitude and seeming intractability of the problem.

A final point is necessary. As I indicated at the start, there have, indeed, been schools that have changed radically and in an excitingly productive way. My hunch is that when this has happened it was a result of a particularly striking and unique person who was able to mobilize people to overcome the resistance that the system reflexively generates.

REFERENCES

Blumberg, A., & Schmuck, R. Barriers to organizational development training in the schools. *Educational Technology*, October 1972, pp. 30–34.

Horney, K. *Our inner conflicts*. New York: W. W. Norton, 1945.

Laing, R. D. *The divided self*. New York: Pantheon Books, 1969.

Likert, R. *The human organization*. New York: McGraw-Hill, 1967.

Sarason, S. *The culture of the school and the problem of change*. Boston: Allyn and Bacon, 1971.

Watzlawick, P., Weakland, J., & Fisch, R. *Change*. New York: W. W. Norton, 1974.

Weick, K. Educational organizations as loosely coupled systems. *Administrative Science Quarterly*, 1976, *12*(1), 1–19.

Woodward, J. *Management and technology*. London: Her Majesty's Stationery Office, 1958.

CHAPTER 3

Using Institutional Conflict to Achieve Change in Schools

MARK A. CHESLER
JAMES E. CROWFOOT
BUNYAN I. BRYANT, Jr.

THE TERMS *conflict* and *change* stimulate powerful emotions and images. These reactions are rooted in learned values and sanctions that lead many people to avoid conflict and to be cautions about change. We ask the readers of this chapter to focus on your own reactions to the ideas presented here and to be reflective about the intellectual and emotional roots of your reactions. It might be helpful to write down your reactions to our ideas, so that they will be available for further reflection.

THE RELEVANCE OF CONFLICT FOR CHANGE

School conflict is a reflection of the natural competition of groups in a pluralistic and heterogeneous society. In this society, rich and poor, white and black and brown, male and female, old and young, Republican and Democrat, manager and worker all compete unequally for their share of material and symbolic rewards. This natural contest may, at times, become rancorous or tubulent in ways that threaten the social fabric and cause personal pain for many or all citizens. When inequality between groups becomes great, and is not adjudicated for long periods, it may create social injustice. Under such circumstances, the potential for turbulance grows. Then powerful groups may try to suppress or destroy less powerful ones, or suppressed people may try to alleviate their condition forcefully. The outcome often is rancorous or escalated conflict that approaches a crisis.[1]

Political and economic structures that comprise the societal context for education place pressures on schools to do certain things and not others. In the process they legitimize prevailing societal patterns, including the privileges and oppressions that accompany widespread inequality. Some of the major societal conflicts that have an impact on U.S. schools involve the clashes between—

1. cultural values of equality and justice *and* historic patterns of inequality and injustice based on race, socioeconomic class, sex, and age. Current struggles attempting to alleviate and change oppressive school patterns and practices (such as desegregation, alternative schooling, finance reform) run up against entrenched elites seeking to maintain their positions.
2. citizen expectations of high school graduation as the gateway to meaningful work *and* current realities of high unemployment, alienating work, and a marked decrease in well-paying jobs entered with only a high school education.
3. historic patterns of local control of relatively accessible schools *and* current patterns of very large schools, organized in complex bureaucratic forms, increasingly influenced by complicated and remote state and federal policies.
4. historically stable patterns of public funding of schools *and* current realities of inflation slowed economic growth and demands for increased teacher salaries and additional school programs.
5. relatively limited expectations of schools (usually phrased as the 3 Rs) *and* demands that schools assist young people experiencing a variety of complicated and rapidly changing societal conditions.
6. traditional expectations of school staff as community servants (traditionally receiving less than average salaries because of altruistic commitment) dependent on community and elite good will, *and* current realities of teacher unionization and demands for economic equality, job security, and increased control over their conditions of work.
7. long-established patterns of child and youth roles without significant input or control in decisions affecting their lives *and* increased pressure by young people and their advocates in courts, communities, schools, and families for fairer treatment, access to critical information, and influence in decision making.
8. citizens and educators viewing education as a technical process involving value neutrality *and* other scholars and citizens viewing education as a political process involving value choices keyed to stability or change.

In each of these areas established patterns are disturbed by changing economic and political conditions, changing relationships between different groups in the society, and changing cultural values. Schools are inextricably involved in these changes since they are a microcosm of the larger society, an arena in which broader societal conflicts are played out. Because of the long period of required education for all citizens, and the deep emotional commitments adults have for the young, schools are at the very center of these shifts. Thus, they are subject to immense conflicts and multiple pressures.

But schools are not simply a passive and neutral stage upon which the drama of social conflict is acted. School organizations also carry within them internal conflicts, such as those—

1. among different groups in the school (teachers, administrators, service staff, and students) over the rights, authority, responsibilities, and rewards of each group.
2. between individuals who must work (teach or learn) together but whose values, expectations, and behaviors do not complement each other (usually because of racial, sexual, class, or other status differences).
3. among advocates of different educational philosophies and methods.
4. between creators (educational staff) and consumers (students and parents) of educational services, often exacerbated by the different racial and class backgrounds of these two groups.
5. between different national and local groups seeking to control schools, or to reallocate power to previously excluded groups.
6. among local alternatives for the implementation of public policies such as desegregation, mainstreaming, etc.

These internal sources of organizational conflict generally are connected to the external and societal conflicts identified earlier. For example, clashes between adults and young people in families and the community carry over into staff and student relationships within the school. Changing citizen expectations about what schools should be doing are intertwined in clashes among professionals over educational goals and methods. The changed community standing of teachers clearly affects the relationships between teachers and administrators within the school. And so on.

Conflict and School Change How are these societal and organizational conflicts related to school change? Virtually all the sources of school conflict listed involve multiple groups with differing desires to maintain and/or change established school practices. The conflicts themselves are signs of struggle over whether the status quo will be preserved or altered, and whether various groups' access to social resources will be reallocated. As such, these struggles indicate commitment and energy for change efforts. In some instances they identify individuals or groups of people who feel strongly about educational issues, while in others they identify issues that can be rallying points for the recruitment and mobilization of concerned peoples. They also identify issues and/or structures wherein the school system itself is vulnerable to change, places where uncertainty or struggle already exists. Thus, these conflicts are useful in identifying *constituencies,* *issues,* and *targets* that people can utilize to escalate an existing struggle or to take advantage of natural organizational contradictions or weaknesses.

What is meant by "change"? All of us have been involved at one time or another in trying to create or resist change, and there obviously are marked distinctions between different kinds of change. Among the important distinctions are those between—

1. alterations in existing programs, rules, structures, etc. that do not alter the rights, responsibilities, and rewards of all groups involved and leave relatively undisturbed basic features of the school; e.g., changing the date of the annual school picnic.
2. alterations in existing programs, rules, structures, etc. that leave most of the school undisturbed but add on new features that affect the rights, responsibilities, and rewards of a relatively small number of school members; e.g., adding an experimental classroom to an elementary building in order to utilize open education techniques.
3. alterations in existing programs, rules, structures, etc. that alter the rights, responsibilities, or rewards of a group or groups involved, but do not necessarily alter basic school features; e.g., ceasing to hire paraprofessionals to supervise children at lunch times and assigning these responsibilities to all teachers.
4. alteration in existing programs, rules, structures, etc. that alter the rights, responsibilities, or rewards of all groups, and that systematically restructures their power and roles; e.g., involvement of community members in sharing school decision making and teaching some classes.

The changes that are easiest to achieve are types 1 and 2. Generally, a consensus can be created so that many different groups will support such innovations and reforms. Changes which fit types 3 and 4 are more difficult to achieve and occur less frequently. They usually involve conflict, since some groups resist the program or role restructuring that alters their responsibilities and rewards, while other groups advocate just such restructuring. Planning, decision making, and implementing these changes generally requires the use of conflict to mobilize new resources and create the pressure for change.

THE PARTISANSHIP OF CHANGE EFFORTS

In the midst of a society and organizations engaged in struggles between various groups, all acts and programs are partisan in nature. When conflict is endemic, there is no real possibility of personal neutrality for anyone involved. All acts and programs result in some comparative advantage to one or another group. If these groups were not in conflict, not engaged in either an overt or covert struggle, then neutral acts certainly could occur. Moreover, we do not mean that all such partisanship is deliberate or intended. To the contrary, however, in a conflict situation even intended neutrality results in actual partisanship—not because of errors in the intellectual approach or behavior of the actor but because of the conflict and partisan structure of the situation.

In conflict situations it also is logically impossible for any one group to define and implement "the general welfare" or the common good. Group conflict creates a situation in which various groups, often unequal in status and power, contend for common resources. In order to justify their cause, each group usually defends its position as being not only in its own interest, but in the interest of others as well. The latter approach is inconsistent with the concept of group struggle: no group can be considered to "stand above" the battle, and to be able to moderate the general welfare without permission and agreement from others. To do so would mean they would have to be *apart* from the system in contest, not *a part* of it.

High-power groups, and especially organizational managers, often use a language and style that suggests neutrality and nonpartisanship; that they have no special interests of their own to pursue; and that they wish to and can seek the general welfare. The use of such language is designed to capture the loyalty of various groups who trust the fair-mindedness of established authority. Thus, it sometimes is difficult to see their bias and partisanship. But management usually is quite concerned with maintaining their control, their view of the organization's place in its environment, and the general public's image of orderly social life. After all, most managers are members of partisan groups: (1) Members of management classes, in educational as well as industrial organizations, generally are adult, white, relatively affluent, and male. They have the moderate to high levels of power and cultural privilege normally accompanying those statuses in the general social order. (2) They are located in organizational positions where they have legitimate authority to define clients needs, client performance, and indeed, the general welfare of a total school organization.

Generally, it is easy to see the ways in which low-power groups pursue their interests with obvious bias and with a concern for their special welfare. They use a language and style that emphasizes partisanship in order to capture the attention and loyalty of others with similar group interests.

Moreover, educational consumers and advocates of low-power groups may have very different orientations to conflict. Rather than trying to maintain order and managerial control, they may seek to utilize disorder, and perhaps escalate conflict, in order to achieve their change goals. By refusing to participate in conventional forms of problem solving, low-power groups make their issues known. Through public (and often noisy) challenges to established authorities low-power groups appeal to their broader constituency. New organizational forms often develop out of these conflicts and crises; hopefully new forms can address problems of inequality and injustice more effectively than do prior procedures.

STRATEGIES FOR CHANGE

Consensus Strategies The attempt to "manage" conflict so as to maintain orderly organizational operations represents the use of a consensus strategy to accomplish change. Here the stress is upon collaborative and cooperative relations between educational authorities, other school members, and parents and students. This strategy assumes people can work together once they identify common problems, and that on the basis of trust, mutual interests will be discovered and met. According to this approach, parents are willing to follow the lead of professional educators, and educators are committed to parents' goals and values regarding quality education. It assumes professional educators and citizens or community groups can and will work together effectively, and that one will not seek to "rip off" or maintain advantage over the other. Different racial and social class groups can overcome the distance and isolation that has been their heritage through a variety of contacts with one another in the school and community.[2]

One major activity consistent with the consensus approach involves the establishment and operation of heterogeneous problem-solving teams. This may include—

• recruiting representations from all segments of the community
• informing the school staff of the need for such teams and soliciting help from them

- holding meetings to prepare/train people of different statuses and groups to work together
- creating a sense of trust among all these people
- developing a list of commonly agreed-on school problems
- reaching agreement on reasonable solutions to these problems

An appeal to managers' values of social justice and educational quality may help change educators' attitudes and practices and represents another consensus approach to changing organizational policies and programs. Such appeals can be facilitated in various ways, but they all require reducing managers' fears of conflict and change, providing ongoing support for new behaviors and programs, and identifying new administrative and educational practices. Specific tactics may include—

- helping demonstrate to managers their own involvement in networks of social conflict
- aiding managers to develop new analyses of how their own tenure is related to the need for change
- identifying new social practices that may close the gap between the "is" and the "ought"
- retraining managers for more democratic or humane instructional technologies—learning new ways to teach and administer
- conducting attitude change programs that seek to resocialize all people
- reducing adults' fears of youth explosiveness
- helping managers examine themselves and conflict situations so as to reduce their realistic fears—"hand holding"
- identifying the "good guys" and giving them lots of stroking and support for their own difficult work

Conflict Strategies Conflict-based strategies of school change often attempt to use, and perhaps escalate, conflict as a means of advocating overlooked interests. The basic process utilized to make changes involves confrontation, pressure, and negotiations or bargaining to influence authorities' responses. When low-power groups and authorities have fairly equal power, they can all make decisions that protect and compromise their own and each others' needs. Without such power parity, authorities do not have to take account of, and respond to, others' agendas.[3]

As oppressed peoples and groups try to change schools, they have attempted some of the following tactics to gathering and appealing to their constituencies.

- identifying inequities or failures in the delivery of services to school clients (or to specific racial, class, and sex-role groups of clients)
- demythologizing the allegedly altruistic and expert bases of school management
- organizing interest groups based on peoples' subjective awareness of alienation and oppression
- specifying and testing coalitions of cross-race, cross-class, cross-sex alignments
- linking student-parent coalitions in ways that prevent educators from forming adult coalitions that exclude youth

Once a group is organized, it is important to consider ways of acting for change. Since the conflict strategy assumes managerial groups will try to retain their power, and thus their privileged share of societal resources and rewards, threats or challenges to the maintenance of such power and privilege are used to persuade them to alter their practices. Specific tactics may include:

- publicizing (gathering and exposing) managers' attitudes and actions, powers and privileges—including those of community groups who control school boards as well as administrators and/or teachers
- publicizing information and interpretations that contradict myths school systems generate about their performance, resources, etc.
- finding out about differences or divisions within powerful groups and trying to "divide and conquer."
- developing programs that challenge the non-school-related activities of managers
- confronting managers' abilities to govern schools through demonstrations, crises, legal action, walkouts, myths, or threats of such activities, etc.
- developing new ways of recruiting administrators and teachers that bypass traditional roles and socialization experiences—and that thereby flood the system with minorities, women, poor people, working class people, and the young

The attempts to mobilize a constituency and challenge authority obviously are complementary components of a conflict approach. Only when a broad and solid constituency (or set of coalitions) is ready to act can the challenge to managers be more than rhetoric; then the threat is backed by strategic power.

Criteria for Deciding between Consensus or Conflict Strategies
Since both consensus and conflict strategies have been successful in different situations, how does one decide which to use?

There is no easy answer. One criterion is the amount of prior cooperation between schools and local community groups. If school personnel
and parents have good working relations, consensus strategies may
work well. But when the school system is derelict and uncooperative,
or when school and community groups are divided on basic issues, the
conflict strategy may be more appropriate.

The following list of advantages and drawbacks of the conflict and

CONFLICT STRATEGY

Advantages

Counter perceived lack of official interest or responsiveness to grievances
Encourage or force an opponent to
negotiate or meet with you
Resolve problems in a win-lose situation, i.e., when both sides cannot be
satisfied by the final disposition
Equalize the power relationship if
you're the weaker party
Obtain or speed up action that has
been delayed
Deal with institutions or agencies with
sharply divergent viewpoints and
interests.

Drawbacks

Conflict can escalate and
produce a strong reac-
tion or backlash that can
deter change.
Outside organizers some-
times enter a communi-
ty and manipulate ag-
grieved persons into
using conflict strategies
that are designed more
to promote external
"movement" goals than
to resolve a community
problem.

CONSENSUS STRATEGY

Advantages

Establish cooperative context for action
Achieve broad community support
Resolve differences among individuals or groups of approximately
equal power and shared values
Resolve issues when compromise is
possible or when all parties can
come out ahead as a result of a decision
Bring hostility out into the open to be
examined, discussed, and alleviated

Drawbacks

Achieving consensus can
be a slow and drawn-out
process, during which
participants and the pub-
lic may lose interest.
Compromise may not solve
the problem.

consensus strategies helps define the conditions under which either approach might be most helpful.[4]

Coser (1956), Himes (1966), Dodson (1960), and others also stress several positive effects the recognition and strategic use of conflict may have on an organization. For instance, it may (1) force the clarification of different needs and goals; (2) generate new ideas about solutions to problems; (3) provide an opportunity for reintegration and a flowing together of previously disparate parties in new and more meaningful relations; (4) establish better communication; and (5) mobilize extra resources for change and organizational renewal.

At the same time, this strategy clearly has potent drawbacks, especially involving hardening the resistance of senior school administrators and staffs. Many sympathetic educators may feel defensive and threatened by challenges, and then overreact to the pressures of a crisis—even if it is nonviolent. For example, some educational leaders have responded to escalated conflict and crisis in particularly ineffective and dysfunctional ways, some of which further escalate a tense situation. Among the common responses of this sort are (1) ignoring or denying protests as accidental or meaningless events not connected with real school problems; (2) cooling off by sitting quietly and listening or talking at length with individual student or community leaders; (3) labeling or defaming protesters as troublemakers, pathologically inclined, or disruptive; and (4) controlling or suppressing challenges with inappropriate educational or civil coercion.

Managerial efforts to ignore or cool-off conflicts are reflections of the consensus approach to organizational decision making and change. They suggest the need to maintain an appearance of internal consensus, partly by noting that alternative statements of school problems are somehow unreal or irrelevant. When problems are so overwhelming that they cannot be denied, it is assumed they can be talked through to a satisfactory conclusion. Such conversations sometimes decrease false rumors; sometimes they lend visibility and legitimacy to student or community concerns. For this response to be effective, however, talk must be followed with action; otherwise it will lead to reescalation.

Managerial efforts to label or suppress challenges more nearly reflect adoption of a conflict mode. Here management is attempting to use its own power to resist change and overwhelm its opposition, either directly or indirectly. This is quite different from consensus-based dialogues, problem-solving efforts, or organizational change programs. But all too often managers utilizing aspects of a conflict strategy represent themselves as the only legitimate party; thus, they deny certain assumptions of the conflict approach that would grant legitimacy to both (or all) parties to the conflict.

Educational managers who do recognize the legitimacy of change efforts and appreciate conflicting educational values and goals have some different options in responding to pressure and conflict. They can pursue social or educational justice by attempting to redress racism, sexism, class elitism, and ageism. Such action might free educators from the psychological and physical burdens of carrying out constraining rules and regulations, corporal punishments, and humiliations of various sorts; it might well relieve them of their own sense of resignation and defense against attack. Tactics consistent with the conflict approach and with change goals of this sort might include:

- Aiding the empowerment of oppressed groups
- Publicly legitimating oppressed groups' agendas with statements of agreement and offers of negotiated settlements
- Aiding dominant groups to understand and analyze the monoculturalism and oppression they maintain and the costs to all people involved.
- Acting unilaterally to reduce social oppression or injustice in schools
- Organizing other managers or elite members to support these priorities

School managers pursuing social justice objectives also must be part of a coalition with other school and community groups sharing these goals. Unless oppressed groups play major roles in determining and supporting change goals and strategies, community support is not likely to occur. And both school and community groups have vital resources to contribute to the fight against injustice in schools. Without the pressures and resources brought by a larger movement, efforts to change schools generally cannot be maintained by themselves. Managerial participation in such coalitions requires their sharing skills in ways that are accountable to community groups and their concerns.

School managers working for change also will require support from like-minded peers and colleagues in schools. Selected colleagues can support new behaviors, provide emotional sustenance in the face of uncertainty, procure needed resources not typically available to a single manager, and protect innovative managers who become the objects of resistance and perhaps repression by established centers of power. Such support groups require overcoming the typical isolation of school leaders, and combatting individual competition, attempts to remain invulnerable, and other established administrative patterns.

ISSUES FOR CONSULTANTS ACTIVE IN SCHOOL CHANGE[5]

Many school change efforts involve not only educational managers and consumers but outside consultants as well. These consultants frequently are relied on to provide diagnosis, recommend change strategies and tactics (such as those discussed above), and perhaps even devise new programs. Often they present themselves, and/or are perceived by others, as "the experts" on school change. In such contexts consultants' roles are quite powerful: thus it is important for consultants to examine carefully their assumptions and roles in school change, and for users of their services to be prepared to be critical of consultant actions and consequences. Some of the key choices consultants make (or are made for them) as they act for school change can be categorized as alternative goals, constituencies, roles, and socialization experiences.

Goals The first decision an educational consultant makes concerns the application of her or his values and goals around social stability and social change, social oppression, and social justice. The attempt to be goal-less, or to accept the system's values as one's own, is in itself a partisan goal statement. In our view, the policies and operating procedures of schools systematically support societal racism, sexism, class elitism, and adult oppression of the young.[6] Not all educators working in these systems personally champion these values, but current organizational procedures and priorities nevertheless lead to such outcomes. The consultant has a choice of whether to serve such priorities or to work in ways that challenge, subvert, or otherwise alter these goals in the direction of social justice.

Closely related to end-goals of change are the various means or approaches to change favored by various consultants. Here the consensus-conflict dichotomy or continuum is relevant again, and even unconscious ideological and/or strategic preferences must be clarified. As noted in our earlier discussion of these approaches, it appears to us that most professional consultants implicitly or explicitly lean toward a consensus approach. Some of the reason for this tendency are highlighted in the following discussions.

Constituencies In addition to the problem of goals or values, action in multiparty conflicts requires resolution of the problem of which constituency(ies) a consultant is serving. Every group pursuing its interests, or which feels its interests threatened, initiates partisan action to change or maintain the social structure so those interests are met. Leadership of every government agency, corporation, and school system fights for its definition of unique and systemic interests, and sometimes it hires consultants to help achieve these ends. Consultation with management groups is a partisan activity in support of an established order and the elements of that order that control a particular organization. Even if the managerial group advocates change, it is likely to be a certain kind of change—one the established hierarchy feels it can accept.

We know of educational consultants in various school crises who served principals and administrative officers, board members, teachers and teacher groups, student groups, the white community, the black community, the Hispanic community, the poor community, community elites, etc. Each of these choices generally involved different definitions of educational goals and value priorities and different notions of just and orderly processes in schools. In each case the consultant had to settle some problems of his or her own credibility in entering into a durable and trusting working relationship. In some cases the consultant concerned with serving a particular group had to help develop that constituency. The recruitment and mobilization of a latent or quasi-group into an organized interest group often was an essential precondition for making effective partisan and value-laden use of knowledge and expertise.

Roles and Styles   One very useful set of distinctions among consultant roles in conflict situations has been presented by Cormick and Laue (forthcoming). The central alternatives they present include: activists, advocates, and mediators.[7] Activists are members of oppressed/powerless or powerful/elite groups and usually are involved in direct organizing efforts. Advocates are not members, but are outside advisers to such groups. They may be funded by governmental or foundation agencies or by local fund-raising efforts; they are accountable either to the elite group or the oppressed group—whichever they are advocating for. Mediators (Cormick and Laue's favorite) are independent of all parties to a dispute, but they are considered as acceptable and helpful by all of them. Cormick and Laue stress that even the independent mediator is not really impartial or neutral; she or he should advocate mutual empowerment of all parties—a key element in their conceptualization of social justice.

Consultants or change agents may play these roles in the service of varied values and constituents. *Activist* members of elite groups may work in ways that consolidate elite power and control of the local schools' structure and culture. On the other hand, activist members of community groups may work to elect new school boards, introduce new curricula, gain parent control of hiring policies, or establish new schooling patterns inside and outside of the traditional school. *Advocates* of elite groups may help them improve organizational procedures, sanitize and humanize control practices, increase their information about community hot spots, raise their skill level, lower their fear or rage levels, etc. Advocates of low-power groups may help students organize to contest grading policies, minorities to generate alternative curricula on race and ethnicity, poor people to include work-study programs for early employment or placement, etc. *Mediators* may be prepared to work with various groups at the point of community contest or crisis. Prior to an actual crisis, they may help generate patterns of mutual empowerment (or its correlates, vulnerability and accountability), and thus may work actually as advocates of previously low-power groups.

Social Background and Socialization   One reality that helps determine the range of possible consultant roles is that the overwhelming majority of the profession of change agents is white, male, affluent—at present although not necessarily at birth, adult, and heterosexual. Obviously this means they generally cannot operate as activist members of oppressed groups, although they often can work as members of elite groups. The profession also may be ill-prepared to act as advocates for blacks, Chicanos, first Americans, and other racial minority groups; it also may be ill-prepared to be helpful advocates of women's agendas, of issues for lower class people, and of gay people. Above all, it may be ill-prepared to share and advocate the agendas of young people. In all these areas the profession as a whole is not categorically and inevitably unable to act as positive advocates, but ill-prepared as a function of demographic background, socialization experiences, and current status.

Although race and sex clearly are immutable, some class mobility does exist in the society, and some consultants committed to social justice goals have renounced their affluence by taking vows of poverty and working as activists for subsistence wages. Others have found it possible or necessary to develop new forms of white or male/affluent consciousness that are less exploitative than previous commitments and styles. It is probably impossible for whites to realize an antiracist identity in full (or males a completely antisexist identity, etc.), but one may be resocialized to *relatively* nonexploitative modes of advocacy or mediation in social justice movements with and on behalf of Third World groups, poor people, and women.

Resocialization is time consuming, painful as well as joyful and not always successful. Is the risk worth it? What kind of retraining is needed? Who should conduct this retraining? Any such changes in personal attitudes or behavior would be facilitated greatly by new role structures that provided low-power consumers greater control of consultants' actions.

SCHOOL CHANGE AND THE CONFLICT APPROACH: ACTION AND RESEARCH

Large-scale movements for educational change, such as desegregation, community control, and students' rights, have occurred, and conflict approaches have been central in these movements and related projects. Even so, no major revolution has occurred: Whether meaningful change in educational quality will follow physical desegregation is an open question; the community control movement has shifted to localized efforts without widespread impact on the prerogatives of educational professionals; and the power and roles of students in our schools have not changed much.[8] But there also is evidence that conflict strategies have created a small number of significantly changed schools, many occurring without corollary changes in larger systems. Moreover, these changes often have been temporary, and traditional procedures have reasserted themselves. But given the basically stable context of American society, we should not expect major changes in elementary and secondary schools throughout the country.

Many local groups have had to spend too much time getting their own act together to be able to make a major difference in local schools. Developing a highly committed action group out of a large mass of people with objectively common interests is no easy task. It involves overcoming inertia, hopelessness, and critical lacks of information. It also requires substantial skill and organizing energy, as well as highly visible and attractive issues. As a result, conflict-oriented groups often have relied on single-issue campaigns rather than on multi-issue organizations and coalitions for sustained pressure on schools. In the same vein, there usually are insufficient resources available to low-power groups, which are the most likely to use conflict strategies. Sometimes this is a direct consequence of a lack of skills and effective organization, but in other cases it has resulted from federal funding priorities as well as carefully planned managerial resistance.

Influence of Mass Media All groups concerned about social change have critical needs for information—both in order to inform and guide their own decisions and to shape broader public support for their efforts. One major source of information about schools and school change is the mass media. But managers of the media and other myth-making institutions have vested interests in gathering and interpreting data in particular ways. Often these predispositions are based on consensus assumptions and are not compatible with the needs of people learning to use conflict strategies. For instance, users of conflict strategies need to know the biases of educational and civic leaders and the details of their strategies for maintaining control of economic, political, and educational institutions. In particular, they need to understand the plans and actions by which elites resist the initiatives and efforts of newly organized groups of citizens. The mass media typically are owned by or dependent on local elites and usually present a selective picture of elite goals, methods, and interactions with challenging groups. Often the media do not interpret the actions of groups using conflict strategies as being legitimate responses, but construe these events in ways that portray these groups as dangerous, irrational, irresponsible, self-serving, misinformed, etc. Or, they may simply ignore the events in which such groups are involved. These responses discourage more people from learning how and when to use conflict strategies.

Role of Social Scientists

Social scientists sometimes play a similar role, especially if the funds for creating and studying changes only are available through collaboration with educational managers. One of the many examples of this pattern is that desegregation assistance centers cannot enter a school system unless invited by superintendents and/or school board officers. The dominant functionalist paradigm underlying much of social system analysis, and the prevailing methods of inquiry, systematically downplay the use and payoffs of conflict in social system change. Thus, social scientists have been a limited resource for learning about conflict strategies of planned social change.[9]

Much of the social scientific and related journalistic efforts to assess school change have searched for significant new student outcomes as the measure of success. The data have been large samples using measurable shifts of student achievement as indicators of change. The use of such indicators may mask other important payoffs that are more likely to be found in purposefully selected cases where the data gathered include extensive efforts to document and understand the feelings, experiences, understanding, and new attitudes and skills acquired by participants. For instance, many groups active in the struggle for fundamental school change have reported an increased sense of their power and skill and a greater understanding of school change processes. Protesting groups have discovered new coalitions and developed increased capability in exchanging information and other resources. In other instances the gains made from struggle are reflected in court-ordered desegregation and its effective implementation; in adult defense of student rights; and in improved recognition of the major role blacks and other minorities have played in American history. These are all important payoffs, and the intentional use of conflict strategies has helped accomplish them.

The investigation of special cases calls for multiple inquiry techniques, including observational methods and extensive interviewing of individuals and parties involved in the change effort. The course of such examination also requires critical analysis of the assumptions of investigators, and the ways their own socioeconomic, racial, and sex backgrounds interact with the change processes being investigated. These investigations will also require agreements between researchers and change practitioners who pay more attention to the impact of research interventions—researcher assistance to change projects—than to the needs for consumer input and influence over final research interpretations and dissemination of research findings. The sheer cost of change work, and particularly work utilizing conflict strategies, makes it essential that some research tasks be done by volunteers—people other than professional social scientists. Research tactics then must be modified to take advantage of the strengths of lay researchers, as well as the limitations on their time and energy and skill.

Need to Create and Share Information As a result of these contradictions and dilemmas in the roles and methods of consultants and social scientists, people developing conflict-oriented change strategies will have to create and share relevant information on their own. They need to expand current information networks, increase discriminating analyses about who can be served best by alternative change strategies, and become more active in challenging misconceptions and partial information about conflict strategies of school and community change. Otherwise, they will continue to be locked into consensus-oriented approaches to school reform and restructuring. The media, consultants, and the scientific community all have helped emphasize the consensus approach to such a degree that it often appears as the only viable and legitimate option. While we have no inherent objection to this approach, it is clear it is a limited option, and an option that works only under certain prescribed circumstances. Under other circumstances, low-power groups in particular must know about, be able to use, and find help in implementing other strategies of school change.

NOTES

1. We distinguish conflict from rancorous conflict or crisis to clarify the difference between a natural and endemic state of social system conflict and the result of continued injustice, oppression, and more or less self-conscious responses to it that appear to threaten the social order (rancorous conflict or crisis).
2. A variety of scholars and practitioners have operated on these assumptions in planning and implementing educational change. Popular labels include most organizational development efforts, human relations' training, group problem solving, management awareness, system "4," etc. Significant writers of research and praxis efforts include: Buchanan (1964), Benne, Bradford, Gibb, and Lippitt (1975), Havelock (1969), Rogers and Shoemaker (1971), Rubin (1971), and Schmuck and Miles (1971).
3. Several educational scholars and practitioners have operated on these assumptions in change efforts known as community mobilization, citizen control, student protest, multiparty bargaining, power-coercive, etc. Significant writers of research and praxis efforts include: Alinsky (1971), Fantini, Gittel, & Magat (1970), Lurie (1970), Postman & Weingartner (1969), and Schaller & Chesler (1977).
4. Taken from American Association of University Women (1972). Other articles that compare these strategies and their advantages in various situations include Baldridge (1972), Chin & Benne (1975), Chesler, Crowfoot, & Bryant (forthcoming), Paulston (1976), and Warren & Hyman (1966).
5. Since consultants, potential consultants, and users of consultants constitute a major audience of this book, the topic assumes critical importance.
6. Several critical analyses of schools which support this perspective are available in recent scholarly literature. Among the most provacative are Carnoy (1974), Gintis (1970), Frazier & Sadker (1973) Hamilton (1968), Rowntree & Rowntree (1968), Sedlacek & Brooks (1973), and Spring (1972). Many other analyses, of varying academic tone and quality, make the same point. To be sure, many other scholars disagree with this analysis: although they acknowledge problems do exist and changes are needed, their general findings and interpretations are substantially less critical of the entire educational institution.
7. They also suggest roles for researchers and enforcers, but these are not of critical import to us here.
8. Of course, several reports describing or evaluating school change efforts proceeding from a consensus approach also conclude that little long-lasting change appears to have occurred (Gross, Giacquinta, & Bernstein, 1971; Levin, 1974; Miles, 1961; and Sarason, 1971).
9. Some of our own experiments with federally funded school change projects were excluded by a prestigious social scientific research institute because the projects involved interventions serving students and parents directly and conflict relations with educational managers. These projects also called for greater balance between action and research and greater researcher involvement in action than is the traditional scientific pattern.

REFERENCES

American Association of University Women. *Tool catalogue: techniques and strategies for successful action programs*. Washington, D.C.: Author, 1972.

Alinsky, S. *Rules for radicals*. New York: Vintage, 1971.

Buchanan, P. *The concept of organizational development, or self-renewal, as a form of planned change*. New York: Applied Behavioral Science Research in Industry, Monograph #23, 1964.

Baldridge, V. Organizational change: the human relations vs. the political systems perspective. *Educational Researcher*, 1972, 4–10.

Benne, K., Bradford, L., Gibb, J., & Lippitt, R. (Eds.). *The laboratory method of changing and learning: theory and application*. Palo Alto, Calif.: Science and Behavior Books, 1975.

Carnoy, M. *Education as cultural imperialism*. New York: David McKay, 1974.

Chesler, M. Crowfoot, J., & Bryant, B. *Institutional contexts of school desegregation: alternative paradigms for research and action*. (forthcoming.)

Chin, R., & Benne, K. General strategies for affecting change in human systems. In W. Bennis, K. Benne, & R. Chin (Eds.). *The planning of change*. New York: Wiley, 1961.

Cormick, G., & Laue, J. The ethics of intervention in community disputes. In H. Kelman, D. Warwick, & G. Bermant (Eds.). *The ethics of social intervention*. (forthcoming)

Coser, L. *The functions of social conflict*. Glencoe, N.Y.: Free Press, 1956.

Dodson, D. The creative role of conflict re-examined. *Journal of Intergroup Relations*, 1960, *1*, 5–12.

Fantini, M., Gittel, M., & Magat, R. *Community control and urban schools*. New York: Praeger, 1970.

Frazier, N., & Sadker, M. *Sexism in school and society*. New York: Harper & Row, 1973.

Gintis, H. New working class and revolutionary youth. *Socialist Revolution*, 1970, *1*, 13–44.

Gross, N., Giacquinta, J., & Bernstein, M. *Implementing organizational innovations: a sociological analysis of planned organizational change*. New York: Basic Books, 1971.

Hamilton, C. Race and education: a search for legitimacy. *Harvard Educational Review*, 1968, *38*, 669–684.

Havelock, R. *Planning for innovation*. Ann Arbor: Mich.: Institute for Social Research, 1969.

Himes, J. The functions of racial conflict. *Social Forces*, 1966, *45*, 1–10.

Levin, H. Educational reform and social change. *Journal of Applied Behavioral Sciences*, 1974, *10*, 304–321.

Lurie, E. *How to change the schools*. New York: Vintage, 1970.

Miles, M. B. (Ed.). *Innovation in education*. New York: Teachers College Press, 1964.

Paulston, R. *Conflicting theories of educational and social change: a typological review*. University of Pittsburgh, Center for International Educational Studies, 1976.

Postman, N., & Weingartner, C. *Teaching as a Subversive Activity*. New York: Delacorte, 1969.

Rogers, E., & Shoemaker, F. *The communication of innovations*. New York: Free Press, 1971.

Rowntree, J., & Rowntree, M. The political economy of youth. *Our Generation*, 1968, *6*, 1–36.

Rubin, L. *Improving in-service education*. Boston: Allyn & Bacon, 1971.

Sarason, S. *The culture of the school and the problem of change*. Boston: Allyn & Bacon, 1971.

Schaller, J., & Chesler, M. *Students and youth organizing*. Ann Arbor, Mich.: Youth Liberation Press, 1977.

Schmuck, R., & Miles, M. (Eds.). *Organizational development in schools*. Palo Alto, Calif.: New Press Books, 1971.

Sedlacek, W., & Brooks, G. Racism and research: using data to initiate change. *Personnel and Guidance Journal*, 1973, *52*, 184–188.

Spring, J. *Education and the rise of the corporate state*. Boston: Beacon Press, 1972.

Warren, R., & Hyman, H. Purposive community change in consensus and dissensus situations. *Community Mental Health Journal*, 1966, *2*, 293–300.

PART TWO

Change: Impact and Approaches

AN OFTEN-QUOTED STUDY by Mort and Cornell (1941) about the 1930s concluded that once an innovation was developed it took about fifteen years before *3 percent* of our nation's schools would implement it. Further, assuming that the innovation worked it might take up to fifty years from initial introduction before it would be widely implemented.

By the mid-1960s Miles (1964) concluded that the process of diffusion was being speeded up significantly. His review of studies of innovations in the 1950s and early 1960s found that such innovations as programmed instruction, language laboratories, teacher aides, team teaching, and modifications in various curricular areas were being adapted by approximately *10 to 20 percent* of the country's school districts within fifteen years of their development.

If anything, the impetus for change has increased even more rapidly since the mid-1960s. The federal government has stepped up its involvement in the change arena with a broad application of categorical grants in areas such as compensatory education and mainstreaming. In piggyback fashion many states have employed these grant programs to urge school districts to implement innovations that have been concocted at the state level. Some states have instituted categorical programs of their own; for example, in the area of reading enrichment. Population shifts toward suburbanization have also led to a variety of grass roots innovations, both in affluent suburbs that expect "more" in the way of education for their young and in relatively poor urban districts that must meet the needs of a changing student population. More widespread sophisticated use of our media system has created a multiplier effect, making innovations that are attempted in one place known to other places quite rapidly.

In short, this has been a most hectic era in the life of America's schools. We have heated up the system to the point that it is now more susceptible to change than ever before. While there may be some doubt about the impact of these changes, there is little question that schools and school districts are increasingly participating in change programs of one sort or another.

How well have we performed in this challenging time? Have schools found means of institutionalizing innovations? Have we developed strategies that support school leaders in their efforts? Do we know how well change programs are proceeding?

This part begins with contributions that summarize two massive studies that have attempted to establish the impact of this flurry of activity. The first, by the Rand Corporation (Greenwood, Mann, and McLaughlin, 1975), reviews the outcomes of the federal government's efforts to change schools. Miles, Fullan, and Taylor (1978) zero in specifically on a major change strategy, organization development, and its applications in the schools.

Berman and McLaughlin report findings from the Rand studies. Their overall conclusion is that there is not much evidence that most change programs have been effective, and that even where such programs are initially implemented, there is relatively little continuation. However, they do find that there are variations on the theme and that these variations have much to do with responsiveness at the local level. For example, it makes a great deal of difference if the central office and the principal involved are supportive of the change effort. Similarly, it matters whether teachers feel challenged by the change program and are actively involved rather than treated as passive receptors. In other words, there are elements that do seem to make a difference and that these elements, if taken into consideration by would-be change agents, can significantly improve the chances of effective introduction and implementation of innovations.

Miles and Fullan next report findings from their extensive survey of school districts that have attempted one or more organization development projects (they even provide an excellent definition of OD). Admittedly their data are skewed because they talked only with those who valued this approach sufficiently to put in the time and energy required. Still, the outcomes of the study are relevant. They conclude that districts attempting such projects are fairly satisfied with the results, but that institutionalization of outcomes requires continued energy, resources, and an awareness that it will require about five years to to significantly affect a school's potential to be "self-renewing." They found that about 1 percent of the school districts across the country are presently involved in such efforts. This is far less than a critical mass, so it is unlikely that OD will be widely diffused in the very near future. In addition, they fear misrepresentation of OD, and the schools' desire for quick and easy solutions will make it difficult at best for OD to fulfill its promise.

Because OD as a change approach is being widely debated, this part of the book will explore several major approaches to it. Arends, Schmuck, and Arends, on the basis of extensive experience in the development of OD strategies at the University of Oregon, propose transferring these learnings to projects that focus on students. They argue that students can be a vital force in school improvement and that OD stategies can well be applied to include this disenfranchised group in the governance of schools. In their view students can easily "become alienated when their ideas and energies have not been used." Their contribution includes a review of concepts from social psychology that help us to understand the potential for students' participation in school governance; a summary of their own efforts to involve students through OD approaches; and the difficulties we will probably encounter and some directions that we must pursue if we want to increase involvement of students.

Bassin and Gross describe a major OD effort that has involved self-renewal at various levels—administrative cabinets, departments, students, and school-wide—in a number of New York City schools. One can hardly imagine a more difficult place to attempt substantial changes than in the inner-city schools of New York. Yet Basin and Gross have devised a six-stage process of self-renewal (entry, diagnosis, planning, implementation, evaluation, and maintenance) that appears to have an impact on these school settings. They conclude their description with an estimation of outcomes, constraints, and factors that seem to be vital if this complex change approach is to be effective. Their conclusions are supportive of the findings presented by Berman and McLaughlin.

The final contribution to this part, by Schwartz, focuses in on an area of growing interest for both researchers and practitioners; i.e., Can we produce accurate evaluations of change programs? She sees accurate evaluations as a means "of satisfying cries for accountability of resources—time, money, and effort." She surveys the field of planned change and, organizing the presentation around the stages of change, explores the difficulties involved for both the change agent and the evaluator of such programs. Not only are change efforts moving targets, but the needs of change agents and evaluators are sometimes in conflict. They often even serve different masters. For example, the change agent may be engaged by those actually involved in the change at the local setting while the evaluator may be supported through funds that are supplied externally. In this light, change agents often work under conditions of confidentiality while evaluators require access to sensitive information and may even need to use such information as feedback for resource providers. Often evaluators can end up as the outsiders, viewed by change agents and those who are to be changed as an impediment; they are interested in the process and the evaluators are interested in measurement. With such different purposes they may well end up in conflict. Schwartz concludes the chapter with several suggestions for reducing the gap and improving chances for accurate evaluations. It is probable that meaningful evaluations will become central features of change programs, so her suggestions should be relevant.

REFERENCES

Greenwood, P. W., Mann, D., & McLaughlin, M. W. *Federal programs supporting educational change*. Vol. III: *The process of change* (R-1589/3–HEW). Santa Monica, Calif.: Rand Corp., April 1975.

Miles, M. B., (Ed.). *Innovation in education*. New York: Teachers College Press, 1964.

Miles, M. B., (Ed.). *Innovation in education*. New York: Teachers College Washington, D.C.: National Institute of Education (Contract 400–77–0051,0052), 1978.

Mort, P. R., & Cornell, F. G. *American schools in transition*. New York: Bureau of Publications, Teachers College, Columbia University, 1941.

CHAPTER 4

Factors Affecting the Process of Change

PAUL BERMAN
MILBREY WALLIN McLAUGHLIN

FEDERAL FINANCIAL AID now makes up an important fraction of many local school district budgets, but its effectiveness in improving local educational practices is uncertain. Federally sponsored evaluations reveal inconsistent and generally disappointing results, and, despite considerable innovative activity on the part of local school districts, the evidence suggests that:

- No class of existing educational treatments has been found that consistently leads to improved student outcomes (when variations in the institutional setting and nonschool factors are taken into account).
- "Successful" projects have difficulty sustaining their success over a number of years.
- "Successful" projects are not disseminated automatically or easily, and their "replication" in new sites usually falls short of their performance in the original sites.

Consequently, although federal support for local school services has become well established, the "decade of reform" that began with the 1965 Elementary and Secondary Education Act (ESEA) has not fulfilled its expectations, and questions continue to be raised about what might be the most appropriate and effective federal role in improving the public schools.

We believe that these questions can only be answered by research that looks closely at how the process of change works in classrooms, schools, and districts. We were able to conduct such research under a contract awarded to the Rand Corporation to study a national sample of educational innovations funded by four federal programs: ESEA Title III; ESEA Title VII; Right-to-Read; Vocational Education Act, 1968 Amendments, Part D. Through interviews and observations in almost three hundred local change agent projects, the study described how the process of innovation works in its local setting, and identified factors that affect the innovative process and its outcomes.*

In particular, we measured several different project outcomes (successful implementation, teacher change, improved student performance, and continuation of project methods and materials) and examined the relationship between these outcomes and federal policies, project characteristics, and institutional setting. This chapter discusses how much each factor influenced what happened to local innovations.

FEDERAL POLICIES

Our overall findings here can be stated simply. Federal change agent policies had a major effect in stimulating local educational agencies (LEAs) to undertake projects that were generally consistent with federal categorical guidelines. This local response resulted from the availability of federal funds and, in some programs, from guidelines that encouraged specific educational practices. But the adoption of projects did not insure successful implementation; moreover, successful implementation did not guarantee long-run continuation. Neither those policies unique to each federal program nor those policies common to them strongly influenced the fate of adopted innovations. In sum, the net return to the federal investment was the adoption of many innovations, the successful implementation of few, and the long-run continuation of still fewer (with the exception of the special case of bilingual projects, where federal and state funding continues to be available).

PROJECT CHARACTERISTICS

The initiation of an innovation produces an adopted project, consisting of a series of decisions about what is to be done and how to do it that together define the characteristics of the project. We find it convenient to divide these characteristics into the project's educational methods (also called the treatment or educational technology), resources, scope of proposed change, and implementation strategies.

*The findings from the Rand study are reported in eight volumes under the general title, *Federal programs supporting educational change*. This chapter draws on Vol. III: *The process of change* (R-1589/3-HEW).

Educational Methods   School people rarely adopt an innovation from outside their district without changing it. Whether they wish to replicate a specific project they saw or heard about elsewhere, or apply a general educational concept such as differentiated staffing, project designers tend at the beginning to adapt the innovation to the local setting as well as to their own interests. For example, a mastery learning project that was successful elsewhere may incorporate materials that are not appropriate for the staff or students of an adopting district. Or, district staff may like the reading instruction strategies of one project but prefer to use the classroom organization methods of another. As a consequence, the project adopted often comprises an amalgam of educational techniques and strategies that may be virtually unique to the district.

Nonetheless, change agent projects also have certain central characteristics or foci. The projects in our sample tended to center on one, and sometimes a mix, of the following general types of educational approaches: individualization (or student-centered) techniques; classroom organization change; curriculum revisions; community involvement; administrative changes; general enrichment; and use of specialists for student needs. Our analysis explored two questions. First, to what extent did the educational approach or method of a project influence its implementation, its effects on teachers and students, and its continuation? The answer for our sample is that it did to some extent but not very much. Second, did some educational methods have more significant effects on project outcomes than others? The answer is that they did, but the differences were not great.

We found that the educational method chosen determines a project's implementation, effect, and continuation to only a small and limited extent. Projects with essentially the same educational methods can be, and usually are, mobilized and implemented very differently and thus more or less effectively. In short, *what* the project was mattered less than *how* it was done.

Project Resources   Our findings about the effects of project resources are similar to those about educational methods: More expensive projects were generally no more likely than less expensive ones to be effectively implemented, elicit teacher change, improve student performance, or be continued by teachers. Nor did variations in the number of project schools per district or in the funding per student strongly affect project outcomes in most cases.

The variants of these general findings are noteworthy. The greater the number of schools in a project, the higher was the proportion of project materials continued, because these large projects typically involved new curriculum material or educational hardware that districts retained after the end of the federal grant. In such cases, teachers made some use of the materials purchased with federal money, but they did not change their teaching behavior. Moreover, the continued use of project materials was often not accompanied by a continued use of project methods, and overall district continuation tended to be *pro forma*. In short, some districts used the federal grant more to purchase up-to-date materials and technologies than to promote basic educational reform.

Another significant variant involved the concentration of project funding: Projects having a higher funding per student tended to produce a greater improvement in student performance than projects with less concentrated funding. However, this effect comes primarily from remedial projects that focused on individualization, which were located in schools in areas of lower socioeconomic status and sought to increase the performance of students who were below-average achievers. The heavy concentration of funding for these remedial projects paid for classroom aides, many of whom were not kept on after the end of federal funding. The teachers in these projects indicated that they had not changed their styles very much, nor did they continue using project methods or materials extensively after the end of federal funding. In short, these remedial projects improved student performance, but we suspect this effect will be short-lived. Successive generations of students are unlikely to benefit, and the federal money spent for aides will have had only a fleeting effect on district practices.

In terms of district financial support, the more expensive the project was, the more likely it was to be cut back when "soft" money had run out. Projects with a high funding per student were particularly likely to cut back or eliminate aides to the teaching staff. Projects that spanned both elementary and secondary schools were likely to be discontinued or reduced to a less inclusive project—e.g., to only one junior high school. Not only did these comprehensive innovations spread their financial resources thin; they also seemed to be trying to accomplish too much too soon.

Scope of Proposed Change The scope of a change agent project—how much it seeks to accomplish relative to its setting—concerns local officials as well as federal and state planners. Should ambitious and comprehensive innovations be supported, despite a possible high risk of producing no change at all, or should narrow, presumably "safer" bets be backed? Our analysis shows that this question does indeed deserve serious attention, because the project's scope influenced implementation and continuation in many ways. Though we did find more difficulties associated with more ambitious efforts, these projects also accomplished more in terms of teacher change and were more likely to be continued.

One major reason for the significance of the project's scope was its effects on teachers in their daily classroom practice. At this level, two related aspects were particularly important: the *type* of change required in teaching practice and the *amount* of extra effort required of teachers. Project designs that called for a change in teaching behavior from standard or traditional practice were more likely to achieve such change than other projects. Similarly, the more extra effort asked of teachers, particularly during the hectic first year of implementation, the more likely they were to respond positively; they were more likely to change their own practices and to truly assimilate and therefore continue using the project's methods. Such ambitious and demanding projects did create short-run problems for both teachers and administrators; yet, by the end of the federal funding period, they were no more or less likely to fail (or to succeed) in meeting their objectives or in promoting improved student performance than were more narrowly focused or less ambitious projects. In other words, attempting less does not necessarily assure more effective implemenation, but it can foreclose teacher change of a lasting variety.

Our data indicate that teachers rise to challenges. Ambitious and demanding innovations seem more likely to elicit the commitment of teachers than routine projects. This is so in part because these projects appeal to the teachers' professionalism; that is, a primary motivation for teachers to undertake the extra work and disruption of attempting change is their belief that they will become "better" teachers and that their students will benefit.

Implementation Strategies   In terms of import, a major finding of this study involves implementation strategies—the local decisions and choices, explicit or implicit, about how to put an innovation into practice. We found that these strategies could spell the difference between success or failure, almost independently of the type of innovation or educational method involved; moreover, they could determine whether teachers would assimilate and continue using project methods or allow them to fall into disuse.

Our evidence clearly indicates that some strategies *usually* did not work and, indeed, could hurt the project's outcomes and chances for continuation. We underscore "usually" because we wish to make it clear that these generally ineffective strategies could help in a few rare and special instances, but their probable ineffectiveness is due to their mismatch with the typical reality of school district life and with the dominant motivations and needs of teachers. The reasons for the ineffectiveness of implementation strategies follow:

OUTSIDE CONSULTANTS. Project staff typically saw the assistance offered by outside consultants as too general, untimely, and irrelevant to the problems of their classrooms. Effective implementation requires the adaptation of project strategies to the particularities of each school and classroom, but most outside consultants had neither the time nor the necessary information to tailor their advice to the individual school or classroom. Furthermore, because the use of outside consultants typically involves considerable advance planning and scheduling, and because outside consultants are generally not available on an on-call basis, the help provided by consultants often cannot be delivered in a timely fashion, i.e., as problems arise during implementation.

PACKAGED MANAGEMENT APPROACHES. Packaged approaches to planned change typically were too inflexible to permit the local adaptation necessary to effective implementation. No matter how comprehensive the "road maps" provided by educational packages were they could not anticipate those local conditions or events that require project plans and practices to be modified. Packaged approaches to change also tended to overstate the role of technology or of a new practice in improving education delivery, neglecting the much more important elements of classroom management and teacher commitment. Even if packages could increase the efficiency of implementation, they seem to pose a severe problem for continuation, by depriving the staff of a necessary sense of ownership of the materials.

ONE-SHOT, PREIMPLEMENTATION TRAINING. Projects that concentrate all of their training efforts in one intensive session, or in sessions prior to project implementation, often do so out of concerns for efficiency and economy. However, for many projects, training of this nature was unable to provide the assistance teachers needed during implementation. The training and assistance needs of teachers change over time as they encounter new problems in their classrooms and usually cannot be accurately anticipated. But even if it were possible to forecast the nature of staff training needs, training that treated issues before they became problems was usually not meaningful to project staff.

PAY FOR TRAINING. Extra pay for training either was not significant or tended to be negatively related to implementation effectiveness, teacher change, student improvement, and project continuation. This strategy fails because it seriously misconstrues the motivations that lead most teachers to want to change their practices. Teachers typically elect to spend the time and energy necessary to carry out a new practice primarily out of professional concerns—because they believe these efforts will help them to become better teachers. Extrinsic rewards such as pay for training cannot stimulate the commitment of teachers if they do not see it to be in their professional self-interest.

FORMAL EVALUATION. It is usually assumed that formal project evaluations will provide summative data for decisions about continuation, but they rarely served their intended function. Except in instances of patent "failure," evaluation findings were generally not the most important factor in district decisions about project continuation after federal funding ended. Local bureaucratic and political concerns significantly influenced these decisions: Do the parents want the project? Does it bring visibility to the district? Is there pressure from teachers to continue project activities? Moreover, where commitment to continue a project existed, district officials often dismissed disappointing evaluation results as "premature" or "badly measured." Formal evaluation activities also failed to serve a formative purpose during implementation. Because formal evaluations rarely assessed process issues (adequacy of training, communication between staff, and so on) and because they were seldom conducted on a routine or regular basis, they did not provide timely and appropriate data that would help project participants to modify and refine project activities.

COMPREHENSIVE PROJECTS. Comprehensive projects often failed because they attempted too much too soon. K-12 projects, for example, encountered difficulty because project strategies were insufficiently discriminating between the very different needs, motivations, and interests of primary and secondary school teachers. Similarly, projects that included a large number of district schools or classrooms typically offered a uniform or standard project strategy that could not accommodate the needs and priorities of particular schools or classrooms. In addition, some district-wide projects spread project staff and resources too thin, thereby (a) foreclosing the possibility of creating a "critical mass" of participants in any one school—i.e., other colleagues who can provide support and encouragement—and (b) diluting the quality of project support (e.g., readily available technical assistance, formative evaluation, and project director involvement) that is important to effective implementation. These projects were usually sharply reduced after the end of federal funding.

In contrast to these generally ineffective strategies, effective implementation strategies promoted *mutual adaptation*, the process by which the project is adapted to the reality of its institutional setting, and teachers and school officials adapt their practices in response to the project. In terms of individual classrooms, the process consists of each teacher developing new methods and practices while adjusting the project design to classroom conditions: It is essentially "learning-by-doing." Effective implementation strategies foster mutual adaptation by providing each teacher with necessary and timely feedback, allowing project-level choices to be made to correct errors, and encouraging commitment to the project. These effective strategies *usually* contributed positively to project outcomes and chances for continuation. This time we underscore "usually" to qualify the findings in two important respects.

First, these strategies are not a panacea. They obviously do not work if they are poorly executed, as was often the case when they were routinely applied. For example, though frequent and regular project meetings could promote mutual adaptation (for reasons discussed shortly), they also could be extremely boring and serve no purpose other than administrative routine. Indeed, we found that frequent, unproductive meetings actually impaired project implementation. This dominance of quality over quantity held for all the implementation strategies: When they were useful, they were very, very useful; when they were bad, they were a waste of time, money, and energy. The "quality" of these strategies primarily depended on two elements: the skill and leadership of the project director, principal, and district staff, and the "practicality" of the strategies.

Second, effective implementation strategies work best when applied in concert with other effective strategies; indeed, they may not work at all when applied separately. Thus, rather than referring to several *strategies*, it seems more appropriate to speak of the project's overall implementation *strategy* and, accordingly, to analyze the *elements* of the strategy that support mutual adaptation. The following elements, when well executed, had major, positive effects on project outcomes and continuation.

Concrete, Teacher-Specific, and Ongoing Training. Teachers required concrete, "hands on" training in translating often very general and fuzzy project guidelines into classroom practice and adapting project concepts to the reality of their particular situation. However, because they are one step removed from classroom operations, even insightful and talented project directors cannot always accurately predict the type of training teachers require; thus, training that was determined in large part by the project participants themselves seemed most likely to aid implementation. Mutual adaptation was fostered, especially on complex projects, by training that continued during and beyond the project's first years.

Classroom Assistance from Project or District Staff. Local resource personnel promoted mutual adaptation by offering relevant, practical advice on an on-call basis. Furthermore, because local resource personnel were able to furnish frequent, though short, on-the-spot assistance, they were less likely than outside consultants to preclude important learning opportunities for the staff; consequently, projects providing effective classroom assistance were more likely to be continued by teachers.

Observation of the Projects in Other Classrooms or Districts. Project staff in our sample usually did not observe other operating projects. But when they did visit other schools or districts (for at least a full day), their experience seemed to aid implementation, particularly for amorphous innovations such as open education. Peers were generally the most effective counselors when it came to advising implementers-to-be about problems they could expect, suggesting ways to remedy them, and encouraging new project staff that "they can do it too."

Regular Project Meetings. Regular meetings of project staff that focused on practical problems, not administrative or routine matters, often provided (a) a forum for the feedback necessary to adaptation, (b) an opportunity to share successes, problems, and suggestions, and (c) a vehicle for building the staff morale and cohesiveness important to effective implementation. However, meetings were seldom effective without a supportive school climate.

Teacher Participation in Project Decisions. Teacher participation in decisions concerning project operations and modifications was strongly correlated with effective implementation and continuation. The reasons for this powerful effect were easy to uncover. Teachers, who are the closest to the problems and progress of project activities, are in the best position to suggest remedies for perceived deficiencies. Moreover, where project activities and objectives reflected significant teacher input, the staff were more likely to invest the considerable energy needed to make the project work. The project, in short, was "theirs."

Local Materials Development. The local development of materials for the project provided staff with a feeling that their professional judgment was valued, with a sense of project ownership, and with an opportunity to learn-by-doing. Thus, the contribution of this activity to project implementation extended beyond the quality of the resulting product. The *process* of materials development promoted the clarity and commitment necessary to effective implementation and long-term continuation.

Principal Participation in Training. The active support of the principal was vital to the project's implementation and especially to its continuation, as the next section discusses. One measure of that support was the extent to which principals participated in project training activities. Involvement of the principal in staff training provided the information and skills needed to help teachers implement the project and sustain project activities in the face of eventual staff attrition. More important, it signaled the staff that their efforts were supported and valued.

INSTITUTIONAL SETTING

Practitioners will not be surprised to learn that the local institutional setting had the major influence on project outcomes and continuation. The three components of the institutional setting that we examined were climate and leadership, school and teacher characteristics, and district management capacity and support.

Organizational Climate and Leadership
Three elements of a school's organizational climate powerfully affected the project's implementation and continuation—the quality of working relationships among teachers, the active support of principals, and the effectiveness of project directors. Each played somewhat different roles and had somewhat different effects.

RELATIONSHIPS AMONG TEACHERS. The development of good working relationships among project teachers enhanced implementation and promoted classroom continuation of project methods and materials (but had no strong effect on student performance or teacher change). When teachers worked well together, they formed a *critical mass* that could overcome both task and emotional needs. For example, by openly sharing their implementation problems and individual solutions, teachers learned from each other and could support each other. Of course, good project relationships did not develop in a vacuum; they occurred in schools that already had high morale (i.e., in schools that teachers felt were good places to work in and had good *esprit de corps*) and in projects in which teachers participated in decisions about adaptation. The sense of ownership that evolved in these cases is a basic reason why good working relationships were strongly correlated with the teachers' continued use of the project.

THE ROLE OF THE PRINCIPAL. The importance of the principal to both the short- and long-run outcomes of innovative projects can hardly be overstated. When teachers thought that principals disliked a project, we rarely found favorable project outcomes. Some projects with neutral or indifferent principals scored well, particularly in the percentage of goals achieved; but these projects typically focused on individualization or curriculum revision and had highly effective project directors who compensated for the lukewarm principals. Projects having the *active* support of the principal were the most likely to fare well. In general, the more supportive the principal was perceived to be, the higher was the percentage of project goals achieved, the greater the improvement in student performance, and the more extensive the continuation of project methods and materials.

The principal's unique contribution to implementation lies not in "how to do it" advice better offered by project directors but in giving moral support to the staff and in creating an organizational climate that gives the project legitimacy. This role is particularly demanding for ambitious projects. Such innovations as open education can be viewed as a radical and undesirable departure from the school norm unless the principal actively supports them and runs interference against disapproving nonproject teachers or parents.

The principal's support was also crucial for continuation. This relationship is understandable, considering that the principal typically sets the educational style of the school. Teachers were unlikely to continue a full array of project methods without the approval of their principal, even if the methods were successful and had been assimilated. To do so would not only be difficult in light of the sometimes subtle, sometimes blunt means that principals often employ to establish a uniform "school style," but also would appear contrary to professional self-interest. Moreover, after the end of federal funding, many districts took a laissez-faire attitude, letting the principals decide the fate of the project within their schools. Unless principals actively promoted the project, particularly when it came to replacing staff and seeking district financial support, even "successful" projects could wither away. All told, the principal amply merits the title of "gatekeeper of change."

Our data leave little doubt that an effective project director greatly enhances the implementation of a special project. But in sharp contrast to the findings about principals, project directors had no significant effect on continuation for our sample of projects.

THE ROLE OF THE PROJECT DIRECTOR. Why does the project director matter for project implementation but not for continuation? The answer can best be understood in light of the different tasks and activities in the implementation and continuation phases. A central aspect of implementation is the teachers' acquisition of new skills, behavior, and attitudes; this task-specific learning can be greatly facilitated by an effective project director. The director's special skills and knowledge can clarify project goals and operations, minimize the day-to-day difficulties encountered by classroom teachers, and furnish the concrete information they need to learn. Once federal funding ends and continuation begins, however, task learning is no longer a major staff activity. (If teachers have not learned project strategies and methods by then, it is unlikely they ever will.) The activities central to continuation require integration of project precepts into routine classroom activities and, in some cases, the modification of standard institutional procedures. Thus, in this phase, the specialized skills and knowledge of the project director become less important to project teachers than the institutional support of the principal and other district staff. In fact, it is not unusual for project directors to assume an entirely new role after the end of federal funding. Many either resume their former positions in the district, go on to head innovative projects in other districts, or, in the instance of Title III "validated" projects, launch a heavy schedule of project dissemination.

School and Teacher Characteristics

We gathered data on a wide variety of school characteristics. For example, we collected information on the academic, ethnic, economic, and social makeup of the school's student population, the size of the school and stability of the staff, and the school's experience with other innovations. (Similar data were gathered at the district level.) None of these "background" or structural characteristics strongly affected any of the project outcome or continuation measures. However, two other characteristics do seem important—whether the school is at the elementary or secondary level and the attributes of the teaching staff.

Change was typically harder to obtain and continue at the secondary level. The reasons for secondary schools' difficulties are too numerous to detail here, but perhaps it is worth citing the problem most mentioned by practitioners. In the words of one superintendent commenting on difficulties encountered on a career-awareness project, "[high school] teachers are simply unwilling to vacate [what they see] as their responsibility to subject matter in adjusting to supplementary materials." In short, secondary school teachers may be "subject-oriented" in contrast to the "child-centered" orientation attributed to elementary teachers.

Three teacher attributes—years of teaching, sense of efficacy, and verbal ability—significantly affected most project outcomes. We found that years of teaching and teacher sense of efficacy had strong and significant, but very different, effects on most of our outcome measures. Specifically, the number of years of teaching had *negative* effects: The longer a teacher had taught, the less likely was the project to achieve its goals or to improve student performance. Furthermore, teachers with many years on the job were less likely to change their own practices or to continue using project methods after the end of federal funding.

The teacher's sense of efficacy—a belief that the teacher can help even the most difficult or unmotivated students—showed strong positive effects on all the outcomes. Teachers' attitudes about their own professional competence, in short, may be a major determinant of what happens to projects in classrooms. In contrast, teachers' verbal ability had no relationship to project implementation, outcome, or continuation with the exception of its positive correlation with improved student achievement.

These results raise questions about the design of change agent projects: Is it possible to instill a new willingness to change in veteran teachers? If not, our findings imply that innovative projects should be staffed with efficacious, less "resigned" teachers. That raises a further question: Is it possible to enhance teachers' sense of efficacy? Districts can always handpick staff for pilot projects, of course, but that amounts to a delaying strategy if the eventual intent is to spread innovations or to maintain them among the general run of teachers after the original cadre of teachers moves on to other tasks. Our field experience suggests that staff development activities could be used to raise the sense of efficacy and rekindle the enthusiasm of many teachers.

District Management Capacity and Support Districts differ sharply in their capacity to manage change agent projects and in their receptivity toward them. Though we could not measure these factors with precision, our observation and interview data leave little doubt as to the importance of constant and active support from LEA officials and specialized staff for the project's short-run outcomes, and especially for its long-run fate.

During the mobilization or initiation phase of the project, the support of the central office staff can determine whether planning for the project is adequate and whether teachers and administrators become committed. For example, an opportunistic attitude or top-down district approach communicates to the staff that the district does not care about the project or does not value the project's implementation.

It was not unusual for LEA officials to neglect projects during implementation. At the time of the continuation decision, however, the support of central officials becomes crucial again, and their attitudes, pro or con, often had not changed since the project's beginning. Their continuation decision seemed to rest on how important the project was to the district's educational priorities and on local political and organizational concerns, not necessarily on how successfully the project had been implemented. However, once a decision was made to continue a project, district officials had to provide active support if the innovation was to be sustained.

More specifically, supportive districts designed from the beginning continuation strategies that were aimed at maintaining the project in the face of financial, personnel, and political uncertainties. The exact nature of these continuation strategies (as well as their effectiveness) depended on the particular attributes of the local setting, but the broad outlines of their objectives can be seen.

They aimed to smooth the project's transition from its special status to its institutionalization (i.e., to becoming a regular part of the district operations). In the budget area, the project had to change its status from a special line item to a standard activity absorbed in the district's operating budget. Political groundwork typically had to be laid to convince school board members of the project's priority. In the personnel area, a procedure for replacing key personnel had to be established; for example, some LEAs use project participants as a "training cadre." In the area of curriculum support, staff training and development needs had to be incorporated into regular in-service activities so that new project members would be integrated smoothly and older ones kept fresh. In the instructional area, projects had to replace existing practices, which meant that district officials once again had to mobilize the support of principals and teachers.

The major findings of Rand's Change Agent study can be stated simply:

- *Implementation* dominated the outcome of planned change efforts.
- The course of project implementation is primarily determined by *local* factors—not by the adoption of a particular technology, the availability of information, the level of funding, or the particular federal program sponsorship.
- Effective implementation is characterized by a process of *mutual adaptation* in which both the project and participants change over time. There is, in successful practice, no such thing as a completely prespecified or uniform "best" treatment.

Taken together, these findings mean that the mere adoption of a "better" practice does not automatically fulfill its promise of "better" outcomes. Initially, similar programs installed in different settings undergo unique alteration; outcomes cannot be predicted on the basis of technology alone. Nor does "more money" necessarily buy the things that matter—staff commitment, administrative support, or implementation strategies that promote the assimilation and adaptation of project methods and concepts. The Change Agent study supports a conclusion that the problem of change is fundamentally a management problem. External resources may be a necessary condition for successful change, particularly in isolated or financially beleaguered districts. But the result of more money or better ideas ultimately depends on local choices about how the money should be spent and how the new ideas should be implemented and sustained. From the beginning to the final stages of a project, a supportive institutional environment was necessary for a project to be effectively implemented and to take root.

CHAPTER 5

The Nature and Impact of Organization Development in Schools

MATTHEW B. MILES
MICHAEL FULLAN

ORGANIZATION DEVELOPMENT (OD) is a strategy for improving organizational capacity, health, effectiveness, and the like. Typically, it is a deliberate, long-term effort in which change agents, rather than technocratically prescribing solutions, work to facilitate the system participants' efforts to study and experimentally improve the organization themselves with the guidance of behavioral science concepts.

Typical OD tactics include *team-building* sessions, where a working group of subordinates and their superior identify and work explicitly on the issues that are hampering their effectiveness; *process consultation*, in which a change agent observes and gives steady feedback on how meetings or interpersonal transactions are going; *survey feedback*, in which departments or work groups examine the results of an organization-wide questionnaire and work on solutions to the problems surfaced; and *confrontation*, in which groups previously out of communication with each other are brought together for problem solving.

Later in this article we will return to the question of OD's defining characteristics, as illuminated by our data. But this starting definition is useful enough for now.

OD was originally created in industrial settings. The first application to schools was not until 1963.[1] Since then, there have been a half-dozen or so studies annually reporting on OD work with schools, but the actual amount of OD use in schools has remained uncertain. A moderate amount of good quality research on OD in schools has accumulated, notably that carried out at the University of Oregon (Runkel & Schmuck, 1976) that suggests its promise in improving the quality of life and learning in the special sort of organization called a school. But there has been no systematic assessment of how many schools are actually doing OD, exactly what they are doing, and what the consequences are (Fullan, 1975). The fact is that we really do not possess answers to some basic questions:

1. What is the actual extent of OD work in school districts across Canada and the United States?
2. What are the different types of OD approaches or programs in operation?
3. What are the conditions or factors associated with sustained, successful OD efforts compared to less successful ones?
4. What do we know about the impact of OD programs?

This chapter addresses these questions based on a larger study we conducted to assess the state of the art of OD in education (Fullan, Miles, and Taylor, 1978; Miles, Fullan and Taylor, 1978, vols. I-V). Our main focus here involves an analysis of two related parts of our study: (1) an examination of the nature, conditions of success, and impact of sustained (eighteen months or more) OD programs in seventy-six school districts in Canada and the United States—districts that we located as having major OD programs; and (2) an analysis of three case studies drawn from our sample of seventy-six, in which we investigated in more detail the operation of three different types of OD programs.

Four main sections follow: a brief commentary on what OD is, including problems of defining the values, goals, and types of OD programs; a summary of the school district data from the seventy-six cases; a summary of learnings from the three case studies; and a concluding section on the future of OD in schools.

DEFINING OD

In reviewing the literature on OD in another part of the study (Fullan, Miles, & Taylor, 1978, vol. II, we found that the key components that characterized OD consisted of efforts involving planned change; long-range efforts toward improving the quality of life of individuals, group and organizational processes, performance, and productivity; the assistance of internal and external change agents; and the use of behavioral science concepts and techniques in a reflexive, self-analytic way.

We noted two major types of problems in published reports. First, many activities labeled OD (e.g., one-shot workshops and the training of individuals and small groups) did not meet the definition of what OD is supposed to be. Simply put, many activities called OD are not really OD at all. This has contributed to confusion about what OD is, and to a reputation that OD is superficial or irrelevant.

The second type of problem concerns possible discrepancy between the intentions or espoused values of OD, and the "values in practice." Some published critiques of the assumptions and actual use of OD have stressed that OD programs may not in fact address the human side of development and the quality of life of organizational members with energy and integrity equal to their efforts to improve the organizational side. OD practitioners, despite their intentions, may not be operating in a value-congruent way, so (a) certain goals may not be achieved; (b) impact may be superficial; or (c) OD may be experienced as inconsequential or as supporting the status quo instead of accomplishing its espoused goals. We also found that many of the definitions of OD were very general and tended to mask the complexities, specific components, and dilemmas involved in its use.

Although OD may have a number of basic characteristics, there are a variety of primary approaches or routes to OD. As we will see later, OD programs can be viewed according to their main approaches. These can vary from classical OD (with strong attention to improving system communication, climate, group functioning, etc.) to those whose primary concern focuses on curriculum change, skills development in personnel, comprehensive school improvement, desegregation, and accountability—e.g., management by objectives (MBO) and program planning and budgeting system (PPBS), which are systematically developed programs for goal setting, planning, and performance review.

It is extremely difficult to assess the impact of OD programs on any kind of organization, let alone schools, but schools are even more difficult to assess than most organizations (Miles, 1967). Their bottom line outcomes are supposedly those of improved cognitive, attitudinal, and behavioral outcomes in students. But these goals are often diffuse, general, and measurable with difficulty. Students also are often not directly involved in OD programs as participants but are expected to benefit somehow in a trickle-down fashion from human-system or educational programmatic changes introduced among and by the adults of the system. Student benefits certainly need not be the only justification for OD's value in schools—adults in schools have a legitimate claim for a better quality of *their* working lives—but they cannot be ignored as a criterion of OD's success in schools. So far, the impact of this sort has been less frequently reported than the impact on adults.

And, as with OD in other settings, the *explanation* of outcomes is weak. We might speculate that coordination problems and "loose coupling" (Weick, 1976) in schools make it even more difficult to link programs to outcomes. Nonetheless, it is possible to gather more direct evaluation information on the operation of OD programs in schools and on reported outcomes, especially if multiple methods of data collection are used. As one contribution in this direction, we set out to gather information on OD programs in school districts including both quantitative analysis and case studies. These results are reported below.

THE STUDY OF SCHOOL DISTRICTS[2]

Sample   We mailed a twelve-page questionnaire to a sample of 390 school districts that had been nominated by one or more OD consultants and/or other school districts. We provided a definition of OD and asked specifically whether such a program had been operating for at least eighteen months since 1964. The definition read—

> A sustained attempt at system self-study and improvement over a period of at least 18 months, focusing on change in organizational procedures, norms, or structures using behavioral science concepts.

After one mail reminder and a phone call, we received a return of 165 responses (42 percent of the total of 390). The incentives we had offered were a list of OD consultants and OD-using districts, plus a report summary. After eliminating responses that were not sustained, not OD, from higher education institutions, or duplicates of other responses from the same district, we arrived at a final refined sample of eligible cases, consisting of 76 school districts in Canada and the United States in which sustained OD programs had been carried out. Phone calls were made to districts in order to verify ambiguous data or to gather more specific information on particular aspects of the program.

A majority (59 percent) of the respondents were local school district administrators (superintendents, assistant superintendents, principals, directors of instruction); staff personnel accounted for 14 percent and internal OD specialists or coordinators for 9 percent. Teachers (3 percent) and others (department and unit heads) accounted for the rest (16 percent).

Seventy-six percent of the districts were in the United States, with the remainder in Canada (Manitoba, Ontario, Quebec, and Saskatchewan). The regional spread was wide; only in the Midwest were there as many as 20 percent in a single region.

The settings were also diverse: thirty-eight percent were suburban districts, long considered more likely to innovate—but 41 percent were urban or metropolitan, and 21 percent towns or villages. Perhaps the most striking property of the settings is that they overrepresented larger districts. For example, only 12.5 percent of our U.S. districts had 1,000 pupils or fewer, while 26 percent of all U.S. districts are this small (U.S. Dept. HEW, 1977). On the other end, though only 1.2 percent of the U.S. districts have over 25,000 pupils, 19.5 percent of our U.S. OD-using districts were this large. One might conclude that larger districts are more likely to (a) have problems of coordination, communication, etc., and (b) be possessed of resources to pay for OD. We also noted that 55 percent said that their expenditures were at the 75th percentile or better for their states, 34 percent said they were about average, and only 11 percent said they were at the 25th percentile or lower. So we have a bias toward above-average district wealth.[3]

The districts in the sample were clearly not restricted in the social class backgrounds of populations served. The median district had 15 percent upper-middle class parents, 35 percent white collar, 30 percent blue collar, and 15 percent semiskilled or unskilled parents. When we characterized districts as to their overall socioeconomic balance, we found that 34 percent had a predominantly middle-class (or upper-middle class) composition, and 61 percent were predominantly blue-collar or working class; 5 percent had no single class level predominating. So if anything, sustained OD seems more frequent in districts with strong working-class representation.

Perhaps most crucially, our 76 districts, a much larger sample than anyone would have predicted existed, constitute a success-biased sample. They had sustained OD work in their systems for at least eighteen months, and liked what they had done enough, in most cases, to continue it. They also liked it enough that they felt free to describe the experience and to take one to two hours to complete the questionnaire. Our sample does *not* include districts who had never heard of OD, or who knew about it but did not try it, or who knew about it, tried it, and discontinued it short of eighteen months.

Nature of the OD Programs The length of OD work in these 76 districts ranged from one and a half years (our bottom-end definition) to ten years, with a median at three. We conclude that once an OD effort gets past the eighteen-month investment, it tends to be sustained. (In fact, as we shall see, 88 percent of our sample said OD was continuing at the moment, and 78 percent predicted institutionalized continuation.)

The targets of attention tended to be several schools (22 percent), total system (18 percent), or multilevel (17 percent). It was rare for the work to be limited to a single school (4 percent) or only administrators (that is, the superintendent plus principals [12 percent] or central office alone [3 percent]). The median total number of different persons involved was in the 300 to 700 range.

At a very general level, what sort of work was going on? We examined the respondents' accounts of their work carefully, noted what sorts of consultants they were using, the materials they cited, and the way they characterized the overall strategy used. Not surprisingly, given our general definition, when districts are asked about "sustained efforts at system self-study and improvement," there are many different varieties, as table 5.1 indicates. Later, we will return to the question of whether different approaches have differing consequences. We might note here that the approaches, when arrayed in the order noted in table 1 (roughly from an indeterminate, person-centered approach to more system-oriented, classical approaches) had *no* meaningful relationship to the size, wealth, socioeconomic status or setting of the district, to the costliness of the OD effort, the proportion of system staff involved, or to the numbers of inside or outside change agents used.

However, classical OD was more likely to start with structural-change problems. Generally, more system-oriented approaches (like those toward the end of the list) were more likely to be used in districts where a good deal of other change was going on and were likely to go on longer. But except for these differences, the approaches did not look very different in terms of general contextual and input features like those above.

At a more specific level, we asked districts to describe the OD activities that had gone on, using a checklist originally developed by Miles and Schmuck (1971). The data appear in table 5.2

So, in general, we note that most of the OD efforts reported clearly transcend "training" and have a strong instrumental (plan-making, problem-solving) emphasis in the approaches reported. But we also note that only about half say that OD-managing task forces are in place, and that only about a third are aimed at bringing about structural change. We will return to these issues.

These activities were aided by external and/or internal consultants in all districts. The number of external consultants involved ranged from one to 187 (yes, that one is verified), with the median number being

Table 5-1
OD Approaches Employed in the School Districts

Approaches	Districts No.	Percent
Indeterminate (workshops, meetings, etc., but approach not clearly defined)	5	6.6
Personnel development (emphasis on skills, personal growth, etc.)	14	18.4
Desegregation (racial attitudes, behavior)	2	2.6
Curriculum change (specific projects, or comprehensive)	5	6.6
Accountability (systematic assessment and planning, often state-specified)	8	10.5
MBO or PPBS (as central feature)*	9	11.8
Comprehensive school improvement models	6	7.9
Classical OD†	27	35.5
Total No. =	76	99.9

*Altogether, 26 percent of our districts said there was some linkage between the OD program and MBO work; 11 percent said the same for PPBS; but 5 percent had both. There were 28 percent of districts where the linkage to MBO, PPBS, or other system-oriented approach was direct, and there were another 16 percent where such programs existed but were weakly linked or not at all. The 11.8 percent figure above refers only to those districts where MBO or PPBS were central.

†Districts classified as having *classical* OD programs ordinarily have reported much attention to issues such as system-level communication, problem-solving, norms, group functioning, and, generally, the human side of the organization. The consultants they used were often those mentioned in Schmuck and Miles' (1971) book on OD in schools; the materials were usually drawn from the general OD literature. A few mentioned the Schmuck et al., *Handbook of OD in schools* (1972).

three. The time spent by the most salient external consultant ranged from 2 to 990 days, with the median being 15 days. If we remember that the median effort time is three years, we can conclude that the usual external practitioner restricts interventions considerably to workshops, off-site sessions, and the like.

The picture for internal change agents is considerably different. The median number of system members involved as facilitators, trainers,

Table 5-2
Number of Times Specific Approaches to OD Were Used

Approaches	Percent Not Used At All	Percent Used Once or More
Training (direct teaching)	26	74
Process consultation	38	62
Confrontation	46	54
Data feedback	30	70
Problem-solving	25	75
Plan-making	16	84
OD Task Force establishment	49	51
Techno-structural activity	62	32

consultants, etc., was eight, so districts were relying quite heavily on internal talent. When asked how much time the most salient inside change agent had put in on the program, forty-three districts answered. The range was from 5 to 1,000 days, with a median of 200 days, more than a dozen times the investment put in by the median outsider. Another finding of substantial interest is that inside change agents tended to be line managers: 81 percent of the districts involved central office administrators as inside change agents, as did 73 percent for principals. Of others involved, 58 percent mentioned teachers and 56 percent central office specialists. Only 33 percent and 15 percent respectively mentioned parents and students. When asked about the two most salient inside change agents in the program, 30 percent of the districts indicated superintendents or assistant superintendents and 27 percent said principals. Only 18 percent of the districts mentioned persons identified specifically as "internal consultants" as being most salient.

Only about half of these insiders were, however, formally trained in OD-facilitative skills; they tended to learn on the job informally. The majority had no colleagues in outside professional groups. Thus, the picture is one of active, sustained work by insiders—mostly line managers—with little sense of support from colleagues. Thus there is much hidden, nonvisible OD occurring, contributing little to the advancement of practice.

The crucial "start" conditions for OD were typically support from a new (or the existing) superintendent and secondarily the existence of organizational problems and the availability of grant funds. The most frequently mentioned start issues were communication (25 percent), reorganization/redesign (11 percent), goals and goal setting (10 percent), and decision making (8 percent). Only 5 percent mentioned student issues as such. When start issues were aggregated into more general areas, we found that 32 percent mentioned task-oriented organizational issues (such as problem solving and coordination), 21 percent were concerned with educational output (goal setting and effectiveness), and another 25 percent with internal educational issues (such as curriculum, classroom climate, programs, finance). A total of 41 percent mentioned socio-emotional issues (communication, trust). Other areas included structural issues (18 percent mentioned items such as reorganization or consolidation); external educational issues such as school-community relations (13 percent); personnel issues (10 percent); and subsystem functioning (4 percent).

Perhaps the most interesting findings here are the emphasis on task-oriented, goal-oriented items, and the educational-programmatic context. Though socio-emotional issues were frequently mentioned, it seems as though where it hurts is "getting the job done."

As programs continued, the instrumental, task-oriented aspects continued to assume importance, while socio-emotional issues decreased. (We note, however, here that socio-emotional outcomes—see below—were the most frequently reported type of result: a to-be-expected result from a human systems intervention method.)

About half of the districts supported the effort with structures or roles such as steering groups, district coordinators, and released time. Actual cadres, or building-level coordinators, were in a quarter or less of the districts.

Supporting materials, primarily printed ones—and most especially training manuals—were seen as crucial for technical support of the OD enterprise.

How much does OD cost? The districts in our sample spent from a few hundred dollars to over a million, but the median amount spent annually (add-on dollars) was only $5,000 to 10,000, a very modest amount. The *time* (and thus hidden salary) costs were more substantial, averaging about ten days a year for at least a quarter of the total staff. And the typical coordinator or OD specialist spent one-third to one-half time.

Finally, only about half of the districts' OD programs had a formal evaluation attached to them, and few of these were systematic or thoroughgoing. The face validity of OD programs, we infer, is the primary issue.

Outcomes   We were naturally concerned to develop a general measure of the success of OD programs, both to see what these programs appear to have accomplished for their users, and to provide a dependent measure against which we could run explanatory variables. The initial criteria of OD "success" we generated were—

1. impact on the district as a system (including impact on students)
2. positive attitudes toward OD, especially those that bear on whether it should be used in schools more generally
3. institutionalization or durability of the OD effort

That is, a successful OD effort is one that makes a difference locally, has become built in, and has partisans who have positive, even evangelistic attitudes that will encourage wider diffusion of the effort to other districts. Although these are self-reported indicators of success, we did find variations. We also used open-ended questions to develop measures of impact based on *specific* descriptions of changes.

It does not seem wise to combine the above three criteria into a single measure; they are only moderately correlated with each other, and the factors that explain their occurrence also vary a good deal.[4]

At the descriptive level, what did respondents tell us?

EXPECTED IMPACTS. The most frequently mentioned hoped-for outcome went to our usual champion, improved communication (20 percent). Other specific expected positive outcomes were planning (8 percent), productivity (8 percent), new educational programs (8 percent), and commitment to change (6 percent). If we use our aggregated categories for the diverse outcomes described, we end up with an interesting finding: forty-seven percent mention socio-emotional improvements in organizational functioning and 37 percent in task-oriented ones. This tends to support the view that successful OD tends to induce a cultural shift (in social processes) along with task-oriented results.

Other frequent categories included organizational output improvement (20 percent), internal educational issues (14 percent), personnel issues (18 percent), and structural changes (13 percent). As seen earlier, direct changes in students are rarely mentioned here (4 percent)—but see below.

UNEXPECTED IMPACTS. To a researcher, *un*anticipated good consequences are always of interest—59 percent of our sample mentioned such changes when asked. The most frequent unexpected gains were spin-off or extension to new participants (16 percent), improved communication (14 percent), and increased acceptance of change (11 percent). For our aggregated categories, we note with interest that 28 percent mentioned unexpected socio-emotional outcomes in organizational functioning, as contrasted with 5 percent mentioning task-related ones: the bluebird of happiness flies in unannounced. Another 17 percent mentioned various unexpected gains related to educational issues, most notably improved school-community relations; we also found 12 percent mentioning personnel issues and 8 percent output issues.

UNDESIRABLE IMPACTS. Our next question focused on whether there had been undesirable or negative consequences of the effort. Though we seemed to be dealing with a population of satisfied users, it turned out that 68 percent could point to at least one negative outcome, a finding that increases the plausibility of the remainder of our data.[5] Twenty-four percent mentioned direct negative consequences of the program activities (such as feelings of threat or work overload) and 35 percent mentioned more general *attitudes* toward the program (such as personal defensiveness, lack of interest, criticism of "games" or outside helpers); only 9 percent saw program weaknesses as such.

IMPACT ON STUDENTS. Since schools are supposed to exist for students, we thought we should ask explicitly whether the OD program had direct (or even indirect) effects on students, in or out of the classroom. Interestingly enough, 70 percent said that such effects had occurred; 18 percent were unsure or said it was too early to tell, and 12 percent left the item blank. Of the fifty-three districts who mentioned student effects, there were 6 percent who said they were only indirect and another 17 percent who did not specify the sorts of student change noted. Over half (53 percent) mentioned various "soft" effects, notably improved learning atmosphere, improved relationships and attitudes; only 13 percent mentioned gains in achievement scores. If we take a skeptical stance, we note that only 37 percent of all districts were specified "soft" student effects mentioned and achievement gains were noted in only 9 percent. Not surprisingly, better-executed programs and those with clear, explicit linkage to the classroom were likely to mention clear student gains.

IMPACT ON OTHER CHANGE EFFORTS. The OD programs in our study were not occurring in a vacuum—39 percent of the districts said that multiple instructional innovations were taking place, another 49 percent mentioned one or two such changes, and only 12 percent failed to mention any other instructional innovations. Thirty-five percent of districts were attempting to cope with some form of mandated change during the time of the OD program (e.g., desegregation, bilingual programs), and 46 percent mentioned concurrent changes in key personnel, including replacement of top management, expansion, cutbacks, and reorganization.

When asked about the pace of educational change efforts occurring concurrently with the OD program, 61 percent said it was faster than usual, 30 percent about the same, and only 9 percent said it was slower. We asked if the OD effort contributed to this. The findings were quite clear: 63 percent said the OD program had directly caused a few (30 percent) or many (33 percent) other change efforts, and *no* respondent said OD had slowed down or blocked other change efforts. So at least as seen from the district viewpoint, OD tends to stimulate other educational change efforts in addition to the direct effects we have already noted. Extensive cross-tabular analysis confirmed these causal attributions; it does appear that improved "organizational health," as Miles (1965) suggested, enables greater innovation at the specific instructional level.

POSITIVE ATTITUDES. Our second major criterion of success concerned whether districts currently held a positive attitude toward the OD program and the dissemination of OD to other school districts. On the whole, they seemed relatively satisfied with the way their programs had been executed. When asked if they would have done anything differently, only 51 percent said yes. The most frequent after-the-fact wish was that the program should have gone more slowly (21 percent), then came the need for better commitment from the top (16 percent) and better planning and preparation (21 percent). Others included more use of outside consultants (10 percent), better involvement of parents (10 percent), and the need for better evaluation (10 percent). The flavor of the first three items is that OD may well have been launched a bit precipitously.

When we asked our respondents whether they thought that OD should be used more widely in this country's schools, 64 percent said they definitely thought so, 26 percent said "Yes, probably," 7 percent were not sure, and 3 percent passed. No one expressed doubt or definite disapproval.

Districts where attitudes toward OD seem so positive, on balance, might be expected to do some proselytizing, a behavior that bears on whether OD will diffuse more widely. We found that of our districts, 60 percent had explained their OD programs at conferences or workshops, 40 percent had sent consultants to other districts, 37 percent had visited other districts to explain their work, 37 percent had sent out reports or materials, and 29 percent had written articles on their OD experiences. These represent proactive dissemination efforts. We also found that 74 percent had had informal contacts with people from other districts, and 51 percent reported that others visited them. So while dissemination efforts are not widespread across our districts, a moderate amount of diffusion effort seems to be occurring. Our sample, by and large, thinks OD is a good idea for schools.

When respondents were asked to predict the future of OD in their districts, 8 percent said it would not continue (or was already terminated), and 14 percent were uncertain. Another 24 percent said that OD would continue, but with some qualifications (go more slowly, or on a contingent basis, or unevenly), 38 percent said it would continue (but gave no qualifications), and 16 percent said it would continue, expand, and get further institutionalized. The gross figure is that 78 percent of districts predicted continuation.

Factors Explaining Success
What might account for our three types of outcome—impact, attitude, and institutionalization?

Regression analyses showed that impact was most likely to be high in programs of larger scale (dollars, time), with good technical support (inside and outside consultants, training materials), and sustained task orientation (including a structural emphasis). Positive attitudes toward dissemination of OD programs were most likely in larger-scale programs, with task and structural emphasis, plus attention to educational content issues as such. The presence of internal coordinators was another positive indicator. Firmer institutionalization was also present in programs with strong educational and structural emphases, supported by training materials and manuals. But the scale of well-institutionalized programs turned out to be moderate, rather than large, with less reliance on external consultants. Large-scale programs were less likely to become institutionalized.

The general approach to OD also made a difference in outcome. Classical OD, plus two other system-oriented, comprehensive approaches (comprehensive school improvement and MBO/PPBS related) were most likely to show clear impact, positive attitudes, and institutionalization. Indeterminate approaches without a clear rationale, personnel development (skill training for individuals), and state-mandated accountability approaches all were inferior on the three outcomes (except that personnel development programs tended to be institutionalized at an average rate). Canadian OD programs, on the average, were less effective on all three outcomes than those in the United States, largely because they were indeterminate or personnel-development oriented, rather than system oriented, and had fewer well-trained internal or external consultants available.

CASE STUDIES
As part of the larger study, we conducted three on-site case studies of successful OD programs drawn from the seventy-six district sample.

We picked districts (none previously appearing in published studies) according to several criteria: successfulness, range of program type, range of district setting and size, and Canadian/American representation. Each site was visited for two to three days in the winter of 1977–78, and case studies were assembled using interview data,[6] observation, and documents; drafts were revised after review by site personnel.

The three cases and supporting documentation run to well over two hundred pages, so we will not even try to summarize them. But it may be useful to present the generalizations we were able to draw from them.[7] The reader should remember that the cases are successful ones (high impact, attitude, and institutionalization) drawn from an already-biased sample of successful efforts.

The Case Study Sites

WINNIPEG, MANITOBA. The district is urban, containing 85 schools and over 2,000 staff for 40,000 students (mostly working class). The OD program falls into the classical OD mode, with a heavy emphasis on survey feedback and professional development, group functioning, and changing organizational norms.

ADAMS COUNTY DISTRICT 12, COLORADO. The district is a medium-wealth suburb of Denver, with a wide socioeconomic range. There are 25 schools, 1,000 staff, and 19,000 students. The OD approach is centered around MBO, coupled with a strong personnel-development strategy.

GARDEN CITY, KANSAS. A growing rural district, Garden City has 15 schools, 4,700 students, and 300 staff. The socioeconomic range is wide. The OD program is a curriculum-based approach to improvement, involving both the creation of a curriculum decision-making structure and the adoption of specific instructional innovations.

Learnings from the Case Studies

INITIATION OF OD PROGRAM. In all three cases it was clear that strong support from the top line manager was crucial. In Garden City, the superintendent provided umbrella support; in Winnipeg and Adams, the superintendent was an active initiator and driver of the effort.

In all three cases, there seemed to be little environmental turbulence; the local community was not presenting acute problems for the district. The basic conditions of the context varied, but they were largely internal to the school district: in Winnipeg, decentralization; in Adams, reorganization; in Garden City, growth.

It also seemed clear that fairly careful front-end planning took place in all three settings: the effort was not launched capriciously or in a piecemeal fashion. This was especially true in Winnipeg and Adams ("You ought to know *why* you are doing it," one central office administrator remarked), but even in Garden City it took two years of planning before the first implementation steps for the curriculum council were taken.

Characteristically, this front-end planning was based on a fairly coherent vision of the projected program's purposes and its underlying values and rationale, especially so in Adams County. In Adams and Winnipeg, the commitment was to system-level change, to increased participation, to careful goal setting, and to redressing the balance between individual and organizational improvement. The goal-setting and participation themes were also visible in Garden City.

GENERAL APPROACH. In Winnipeg and Adams especially, the programs involved direct and explicit attention to organizational variables such as communication, coordination, decision making, and climate. In Garden City this attention was less evident but growing.

All three districts operated under the assumption that structural changes would be needed; all created new operating groups at several levels, linked to each other. None took the structure existent at the time of program initiation for granted.

All three districts also seemed to be assuming that structural change was not enough. All built in direct attention to the content of curriculum in the district and its meaning for delivery of educational services. Curriculum development is not organization development, but these districts, especially Adams, seemed to consider it as a meaningful subtask in the overall effort. For Garden City, it was perhaps the central developmental task.

In Winnipeg and Adams, there was another sense in which "structure is not enough." They included a strong emphasis on skill development for role occupants so they would be able to function more adequately in the new structure. As we have seen, personnel development alone tends to be ineffective, probably because it encourages inattention to needed changes in the organizational setting.

We can also note that the OD programs in all three sites were not a superficial add-on, but a "way of life." For example, in Adams a systematic assessment program was used not only in the hiring of new personnel but as a routine support for goal setting and development planning for role occupants; in Winnipeg the OD program was aimed at helping line administrators do their regular jobs in a change-supportive way; in Garden City the curriculum council was the main means for goal setting and coordinative planning in the district.

It also seemed clear that, especially in Adams and Winnipeg, a good deal of adaptation-evolution occurred in the OD program over time. Approaches developed outside the district (MBO, and a survey feedback approach from General Motors) were revised considerably to fit local needs. And in all three districts, the program was not wholly preenvisioned; it developed organically and eclectically to meet the exigencies of situations. This development did *not* seem to be expedient: it was informed by underlying principles, as we have noted above.

Winnipeg and Adams took the adaptation principle another step: though the insider consultants developed local program packages (such as the survey feedback design in Winnipeg or the MBO program in Adams), there was usually a second adaptive step when the package was used with any particular subgroup such as a building faculty.

CONSULTANT SUPPORT. All three districts used outside consultants they considered particularly competent. Winnipeg and Adams tended to use outsiders selectively, for spot input in early stages of program development and for training of insiders. Outsiders were thus seen as distinctly disposable; once their expertise had been utilized in program development, they tended to be dismissed. Though Garden City used outsiders to help make innovation adoption more lasting, as a sort of extension of their own capabilities, they too made only limited use of outsiders in comparison with the time invested by insiders.

Winnipeg and Adams both had insiders who were strong, quite sophisticated about OD, and well linked to top management by supportive personal and working relationships. In Garden City, the main insider was sophisticated about curriculum development, and well linked to the superintendent.

This finding goes a bit deeper than the idea noted in the district study that insiders, often line managers, are the main change agents. It suggests that a vigorous *partnership* is needed between the top line manager and a strong, sophisticated OD specialist. It helped that all three insiders in our study also had formal line responsibilities themselves—for OD itself, for personnel, or for curriculum.

In both Winnipeg and Adams, the OD specialists played important roles in overall program planning, development of specific program packages, training of others as internal trainers, and brokering outside expertise as needed.

Finally, in all three sites, the idea of multiplier effects was important. OD interventions were not just run by the main change agents—inside or outside—and left at that. Rather, the regular practice, most strongly in Adams, was to develop district personnel who could train others.

Thus, program participants were not just "doing" a program the first time through, but were engaged in second-order learning—learning how to carry out the program with others. The programs thus have a "professionalizing" effect, creating an internal cadre of change agents.

COSTS. In all three districts, the out-of-pocket dollar costs were quite small, typically less than half of 1 percent of the overall budget, and as we have noted, of the same order as funds typically spent on in-service education. Thus, they are presumably not particularly difficult to justify to boards of education.

Specifically, annual add-on costs in Winnipeg were $40,000 (including inside change agents' salaries); in Adams County they were $110,000 (including about half for building-specific personnel development activities); in Garden City they were about $30,000.

The time and energy costs are something else. The programs in many respects became "a way of life." So OD was simply the improvement/change-supportive/developmental aspect of what any particular role occupant was expected to be doing from day to day. So that should not, at least in principle, seem like extra effort. In fact, however, at all three sites, problems of overload and pressure were reported. No matter how routinized OD becomes, it is still something of a strain to confront organizational issues, consider alternatives, learn how to train others, clarify one's goals, plan strategies, etc.—as contrasted with day-to-day teaching or managing. The actual person-days invested for participants most actively involved (central insiders not included), were something like fifteen to twenty-five days a year in Winnipeg (of which half was "contributed" by the participant), a similar amount in Adams, and perhaps fifteen days a year in Garden City (more than half "contributed") on the council work, and from five to twenty days on innovation adoption work. Thus, we are speaking of something like 10 percent of a typical actively involved participant's time being spent on OD activities. In some cases, the interview data suggest that this felt like an "add-on"; people had not been able to let go a particular activity or had not been released from other ongoing responsibilities. Further, the feeling of being "meetinged to death" can arise quite easily, it seems.

The time costs for inside change agents were much larger. In Winnipeg, two change agents worked 100 percent for two years, then half time each for the third year. In Adams the OD director was full time, putting most of his energy on the OD program. In Garden City, the full-time curriculum director probably put in about one-third to one-half time on the council and the innovation adoptions. These figures suggest that an OD program requires something like a full-time inside change agent for every one thousand staff members. Here again, the actual dollar costs are small in relative terms. But the commitment and sustained energy required by the focal change agent or agents must be seen as substantial.

We should note too that the annual time costs we are describing can be expected, judging from these cases, to continue for a matter of three to five years before the OD program is institutionalized and can survive beyond the protective support of its initiators. Further, certain time costs will probably continue on a permanent basis, although they will be in the "lightly scrutinized" part of the budget.

BENEFITS. It seemed evident in all three cases that the OD programs did improve communication, enhance decision-making participation at lower levels, clarify goals, aid coordination, and improve satisfaction and climate. At least this was true for roles and groups who participated actively in program activities. And the testimony of most participants is that the benefits are worth the costs. So the programs work.

But we should note that though in Winnipeg and Adams all, or nearly all, central office personnel and principals had been actively involved, the penetration to the teachers was more limited, with perhaps one-third of teachers involved. In Garden City, though the council nominally involved all teachers, it seemed likely that between it and the innovation-adoption work not more than a quarter of teachers had been active participants.

And the impact on students remained somewhat ambiguous, though it was asserted to have taken place. Even where student affective or achievement data are available, the direct linkage between such outcomes and the OD program's activities was rarely demonstrated. It was clearest where some program component was directly focused on curriculum or teaching methods, as such—but even there, OD programs do not seem to be any more crisply evaluated than are school programs in general.

Though the Winnipeg and Adams programs contained a good deal of short-run testimony-level evaluation, enough to suggest users' satisfaction with what the programs were doing, and outline areas (such as overload, program ambiguity, etc.) where corrective action was needed, neither contains systematic evaluation; Garden City evaluation data were minimal. It can be argued, at one level, that impeccable evaluation data are not necessary; complex and energy-consuming programs of this sort will only survive if they are inherently satisfying to their users. The causal linkage to the OD program as such will ordinarily be taken on faith.[8] Of course, cleaner evaluation data may make some difference in the *diffusion* of OD programs to other districts, especially the diffusion of "proven" program components (such as the Winnipeg survey feedback design or the Adams personnel assessment or MBO programs).

THE FUTURE OF OD IN SCHOOLS

A Revised Definition   As we have seen, the question of what OD "is" is not simple, and one subject to a good deal of debate in the general OD literature. Our present inclination is toward a revised definition of this sort:

> Organization development in school districts is a coherent, systematically planned, sustained effort at system self-study and improvement, focusing explicitly on change in formal and informal procedures, processes, norms or structures, using behavioral science concepts. The goals of OD include *both* the quality of life of individuals as well as improving organizational functioning and performance.

The revisions should be noted. The requirement of coherence and systematic planning may be too normative, but does serve to distinguish OD from haphazard efforts casually labeled OD, as increasingly seems to be the case in our experience. The emphasis on explicitness indicates that OD deals directly with organizational phenomena and their alteration rather than inducing changes indirectly through some other vehicle. The inclusion of both formal and informal organizational issues makes for more thoroughness, and excludes simply "official" rearrangements. The emphasis on quality of life of individuals and on organizational performance highlights the dual goal of OD and potential problems in pursuing these goals in a balanced, value-congruent way. The permissive inclusion of educational content acknowledges that such work is a primary task of school districts, but indicates that curriculum-focused work is not necessarily OD in the absence of the preceding qualifiers. The label "sustained" is perhaps best left unspecified, though the eighteen-month figure is probably useful as a guide, given the year-by-year planning often characteristic of school districts.

The Prospects   Although our study located many more OD-using districts than most knowledgeable people thought had existed, probably not more than 1 percent of school districts in the U.S. and Canada are using OD. The diffusion rate at present is very gradual. OD is a relatively complex, poorly "packaged," poorly understood and labor-intensive innovation, which, if adopted, is likely to cause substantial change in the district. These changes are generally quite positive—but it remains true that the "bureaucratic costs" (Pincus, 1974) of OD are high.

The incentives for adoption are not present in all districts. Our study shows that OD—if it is done right—is a good way to increase instructional innovation, to increase participation by all levels of personnel, and improve task and socio-emotional functioning. But not all districts want to innovate, increase upward influence by teachers, or even improve their functioning.

Some prior analyses (Derr, 1976; Blumberg, 1976; Deal and Derr, 1977) are pessimistic, suggesting that OD in schools has no future, has "come and gone" like other fads, because it is inapplicable to schools' needs, and/or is unwanted, misunderstood, and misapplied. Miles (1976) has countered these views, and the current study provides further empirical support for the idea that OD can have a moderately bright future in schools, given certain conditions.

In brief, our study shows clearly that sustained OD, if competently carried out with a well-developed conceptual framework and aimed at structural change rather than simply individual training, and with strong top-management support, can be very effective. The improvements in district functioning are real, and they include effects at the student level. The negative effects noted do not seem serious. Furthermore, the add-on dollar costs of OD are comparable to what is now spent on in-service education (less than half of 1 percent of budget), and the benefits considerably more substantial. OD does require more personnel time and is unlikely to get durably institutionalized short of five years of work.

Will OD become more widely used in schools? That question is an iffy one, and the ifs are not small. The first concerns the current state of *OD as a field*. Our review of prior reviews surfaced criticisms by OD researchers and practitioners themselves: that OD—in spite of its widespread use—is a young field, with a weak theoretical base and plenty of unclarity in goals and assumptions (Kahn, 1974; Lundberg, 1978), without a strong research base (Friedlander and Brown, 1974; Pate et al., 1977) or good dissemination and exchange of knowledge.

The second "if" concerns *misrepresentation*. Much that is labeled OD could be better termed "OT"—organizational *training*. Our study showed that training efforts aimed solely at benefiting individuals do not achieve the sorts of impact we have outlined above. Authentic OD devotes itself to system-level efforts, in which both organizational effectiveness *and* the quality of life of individuals are improved through long-range, reflexive planned change efforts. Brief workshops that ignore organizational structure and tasks may be useful to individuals, but they are not OD, and calling them that may raise expectations that are doomed to be dashed.

A third "if" concerns *misuse* of OD. Our review of prior reviews showed that the values and the conceptual bases underlying OD are far more important than its specific technology. When these are not worked out, or are casually treated, the slippage between espoused intentions and the actual practice of OD can be substantial. Such slippage is more likely when OD practitioners have inadequate or incomplete training.

The fourth "if" concerns *institutionalization*. Most writing on OD speaks of a three- to five-year period before continuous, self-renewing organizational change efforts can be expected. Our data indicate that five years is likely before OD becomes "a way of life" in the organization, and has a strong OD unit, and/or well-developed capacity of line mangers to utilize the self-analytic, behavioral science-based methods of OD. There are benefits along the way, but strong support from the top and steady energy investment are required. An active, internal cadre of competent change agents must be developed. Our data suggest that something like a minimum of ten days a year is needed from most personnel, and that a district coordinator can expect to spend a third of his time at a minimum; full-time work is desirable in systems of one-thousand personnel or more.

IMPLICATIONS AND ADVICE. Given these ifs, our advice to *local school districts* is (1) become as aware as possible of OD's goals and operating characteristics and connect them with local organization needs (the present study is a good beginning); (2) plan the start of the program carefully, with competent assistance from outside; and (3) expect to make a long-term commitment.

The implications for *state departments of education* and *intermediate service units* are for the development of OD-supportive services, including improved dissemination and awareness development, and supplying and training networks of competent OD consultants, so that a better "infrastructure" can emerge. For state departments with a strong interest in supplying support and facilitation to local districts, OD is a strong capacity-building method. But a better infrastructure is needed.

Universities, given our findings, can be helpful through developing training programs for external and internal OD change agents, stimulating local awareness-interest, and carrying out experimental projects with a strong research component.

Federal support for research and development on OD could, we think, produce at this point a more-than-incremental gain in the responsible diffusion of OD in schools. Specifically, there would be much value in support for review and development of OD-supportive materials; prototype training programs for OD consultants; OD practitioner network development, so that change agents have strong colleague ties; improved conceptualization; better evaluation studies, and research on OD adoption, implementation, and outcome; experimental diffusion and dissemination efforts (case studies, awareness conferences, a clearinghouse).

If there are better support materials and a critical mass of more competent OD practitioners for schools, along with some dissemination effort, we think the resultant extended and improved practice base can in turn lead to more pointed and illuminating research effort. Over the next five-year period, the "ifs" of improved conceptualization and practice, the avoidance of mislabeling and misuse, and a realistic understanding of what good OD requires—and delivers—should become much less prevalent. And many more school districts will have benefited from well-conceived OD programs.

NOTES

1. See Miles and Schmuck (1971) for a historical review and a series of research studies.
2. This is abstracted from Miles, Fullan, and Taylor, vol. III (1978).
3. However, the reader should not jump to conclusions about money and OD. Two findings to be reported later are relevant here: (1) the median district spends under $10,000 annually for OD; (2) though higher annual costs do tend to have more of an impact, it is the *less* expensive programs that are likely to become institutionalized or built into the district.
4. We did discover that *both* high *impact* and the existence of positive dissemination-prone *attitudes* are required before programs are likely to become *institutionalized*. That is, it is rare for evangelism alone to result in institutionalization, and impact alone without positive attitudes is also insufficient.
5. Negative results were *not* more frequent among districts where high impact was reported (the "churning of the system" hypothesis); nor were they more frequent where low impact was reported (the "a little OD is a dangerous thing" hypothesis). Rather, they simply seem to be routinely reported accompaniments of OD work.
6. The interviews, usually totaling fifteen to eighteen, and held with OD coordinators, superintendent, central office administrators, principals, teachers and school board members, focused on: description of the OD program(s), perceptions of the main goals, reasons for success and failure; role of internal and external change agents, consequences and impact of the program, and the future of OD in the district.
7. The full cases and documentation appear in Fullan, Miles, and Taylor, 1978, Volume IV.
8. We might reiterate here a point made elsewhere (Miles, 1976). Though hundreds of profit-making organizations have ongoing OD programs, they are rarely continued (or discontinued) on grounds that they make or lose money for the company. There is only one known instance of a firm's treating its OD program as a trade secret, which if known would reduce its competitive advantage.

REFERENCES

The larger study from which this article was drawn appears in five volumes, under the general heading *OD in schools: the state of the art*, produced for the National Institute of Education in 1978 under Contracts 400–77–0051, 0052. The five volumes are as follows:

Fullan, M., Miles, M. B., & Taylor, G. Vol. I: *Introduction and executive summary*.

Fullan, M., Miles, M. B., & Taylor, G. Vol. II: *Review of reviews*.

Miles, M. B., Fullan, M., & Taylor, G. Vol. III: *OD consultants/OD programs in school districts*.

Fullan, M., Miles, M. B., & Taylor, G. Vol. IV: *Case studies*.

Miles, M. B., Fullan, M., & Taylor, G. Vol. V: *Implications for policy, research and practice*.

Copies of separate volumes are available at cost from Michael Fullan, Ontario Institute for Studies in Education, 252 Bloor Street West, Toronto, Ontario M5S 1V6, Canada.

Blumberg, A. OD's future in schools–or is there one? *Education and Urban Society*, November 1976, *8*, 213–226.

Deal, T. E., & Derr, C. B. "Toward a contingency theory of organizational change in education: structure, processes and symbolism. Paper prepared for Stanford-Berkeley Seminar, 1977.

Derr, C. B. 'OD' won't work in schools *Education and Urban Society*, November 2, 1976, *8*, 227–241.

Friedlander, F., & Brown, L. D. Organization development. *Annual Review of Psychology*, 1974, *75*, 313–341.

Fullan, M. An overview and critique of OD in schools. Open University Course E283, Management of Education, Open University Press, Milton Keynes, United Kingdom, 1975, pp. 43–49.

Kahn, Robert L. Organizational development: some problems and proposals. *Journal of Applied Behavioral Science*, 1974, *10*(4), 485–502.

Likert, R. *New patterns of management*. New York: McGraw-Hill, 1961.

Lundberg, C. The current state of theory in organization development. Oregon State University. Paper read at Academy of Management meetings. San Francisco, August 1978.

Miles, M. B. Organizational health: figure and ground. In R. O. Carlson et al., *Change processes in the public schools*. Eugene, Ore.: Center for Advanced Study in Educational Administration (CASEA), 1965.

Miles, M. B. Some properties of schools as social systems. In G. Watson (Ed.), *Change in school systems*. Washington, D.C.: National Training Laboratories, 1967.

Miles, M. B. Critique: diffusing OD in schools, the prospects. *Education and Urban Society*, 1976, *8*(2), 242–254.

Miles, M. B., & Schmuck, R. A. Improving schools through organization development: an overview. In R. A. Schmuck & M. B. Miles (Eds.), *Organization development in schools*. LaJolla, Calif.: University Associates, 1971, pp. 1–27.

Pate, L. E., Nielsen, W. R., & Bacon, P. C. Advances in research on organization development: toward a beginning. *Group and Organization Studies*, 1977, *2*(4), 449–460.

Pincus, J. Incentives for innovation in public schools. *Review of Educational Research*, 1974, *44*(1), 113–144.

Runkel, P. J., & Schmuck, R. A. *Organization development in schools: a review of research findings from Oregon*. Eugene, Ore.: Center for Educational Policy and Management, University of Oregon, 1976.

Schmuck, R. A., & Miles, M. B. *Organization development in schools*. La Jolla, Calif.: University Associates, 1971.

Schmuck, R. A., Runkel, P. J., Saturen, S., Martell, R., and Derr, B. *Handbook of organization development in schools*. Palo Alto, Calif.: Mayfield Press, 1972.

Schmuck, R. A., Runkel, P. J., Arends, R. I., & Arends, J. *The second book of organization development in schools*. Palo Alto, Calif.: Mayfield Press, 1977.

United States Department of Health, Education and Welfare. *Digest of educational statistics*. Washington, D.C.: Author, 1977.

Weick, K. Educational organizations as loosely-coupled systems. *Administrative science quarterly*, 1976, *21*, 1–19.

CHAPTER 6

Students as Organizational Participants

JANE H. ARENDS
RICHARD A. SCHMUCK
RICHARD I. ARENDS

THE FACULTY OF Bay City Junior High is engaged in an organization development workshop. It is the afternoon of the second day of a five-day event. The faculty has been assigned randomly to a number of small teams. Four of the teams have been designated to take the role of "planners," and the other four teams are to role play "operators" in an exercise to simulate decision making in a school. Some have been asked to team up with consultants as observers of the simulation. Each team of planners has been directed to devise instructions for its respective operating team in assembling a specially packaged jigsaw puzzle.

Teams of four planners are meeting at one end of the school's multipurpose room, and the teams of four operators are seated at the opposite end of the room. Each planning team has been paired with an operating team to simulate the administrators and teachers of the school. The eight faculty members who have been designated as observers are walking about a room that is buzzing with activity. There is tension in the air.

The planners know they can begin giving instructions at any time during the next half hour, but that they must give the operators at least five minutes of instruction and must finish giving instructions and maintain silence after the thirty minutes have passed. Both the planners and

The Program on Strategies of Organizational Change at the Center for Educational Policy and Management (a division of the College of Education) of the University of Oregon has launched a longitudinal study on action research project on the effects of the school's organization on students, and this chapter is part of that work.

operators know that the exercise will conclude when the operators have completed whatever tasks the planners give them. Planners are not allowed to touch the pieces of the jigsaw puzzle to preclude them from doing the task for the operators. Once the operators have started to put the puzzle together, the planners may not help them.

This scenario has been played at OD workshops many times. Indeed the Planners and Operators Exercise has become a standard feature of training designs in OD that we and others use to facilitate school improvement. With the teachers, administrators, or other adult professionals of the participating schools, the exercise has invariably served as a powerful, efficient, and relatively nonthreatening means of teaching at least three important lessons about certain pitfalls that can occur in relation to organizational problem solving and decision making.

1. *Preoccupations of status responsibility.* Planning often becomes a very seductive assignment. The responsibilities of designing a way of assembling the puzzle and of training the operators both raise the planners' excitement and narrow their awareness. The planners often become so involved in their planning that they ignore the very presence of operators until it becomes absolutely necessary to begin giving instructions. Then their instructions are hurried, and the operators feel at loose ends when the planners are obliged to leave.

2. *Alienation of low-power position.* Operators become increasingly restless and frustrated as the minutes pass and they cannot figure out what work the planners have in mind for them. When the operators send notes to the planners (they are not permitted to initiate a face-to-face visit) to ask for information and receive only cryptic answers, if any, their frustration and restlessness increase. They begin to perceive the planners as not intending to be helpful and supportive, and they come to view themselves as helpless, but as opponents nonetheless of their own organizational coparticipants, the planners.

3. *Hierarchical decision making.* Once the instructions have been given and planners must be quiet while operators work on their own to complete the puzzle, the planners often become extremely upset as they observe deviations from what they believe to have been clear and valid instructions. However, the planners realize where they made their mistake in communication and begin to feel angry with themselves for having neglected the operators for so long during the planning period. They come to appreciate the drawbacks of making decisions *for*, rather than *with*, others.

The Planners and Operators Exercise simulates status differences and role distinctions that are typical of schools. Indeed the exercise works well (even better) when the people who in real life actually occupy low-status positions (e.g., teachers) play planners and when those who are really high-status holders (e.g., the principal and department heads) take the role of operators. It is, in other words, status and role differentiation and not the personalities of the participants that makes the game so much like real life in the school district.

TRADITIONAL SCHOOL IMPROVEMENT

Similar to most consultants who have applied the strategies of organization development to school improvement, we have consulted almost exclusively with groups of adult professionals. We have helped entire faculties, administrative cabinets, teaching teams, departments of central offices, and advisory or policy-making committees to specify more clearly organizational goals, improve meetings, clarify communication, manage conflicts, and develop innovative procedures and structures for solving problems and making decisions. All these OD activities treat the adult professionals as synonymous with the school organization. In fact, consultation for organization development, as we and others have practiced it during the last decade, has a well-documented capacity to enhance interpersonal skills, group norms, and organizational structures as they pertain to adult professionals in schools.

While it may be the case that some OD consultants have worked with nonprofessional adults such as parents or interested citizens in the school community (e.g., parent advisory groups associated with Title I schools, parent-teacher groups wishing to start alternative schools or programs, or citizens who volunteer to work as tutors or instructional aides), the instances of such interventions are isolated and they typically have not been documented or evaluated. Perhaps the primary reason for the scant number of OD interventions involving parents has been that such collections of adults are usually unstable, having few regular members who can represent organized and permanent constituencies. Nonetheless, there have been a handful of efforts to apply OD to parent groups, and if some common logistical and practical difficulties can be overcome, the instances of successful applications will undoubtedly increase.

Students as Organizational Participants It is in relation to students as organizational participants, however, where OD consultants have been most myopic. The theory and practice of OD only rarely has given weight to students as clients. OD consultants along with adult clients have typically regarded students as products of the educational system to be acted upon and shaped, as juveniles (not yet responsible citizens) who need to be controlled or protected, or as consumers who occasionally want to express their reactions and preferences. Almost never have consultants, educators, or parents viewed students as full-fledged organizational members who do, can, or should participate in school planning, problem solving, or decision making. We know of no school where students are viewed as having legitimate influence over the school's curriculum, grading policies, teacher evaluation procedures, budget, and the like.

Many adult-focused school improvement efforts have faltered when students intentionally or unknowingly have sabotaged attempts by the adults to work in new ways together. For example, we have consulted with elementary staffs that were attempting to move from a self-contained structure to team teaching. In some of these schools the students' expectations to have their own homeroom teacher were so strong that they resisted going along with the teachers' efforts at individualizing instruction and platooning the students into various groups. As another example, we have worked in secondary schools in which the staff's best-laid plans for student government went awry because of student apathy and noninvolvement.

An explanation for the ability of students to sabotage school improvement efforts may be the failure to adhere to a fundamental tenet of organization development, which argues that consultation should be provided to important and intact subsystems of the school—to groups of role takers who perform important tasks or sets of related, interdependent tasks. Since in schools students outnumber adults by a substantial margin, many of the most important subsystems—classrooms, for example—have student members. The lack of living up to the subsystem tenet has often hindered attempts at school improvement and has constrained the progress of consultations that are aimed at building the school's organizational capacity to solve problems. By virtue of excluding students from the set of organizational participants, consultants and their adult clients sometimes have had difficulties uncovering and managing important and generic problems with the way work gets accomplished in the school. OD consultants have sometimes been unable to gain access to students' views about how the school functions and affects them, while teachers and administrators have been unable to predict how students will react to their new plans.

The consequences of failing to consider students as organizational participants and to involve them in school improvement efforts can lead to outcomes that are similar to those of the Planners and Operators Exercise. Teachers and administrators can become so preoccupied with their own "important" work and heavy responsibilities that they begin to exhibit insensitivity to students' preferences and experiences. Consultants, too, can concentrate so much on the adult professionals that they get sidetracked from improving the quality of education for the students. Teachers also can feel powerless to discipline students and burdened by the extent of the responsibilities they have assumed. Students, for their part, can feel "put down" by imposed rules and become alienated when their ideas and energies have not been used.

In many schools, particularly in troubled urban schools in which the organizational problems are severe and myriad, alienation of adults from other adults and from students is often very high and dysfunctional. Moreover, within and across the different age groups that spend their time in schools, we have observed a strong association between alienation and mediocrity. Teachers, administrators, students, and consultants alike have sought the lowest common denominator to avoid debilitating and unproductive disagreement over different values that are important to each.

We are not suggesting that all problems of schools or the difficulties faced by OD consultants can be solved simply or easily by bringing students in as full-fledged organizational participants. In fact, we admit that such a strategy is largely untried and that consultants, teachers, and administrators lack experiences upon which to ground their theories and technology for work with students. Since we believe the idea of bringing students and adult professionals together as co-clients in school improvement efforts has enough merit to warrant exploration, the major goal of our research and development work in the Program on Strategies of Organizational Change at the Center for Educational Policy and Management over the next few years will be in this direction.

We will delineate what we know and do not know now about the potentiality of bringing students into the center of school change. Three sections follow. In the first, we present some concepts from social psychology that are relevant to understanding students as organizational participants in schools. The second describes some recent efforts at consultation and workshops in which students were involved and from which some lessons can be derived for future school improvement efforts. The third section considers what we need to learn to actualize the concept of students as participants in planned efforts at school improvement.

UNDERSTANDING STUDENTS AS ORGANIZATIONAL PARTICIPANTS

Three sets of concepts can be helpful in understanding students as organizational participants. These can be conceived as being related in the following manner: The capacities of students interact with the norms and structures of the staff to foster some amount of student participation in organizational problem solving and decision making.

Capacities of Students

We use "capacity" to indicate combinations of interpersonal skills, understandings, experiences, and attitudes that students may possess or aquire as organizational participants. The three capacities worthy of emphasis that match three sets of motivations that students, like adults, bring with them to organizational life are motivations for *affiliation* with others, for *power* over their destinies, and for *achievement* of valued goals. In efforts to satisfy these motives, students will typically strive to experience friendship and trust more often than rejection, influence in relation to others rather than powerlessness, and competence more often than feelings of disability. The lack of gratification of these three motives can reduce the student's self-esteem and lead to alienation from the school.

A student's capacity to affiliate effectively includes skill at interpersonal communication: knowing how to describe others' behaviors and his or her feelings about them, to paraphrase another's messages to show understanding, and to express empathy by checking impressions of another person's feelings. The affiliative capacity may be exhibited when students help one another take part in a class discussion, act as tutors for their peers, help new students to learn about the school, form teams to complete assignments, represent the school in athletics or music, and the like.

Keys to students' capacities to exert power over their own lives are knowledge of their own values and an ability to assert themselves to accomplish their own self-interests. Students exercising this capacity act as advocates or spokespersons for a constituency, negotiate with others when conflict occurs, and act as arbitrators or third parties when others disagree. This capacity is executed by groups of students when, for example, they organize to canvass voters for a school budget election or launch a campaign to clean up the school grounds.

The lion's share of formal programs in most schools are established to foster students' capacity to achieve. As students are helped to acquire academic skill and to learn concepts in a number of disciplines, at the same time they are developing the willingness to take risks, abilities to think creatively, to question what they observe, to mobilize their own energy, and to reach out for the resources that others possess. In student groups, the capacity to achieve is exhibited with skill at convening meetings, brainstorming creative ideas, preparing proposals and action plans, conducting surveys, and the like.

Norms and Structures of the Staff
The way in which most schools are organized, however, offers students little opportunity to use or perfect their capacities. While individual students may become leaders of informal groups of students, it is rare that large numbers of students are called upon or allowed to exhibit their capacities in relation to the school.

The nature of school organizations in public education is such that students cannot use their capacities to affiliate themselves with the school or wield influence on how the school is run without the presence of supportive norms among the staff. The sorts of norms we have in mind are similar to those that are characteristic of democratic groups and what Tannenbaum (1968) has termed the "polyarchic influence structure." Examples of these norms in support of widespread influence include: (1) implicit group agreements that every individual, regardless of status or role, is an important part of the organization; (2) shared expectations that collaboration across organizational levels is preferred to either competition or independent action; (3) group agreements in support of proactivity and thinking ahead instead of "coping" or "fire fighting;" (4) shared support for continuing communication under conditions of conflict, even across organizational levels; and (5) routine attention to group and organizational processes through formal diagnoses and problem-solving discussions that involve all organizational members.

As OD consultants, we have learned the importance of another norm; which supports noting and accepting differences of opinion and feelings and downplays operating on interpersonal and intergroup stereotypes. When such a norm exists on a school staff, opportunities to participate in problem solving are created for persons of both sexes, of any race or ethnicity, and regardless of level of experience, salary, title, or the like. While this norm is rarely strong in schools, we have seen it take hold among adult staff members that have taken part in organization development projects. However, another norm—one that supports stereotyping on the basis of age—has largely been inimical to alteration, even in the most successful OD schools. In most schools, even after extended consultation, there remains a decided gap between adults and students in relation to how the school should be run, and the motivation and cognitive capacities of students are ignored or undervalued. Where such a norm is pervasive and salient, students stand little chance of being viewed as full-fledged organizational participants and therefore of being able to participate in a problem-solving manner with the adult staff.

In addition to the presence of norms among the staff that might support students as organizational participants, certain structural characteristics of the school also seem to be important. We have generalized three from our work as OD consultants with adult groups in schools. First, there are multiple structures for problem solving that are differentiated from structures used for other purposes. In other words, the school participants do not expect a single structure—the faculty, the student council, or the administrative team, for example—to be sufficient to handle the myriad organizational problems of the school. This feature also implies that settings from problem solving are separated from occasions for communicating routine information, for supervising performance, for redressing grievances, or for learning new interpersonal and group skills.

Second, there is clarity about the boundaries of every structure both for the benefit of those who participate in each and for the understanding of those who do not. For example, there is clarity about the limits of parental authority, the faculty's powers, administrators' prerogatives, and the jurisdiction of the student council. People recognize that formal group agreements only emerge from extensive communication and often time-consuming and difficult negotiations, and that to abandon the search for clarity about boundaries in the interest of saving time or avoiding conflict is to render those structures impotent.

Third, there is flexibility and informality within structures used for problem solving. People recognize that rigid and formalized rules about who can say what, procedures for meetings, or what topics are appropriate for the agenda often destroy creativity, create unnecessary smokescreens that get in the way of managing important conflicts, and take the fun out of participation. The school has ways to achieve clarity about the boundaries of multiple structures without firmly or permanently casting elaborate charters, codes, constitutions, role descriptions, and the like.

Participation in Organizational Problem Solving

Not all the functions and tasks that are carried out in a school can or should involve the collaborative actions of adults and students. For instance, in many schools tasks such as maintaining students' records, scheduling classes, requisitioning supplies and books, negotiating teachers' salaries, and completing required reports for the state department may be performed capably and appropriately by adults with very little, if any, involvement on the part of students.

On the other hand, students might more appropriately be brought in on tasks related to problems and programs that require their interest for implementation. Without opportunity to participate, students may express their opinions by "voting with their feet" and staying away from programs they have no hand in designing, by psychologically withdrawing from instruction that they find irrelevant, or by disobeying or ignoring rules that they have had no part in making or that they find oppressive or unreasonable.

Figure 6.1 displays a classification of issues commonly present in schools. Examples in each category of the scheme do not comprise an exhaustive list, but are illustrative of questions that have attracted the interest of students with whom we have worked.

The Classroom

Group Processes and Maintenance

Who will correct the tests or lead the discussion?
What constitutes "helping" that is not "cheating"?
How can friendship, playfulness, and anger be displayed?

Instruction and Learning

What requirements and assignments pertain to which students?
About which topics can students disagree with the teacher?
How shall grades be distributed?

The School

Curriculum and Programs

Which electives shall be offered for next year?
Which books can be checked out for independent study?
When can out-of-school-jobs count for academic credit?

Extracurricular Activities

Which interest groups should the school sponsor?
What arrangements shall support incoming students?
What foods shall be served in the cafeteria?

The School Environment

Neighborhood and Community

Can students go off campus during the day?
What community events will be held in the building?
What procedures must visitors to the school follow?

Other Schools and District

What special programs can the school offer?
What teachers shall be assigned to the school?
How can transfers among schools be arranged?

Figure 6-1   Issues for student participation in organizational problem solving

With respect to any issue delineated in figure 6.1, students may participate at one or more stages of problem solving. They may be called upon to identify and articulate the problems that are most deserving of attention. At another stage of problem solving, they may be involved in generating diagnostic data, brainstorming alternative actions, or designing possible solutions to problems. Once alternative proposals have been developed, they may participate in deciding on the one that shall become policy or procedure. Still later, after a decision has been made, they may assume responsibility for implementation or evaluation of effects.

Students can participate in organizational problem solving within various groups. An individual student may participate as a member of the total student body, as an officer of a grade level, or as a representative of a particular classroom, program, or interest group. Students may act as delegates to faculty senates or parent advisory boards by virtue of their appointment, election, or own initiative, and they may serve as representatives of some constituency on a student council, faculty-student senate, or parent-faculty policy-making body. Of course, some students may participate in several of these ways simultaneously.

At different stages of problem solving, depending on the particular issue, students can participate by being accorded different status or given different levels of decision-making authority commensurate with their participation. A scheme is offered below for rating and coding the degrees of decision-making participation from low to high, which we have often used in our OD consultations with adult groups to create group agreements about who functions and in what manner in relation to a particular issue.

Levels of Participation in Decision Making

I: Is Informed. After a decision has been made, a person or group can be told the result and required to go along with it.

C: Is Consulted. Before a decision is made, a person or group can express an opinion about one or more of the alternatives.

Vo: Votes. A person or group can participate by casting a written or verbal ballot.

Ve: Vetoes. After a decision has been made, a person or group may be able to overturn or ignore it.

In attempting to gain shared understandings about the role of students in organizational problem solving, a multicelled matrix is prepared in which rows are labeled with issues from the above scheme and the columns are titled with persons or groups in the school, e.g., administrators, counselors, teachers, students, etc. The cells of the matrix are coded with the categories of this scheme in order to depict the level of involvement appropriate to each person or group who has a stake in the school. This matrix can be prepared with only the roles and the columns specified and then the adults and students can discuss alternative ways of filling out the matrix with the categories. Table 6.1 presents an illustration of a participation matrix for a high school involved in enabling students to become full-fledged organizational participants.

EXAMPLES OF CONSULTATION FOR STUDENTS AS ORGANIZATIONAL PARTICIPANTS

Now we turn to a description of three tested strategies, each of which aims to help students increase their understandings of how school organization works and to become skillful as organizational participants. These strategies do not comprise a complete list of all that have been tried in schools but instead offer a starting point for planning to achieve school improvement. They represent attempts to make

Table 6-1
Illustrative Matrix for Participation in Decision Making

Issues	Categories of Participants						
	Principal	Other Administrators	Counselors and Specialists	Elected Faculty	Faculty at large	Elected Students	Students at large
Elective classes for next year	I	C	Vo	Ve	Vo	C	I
Out-of-school jobs for credit	C	C	Vo	Ve	Vo	C	I
Interest groups for school sponsorship	Ve	Vo	Vo	I	I·	Vo	C
Students off campus during the day	Vo	Vo	Vo	Vo	Vo	Vo	Vo
Community events in the school	Ve	Vo	I	C	I	C	I

changes away from the traditional hierarchical school in which the adults serve as the planners and the students as the operators toward a more democratic and polyarchic organizational structure.

Changing Classroom Norms Several school districts now regularly receive consultation in organization development from cadres of organizational specialists. The cadres are composed of specially trained teachers, administrators, and counselors working part time as organizational consultants while also carrying out their regular full-time duties. We have trained and studied cadres in Eugene, Oregon and Kent, Washington and are familiar with the operation of additional OD cadres in Polk County, Florida, Santa Cruz, California, and Buffalo, New York.

Members of at least the first two cadres have, on occasion, provided consultation to classroom groups of students and their teachers. The most common designs have involved training the teacher and students simultaneously in the cognitive and behavioral aspects of interpersonal communication, steps and procedures for group problem solving, goal-setting methods, and in the methods of process observation and debriefing in relation to the classroom group. The Planners and Operators Exercise has been used to highlight the dysfunctions of classroom hierarchy while other exercises such as the Five Square Puzzle or the NASA Consensus Activity (Cost on the Moon) (Schmuck et al., 1977, pp. 131–133, 344–347) have been used to help class members and the teacher test out new ways of carrying out joint problem solving and collaborative decision making. After several hours of this training, the cadre members then have helped the students and their teacher to explore the most potent norms that govern how work gets accomplished in their classroom, how students and the teacher relate to one another, and how rewards and punishments get distributed. The analysis of existing classroom norms has served as a springboard for establishing new norms that were desired and for creating new structures and processes to make the classroom a more enjoyable and effective environment for teaching and learning. The basic design has sometimes been embellished with elements described by Schmuck and Schmuck (1979). These elements have included activities in relation to the sequential stages of group growth, classroom leadership, interpersonal communication, and group cohesiveness. Some form of a design to refurbish group norms has been tried with a high school band, a high school art class, elementary school classrooms, and junior high homerooms and guidance groups.

Our evaluations of these cadre interventions indicate that many target groups have developed a more open climate both in terms of support for learning and for personal development—a climate where students help set their own learning goals, work toward accomplishing their goals in collaborative rather than competitive ways and are involved in assessing their own progress. In classroom groups where extended interventions have occurred, new norms have been built in support of promptness and completeness of assignments, helpfulness to younger children, cleaning up materials and equipment, and talking about feelings rather than acting them out.

However, in some schools, particularly those where students do not spend the entire day in a self-contained classroom but rather move into different groups and are with different teachers, some problems have resulted from consultation to change the norms of one or a few classrooms. Students have been quick to recognize inconsistencies among the norms of different classes and have caused or been caused to have problems as they repeatedly had to adapt to widely differing rules and expectations. Teachers and students alike have found it confusing and upsetting when, in some classes, student participation was expected and rewarded and students were encouraged to evaluate and discuss how the class was going, while in other classes the spirit of collaboration was very low, the teacher directed all activities, and the students were expected to keep their evaluations to themselves.

Amending Curricula Another strategy for school improvement that calls upon students to act as organizational participants involves planned change of the formal curriculum. The three of us, along with two secondary teachers and one student, took that approach by developing a short curriculum module for the American Psychological Association's Project on Human Behavior (1977). The fundamental objectives of the module, *Understanding School Life through Organizational Psychology*, were to help students understand the dynamics of the school as a form of social organization, to delineate their roles as potential organizational participants, and to present the students with the skills required to design and implement a sustained school-improvement program.

Through a series of experimental activities, reading, and group assignments, students who participate in the three-week module (approximately twelve hours of instruction) learn how the human motives of affiliation, power, and achievement may be satisfied or frustrated through organizational participation. They have an opportunity to practice some communication skills to facilitate their discussions about interpersonal relations in the school and then explore the roles of individuals, groups, and the organization-as-a-whole in carrying out the school's missions and in satisfying the needs of both the students and the adults. In one activity students prepare "maps" of the informal structure of the school, designating the groups in which students spend their time out of school. They compare the maps with rosters of students in classrooms and discuss the congruence of friendship groups to work groups. In another activity students collect questionnaires about the climate of the school from other students, teachers, and administrators. They analyze the data and present a summary in a colloquium setting for members of their class and interested others in the school. This activity can provide the school with important data for diagnosing the satisfactions and frustrations of all participants in relation to the way decisions are made, how conflict is managed, and how goals are established.

This strategy of amending the formal curriculum by adding a special workshop for some students does not necessarily facilitate normative and structural improvement in the school. It does, however, provide at least some students with understandings and skills that can help them participate more effectively as clients of more comprehensive designs for OD interventions. And in a few instances it has encouraged the development of a special task force that continues on after the module to attempt to design and implement some improvements in the school organization. In one school dissatisfactions of teachers and students with the operation of the student council became the springboard for rethinking how students should be elected to that group, which items were appropriate for its agenda, how its meetings would be conducted, and how its decisions could be transmitted to the student body and faculty.

Improving Student Governance   A third example of efforts to treat students as organizational participants aims at improving the effectiveness of student governance structures within high schools. Within our program, this strategy has been engineered by Medina (1978) who has developed and field tested an instructional system titled *Student Leadership Skills*. Medina's thirty-hour design trains members of student councils to examine their own group behavior, develop more effective interpersonal communication skills, consider new ways of relating to their constituencies, and learn more effective procedures for conducting meetings in which collaborative problem solving and decision making occur. His design requires taking the entire student council and its faculty adviser out of school for approximately one week. Through a series of activities and discussion periods, council members learn new understandings and consider applications of their skills to their roles as student leaders and to the responsibilities of their council as a leadership group in the school.

Evaluations of initial field tests led Medina to conclude that at least two important and new learnings accrued to students who participated. First, they came to understand and appreciate leadership as a set of functions performed by a group instead of as the attributes of particular people. They came to realize that their student council's effectiveness rested on the skills that each of them could and did exhibit. Second, they learned how to observe human behavior, to draw and check inferences from that behavior, and to use their observations to assess the effectiveness and appropriateness of their group's dynamics. According to Medina, students were surprised and delighted to learn how to check one another's skills in paraphrasing, for example, and to watch for behaviors that would signal a problem with making decisions in their meetings.

In some schools, students changed the nature of their council meetings after training. Follow-up investigation of trained students councils, however, showed little transfer and carry-over to other groups in the school and some fade-out of effects over time within the council. As council members were confronted with existing norms and structures of their school, and as there was some turnover in council membership, the new norms within the council were eroded. This led Medina to conclude that a macrodesign of some extended duration with an intensive start-up workshop and a series of follow-up events would be necessary to build a sustained capacity for problem solving into the councils.

SOME PROBLEMS FOR FUTURE APPLICATIONS

The time is right to test out applications of the theories and technology of organizaton development to students as organizational participants. There are, as we have described, both concepts and ideas for consultation that already have been tested against the reality of bringing students into school improvement efforts. In all, we think the prospects look good for applying what we already know to more schools.

But there is a lot that is not known by schools and their consultants. We have identified at least two important gaps in available knowledge that ought to be filled before future applications with students are tried. The first concerns the lack of current knowledge about how students are related to their schools as organizations and the effects that the structures and norms of schools have upon students. The second concerns the lack of comprehensive designs for promoting student participation in problem solving and decision making in schools.

Students in School Organizations   OD consultants work in schools not only to help clients acquire new interpersonal skills, but also to promote effective organizational norms and structures. Few consultants are satisfied if undesired hierarchical norms persist or if new, more collaborative structures fail to take hold. In relation to efforts to make students more integral organizational participants, however, consultants and their adult clients lack knowledge about those dynamics of schools' norms and structures that relate to the interface between adults and students. They need this knowledge to develop their consultative strategies and to monitor their effects.

There has been very little documented experience and virtually no systematic research on the relationship of students to their school organizations. We don't know if or how students are affected by student councils, faculty-student senates, or other structures that aim to enhance their participation in problem solving and decision making in their school. We also don't know much about the dynamics through which informal cliques and scheduled groupings of students facilitate or constrain their participation in the school-as-a-whole. And while we know that it is difficult to do away with the stereotype that all students are inferior to all adults, we don't know the kinds of role relationships among adults that make the stereotype more or less likely to be present. What is required, we think, is some large-scale, longitudinal research to produce information about the relationships of students and schools as organizations.

Such an effort will be part of the work of the Program on Strategies of Organizational Change. We shall look for chains of causes and effects among (1) norms and structures that govern interaction among adults in schools, (2) innovative and traditional arrangements for promoting student participation in problem solving and decision making, and (3) effects on students' perceptions, skills, and accomplishments. We hope that the knowledge we will gain will prove to be informative and helpful to consultants and schools that wish to extend applications of organization development to students.

Macrodesigns for Consultation   Because of the organizational complexities of the many adult and student subsystems of schools, efforts at planned change that aim to help students become full-fledged organizational participants are much larger in scope than the typical OD consultations that have been carried out in schools. A macrodesign involving consultation to change classroom norms has to be repeated many times in a large secondary school where students move from classroom to classroom five or seven times a day. A macrodesign involving an amendment to the curriculum (such as the module described earlier) requires simultaneous work with administrators and other teachers so they can play their respective parts appropriately. A macrodesign including an effort to improve student governance (such as that designed by Medina) requires extensive followup with the group of student clients to prevent fade-out of effects.

Besides the problems of increasing the sheer number of clients and subsystems that need to participate in the school improvement effort, there are further complications that arise in working with students because of their regular flow in and out of the school through matriculation and graduation. A three-year middle school, for example, expects a 33 percent turnover rate each year. Three years, as most consultants know already, represents a very short period of time to build and stabilize new norms and structures in any but the simplest and smallest of organizations.

Macrodesigns for consultation aimed at student participation, therefore, have to be extremely complex and comprehensive. They require more days of consultation by more consultants than is typical of most OD in schools. Consultants who wish to extend applications of OD to students will, we think, find it useful to share ideas about such things as: (1) finding the time to work with students, particularly finding chunks of time that last longer than the class period or school day; (2) supporting adults in the school who act as consultants to student groups; (3) teaching student consultants to help incoming students develop their capacities as participants; and (4) timing and sequencing the various parts of comprehensive designs for training, consultation, feedback, and confrontation.

OD consultants and other change agents in education who aspire to extend applications of their theories to work with students have a major task before them if they are to produce the knowledge needed for school improvement through student involvement. We end, therefore, by noting that the prospects seem exciting, that the problems appear to be many but not insurmountable, and that the opportunity awaits those who will join in finding ways to understand and help students as organizational members who can and should contribute to improving their schools. We hope someday to begin a chapter of another book like this:

> It is the first week of school in 1980 at Bay city Junior High. The entire faculty and student body are involved in a week-long OD workshop to establish a sense of community cohesiveness in the school. During the latter half of the second day some of the students are put into planning teams and teachers along with the school's administrators become operators. The planners have the serious responsibility of training the operators in how to put a complex jigsaw puzzle together. The operators are waiting restlessly for their instructions. . . .

REFERENCES

Arends, R., et. al. *Understanding school life through organizational psychology*. Washington, D.C.: American Psychological Association, 1977.

Medina, G. *Student leadership skills: The development and testing of an instructional team*. Unpublished doctoral dissertation, University of Oregon, 1978.

Schmuck, R., Runkel, P., Arends, J., and Arends, R. *The second handbook of organization development in schools*. Palo Alto, Calif.: Mayfield Publishing, 1977.

Schmuck, R., & Schmuck, P. *Group processes in the classroom*. Dubuque, Iowa. William C. Brown, 1979.

Tannenbaum, A. *Control in organizations*. New York: McGraw-Hill, 1968.

CHAPTER 7

Turning on Big City Schools: Pragmatic, Participatory, Problem Solving

MARC BASSIN
THOMAS GROSS

THE PROBLEMS of inner city schools are well documented in the national press. Indicators such as increasing violence and vandalism (*Phi Delta Kappan*, January 1978) and declining reading and math scores (Ebel, April 1978), coupled with pessimistic perceptions of those within the schools (*Newsweek*, March 1978) paint a bleak picture of these schools as institutions in crisis. At the same time repeated research findings indicate that "no significant differences" are produced by the billions spent on efforts to aid the schools from external research and development centers (National Institute of Education, 1974). This situation increasingly leaves inner-city schools with the necessity of better utilizing their own resources to solve their pressing problems.

CAN SCHOOLS SOLVE THEIR OWN PROBLEMS?

Ten years of experience in the New York City high schools in developing a self-renewal model for just such a process leads to an encouraging and affirmative response. Consider a case in point.

In 1975 renewal began in what may be characterized as a typical south Bronx high school of 5,000 students, 95 percent of them being minority students from lower income homes. Sixty-five percent was the average attendance rate. At least 70 percent of the students were reading two or more years below grade level; in addition, 50 percent of the students dropped out of school by the end of two years.

The teacher union in the school was strong and generally antagonistic, and there have been a succession of three principals in the last three years. Among the problems evident in the school were lack of adequate security, lack of discipline, smoking of pot and cigarettes in the halls, selling of drugs in and around the school, a very low percentage of students passing regents, poor morale and lack of innovation among staff, and an outdated curriculum that had been designed for a different student population ten years previously.

The current principal began to involve his school community earnestly in the renewal process in 1975. Since then the renewal participative problem-solving process has resulted in the following: the establishment of a thriving career education program; a mini-school for low achievers encompassing about one-half of the incoming ninth graders with a specific focus on improving reading skills; Project Return, a program designed to help truants ease themselves back into the school; a computerized attendance program that has reduced absenteeism by about 18 percent; a school beautification effort; a biweekly student newsletter; a student renewal class; a pregnant girls' class; an office skills class that simulates an actual business office; the production of over two hundred lesson plans in English, math, and science to relate to careers; and the revamping of the entire English curriculum to focus more attention on standards.

In addition, the cabinet, which is the administrative body of the school, has engaged in a management development program to improve its effectiveness.

While this school has by no means completely solved its problems, it has engaged more than half of the faculty, the entire administration, many students, parents, and community members in assuming responsibility for systematically working on them. Renewal certainly cannot alone take the credit for the great strides this school has made over the past four years, but is been the major vehicle for talented individuals who are committed to improving their school from within.

This case of attempting to improve a New York City high school exemplifies issues and problems involved with working to improve inner-city schools anywhere in the country. The New York City system is large and unresponsive: there are over one million students. In the High School Division alone there are 111 schools, many of which have 4,000 students. The system is vulnerable to the socioeconomic conditions of the modern city. The middle class continues to flee while increasing numbers of economically disadvantaged minorities move in. At the same time the education budget has been cut over and over in the face of general city-wide budget cuts, causing many of the younger energetic teachers to lose their jobs and lowering the morale of those remaining. In spite of these conditions—and perhaps because of them—renewal has spread rapidly throughout the city so that currently there are thirty-one schools actively engaged in the process.

School self-renewal is a participatory, systematic, planning, and problem-solving methodology calling upon all segments of the school community (administrators, teachers, counselors, students, parents, and others living or working near the school) to collectively identify, analyze, and develop solutions to school problems, according to a specific sequence of problem-solving steps called the renewal model. It represents the longest (ten years, 1969–79), largest, and what we believe to be one of the most successful, models developed nationally to introduce organization development (OD), problem solving and management concepts, and techniques into the public schools.

Several factors indicate the efficacy of the school self-renewal approach to school improvement: the program has expanded from two to thirty-one schools in ten years; the principals in the program support it publicly with their testimony; in spite of severe budget cuts the New York City Board of Education has increasingly assumed financial responsibility for the program; and two externally conducted evaluations of the program conclude that it is a widely successful method of school self-improvement (Sole, 1977; Simmeljkaer, 1978).

This chapter will present the history of the renewal program and renewal model, provide case examples, summarize recent research results, and indicate the major learnings to date about this approach to school problem solving.

HISTORY OF RENEWAL

High School Self-Renewal began as a joint endeavor between the Economic Development Council of New York City, a nonprofit business organization of over two hundred corporate members, and the New York City Board of Education as a pilot in two inner schools in 1969. Known then as the "Partnership Program," it involved the placing of teams of "on-loan" business executives in the schools. In 1970, two additional schools were added. In 1974, the partnership program and the on-loan executives were replaced by the renewal program and the six-person renewal consulting team, which is providing services to twenty-nine high schools and two junior high schools. This successful history of business and school collaboration is evidenced by a shared funding arrangement for the support of this project by the two groups.

THE RENEWAL MODEL

A Pragmatic Approach to School Improvement

Inner-city school people evidence pessimism and little patience with promises of change in their schools. For this reason, any effective school improvement methodology must be pragmatic. The renewal model is based on this recognition and has developed three pragmatic elements: flexibility, political sensitivity, and speed. The model is flexible in that the uniqueness of the individual school is addressed. Each step of the model has a range of alternatives from which the school's renewal participants may select those that are most appropriate to their own situation. Next, the model is sensitive to the political dynamics of the school organization. The renewal consultant is skilled and experienced in preventing and, if necessary, mediating conflict between interest groups or individuals. Finally, the model aims to help the renewal committee establish early credibility through the achievement of speedy results, at least within the first five months of the process in the school. Taken together, these aspects of the renewal approach represent the bottom line pragmatic conditions for introducing this process into a troubled big city school. Without any of these components, the chances of survival for the process diminish substantially.

Underlying Assumptions of the Renewal Model

Certain key assumptions are the basis upon which the methods of the renewal model have been developed. All pertain to the climate of working in inner-city schools. Two basic renewal assumptions are shared in common with OD. The first holds that any organization, including a school, has sufficient human resources to engage in self-help problem solving so that it may improve itself significantly from within (Schmuck, 1974). This assumption is the basis for one school of thought in OD, the "human process" approach to improving organizations (Friedlander and Brown, 1974).

The second assumption relates to another school of thought in OD, what Friedlander and Brown call the "techno-structural" approach, and holds that improvements in organizations should aim at structures and processes so as to produce results as directly as possible. For this reason, contrary to common OD practice, committees are created and are trained by doing renewal rather than first being trained.

The third basic assumption of the renewal model is not found in the literature on OD and is unique to the Renewal Program. This holds that a credible outside agency is necessary to serve as an external catalyst for school improvement. In the case of renewal, the external catalyst has been the Economic Development Council (EDC) of New York City. EDC was the originator of the renewal concept beginning in 1969 and has been a primary source of funds and support over the years. The Board of Education has openly accepted the involvement of EDC due to its professional credibility and substantial resources.

The Six-Stage Renewal Model

The renewal model is a participatory, systematic, planning and problem-solving methodology. It calls for all segments of the school community (teachers, students, administrators, parents, and other staff) to collectively identify, analyze and develop solutions to school problems. The model had six discrete, sequential stages: entry, diagnosis, planning, implementation, evaluation, and maintenance/institutionalization.

ENTRY. This is the set of activities that comprises the school's initiation of the process of renewal. It begins with the nomination of the school to the renewal program by the principal, possibly upon the suggestion of the superintendent. Following that is the acceptance of the school by the renewal program if there is available consultant time. A renewal consultant then meets with the principal to begin to explore which segment of the school should be the first to proceed with renewal. Next, the principal, usually with the help of invited staff members, designs a process with the consultant for selecting an internal renewal coordinator who will oversee the project. The coordinator's first task is to enlist a voluntary committee. Finally, the consultant, the coordinator, the principal, and the committee design the details of the remaining stages of the renewal model in terms of who will do what and when. These prior steps are not rigid and may differ from school to school.

DIAGNOSIS. This is the data collection or needs assessment stage of renewal. The committee decides which segment(s) of the school community to survey and then collects data upon which to make its diagnosis of school problems. Various methods of data collection are used, the most common being survey instruments, group brainstorming, and interviews. All of these methods produce opinion data. Occasionally, baseline, or quantitive data, are also collected, which are used by the committee to establish the planning priorities.

PLANNING. This is the process by which ideas and programs are developed for solving priority problems. It entails several steps:

1. Potential implementers are invited to participate in the planning process so that they may later want to cooperate in implementation because they were included in the plans.

2. Research and development is carried out by examining the relevant effective practices employed elsewhere.
3. The action plan is developed including a carefully specified set of objectives, an accountability scheme, and a time line.
4. The evaluation is designed in advance as a way of creating a vehicle for modifying and improving the project during implementation.
5. Administrative approval is sought in order to assure that the project is consonant with the goals of the schools and also to enlist the support of the administration in facilitating the process of implementation.

IMPLEMENTATION. The planning process culminates in implementation, which involves putting into effect the planned programs or processes.

EVALUATION. Primarily a formative, or ongoing, assessment, the purpose of evaluation is to support, modify, and improve the implementation process.

MAINTENANCE/INSTITUTIONALIZATION. The final step of the renewal model is maintenance/institutionalization, which entails decreased dependence on the external consultant and greater assumption or responsibility by the coordinator and the committee for generating new planning cycles with involvement of new school constituencies. It requires that the renewal committee(s) and processes have credibility in the school based on a successful record of accomplishment and that the committee(s) are considered to be a regular component of the school.

The Four Levels of Renewal: Assuring Flexibility

The renewal model is flexible so that it may be adapted to the needs of each unique school. Introducing renewal to various levels of the school organization is the primary feature assuring this flexibility. Levels may be considered subsystems and for the purposes of renewal include administrators, school-wide staff, students, and academic departments. Each school selects levels for renewal in a different sequence and with a different representation of individuals. If renewal is stymied on one level—for example, due to political constraints—then it may be introduced to another level. This permits the maintenance of renewal in the school and also makes possible the return of renewal to the previous level when conditions become more conducive. Thus, the combination of levels varies from school to school.

Once a level has been selected the consultant and the client group design the activities for each stage of the renewal model to fit the needs of that particular school.

A brief explanation of the characteristics of the four levels of renewal follows:

1. *School-wide renewal*—A committee of staff, students, community, and parents that represent the various constituencies of the school working on school-wide problems (the most common level for beginning renewal).
2. *Student renewal*—Renewal that is carried out independently with a group of students, usually in a class for credit especially arranged for this purpose. The students work toward solving school-wide problems as seen by students.
3. *Department renewal*—Renewal that is done in a subject department where the process is used to examine any aspects of the functioning of the department (usually curriculum).
4. *Cabinet (administrative) renewal*—Renewal with the top and middle management team of the school (the cabinet—the principal and his or her department heads) for more effective management of the school. This in turn has four approaches from which the cabinet may choose, usually one at a time. They may be conceptualized on a continuum ranging from least threatening/least beneficial, to most threatening/most beneficial.

    a. *Seminars:* on management topics such as decision making, accountability, delegation, time management, etc.
    b. *Work on an administrative problem:* use of the renewal problem-solving process to work on a live problem facing the administration such as programming or security
    c. *Improving cabinet functioning (team building):* to improve the functioning of the cabinet as a team through application of OD survey feedback methods whereby the team analyzes itself
    d. *Leadership:* to improve the functioning of each administrator as a supervisor through a process of survey feedback from teachers to chairpersons (subordinates to superordinates)

Key Roles Necessary to Implement the Renewal Model

Carrying out renewal properly involves a commitment of time and energy on the part of the participants to following the sequence of the six stages of the process. While it is not necessary for any individual to devote her or his full time to renewal, during the sequence specific functions are performed by individuals in specific roles.

The principal, having invited renewal into the school, must continue to demonstrate support and commitment throughout this process. This begins by appointing a Renewal Coordinator, a staff member who will receive some release time from teaching to manage and facilitate the renewal project in the school. The coordinator is helped and trained by a Renewal Consultant, an external OD consultant who is responsible for helping the school to learn and institutionalize the process. The consultant guides the coordinator and a Renewal Committee, a voluntary group comprised of members of the school community, through the six-stage process, gradually transferring more responsibility to them. They are also aided by a Corporate Representative, an executive from a company who serves as a liaison between the company and the school so as to provide company resources when possible to support the renewal process. Taken together, these roles provide the impetus and structure necessary to initiate and maintain renewal.*

THE RENEWAL MODEL IN OPERATION: PROTOTYPICAL CASE EXAMPLES

The case examples that follow are intended to provide the reader with some understanding of the wide range of forms renewal takes in different schools. The cases span the continuum from fairly easy, rather successful situations, to extremely difficult, frustrating ones.

It will be noted that, in most cases, the flexibility and resiliency of the model (among all four levels of use) were key factors in getting it to take hold within a school. The cases will be presented according to the four levels since that is the primary macro-level guide for conceptualizing renewal activities.

Case 1: Approaching the Ideal
Renewal has been in this school for only one year. One-fourth of the teachers are actively involved and have met weekly during one of their lunch hours. The coordinator is capable, committed, and well regarded. The principal attends all meetings and is extremely supportive of the entire project.

After a school-wide diagnosis through a questionnaire, five project committees were established. The simplest and first project involved the fixing and changing of bell schedules allowing for reduced traffic and noise in the halls. This early success was followed by the creation of a buddy system to help new teachers to adjust more easily to the school, a social staff newspaper to enhance communications, the production of a student handbook, and the creation of an entirely new discipline and attendance procedure involving all staff in the school.

The committee has enjoyed the participation of a corporate representa-

---

*A more detailed description of the renewal roles may be found in the Renewal Manual, *School Self-Renewal*, by Marc Bassin and Tom Gross, available upon request from the authors.

tive from a nearby company at most of its meetings. In addition to providing a much appreciated point of view, he has arranged for tours of the corporation by students and the printing of the student handbook.

An evaluation committee has been established and a questionnaire designed to evaluate all the projects early next year. Plans have also been made to begin a student renewal class next term with one of this year's committee members as teacher. The committee and principal just spent a half day away from school-making plans to recycle the process next year and are eagerly anticipating implementing their plans.

Case 2: A Waste of Time

After attempting to initiate renewal in some form for a year in this school, we have politely withdrawn. Trouble began with warnings from many people in the school that renewal was not possible here because of an authoritarian principal. Problems first emerged over wording on the diagnostic questionnaire, and were compounded when none of the recommendations of the core group were implemented. A weak coordinator and an outright antagonistic union resulted in a union faculty referendum that showed no support for renewal. An attempt was made to work with a group of students, but the student adviser refused to present any plans to the principal, fearing that they would be thwarted. Under these conditions, after a year's time, we withdrew our consultant from the school. (This is one of the two schools from among the thirty from which we have withdrawn the Renewal Program feeling that no progress was possible at that time.)

Student Renewal—Case 3: Setting an Example:
"If you won't do it, we will"

When we tried to form a core group of staff in this school, we could only get two teacher volunteers. Since the principal was very interested we began to work directly with the cabinet (administrative team). They were somewhat reluctant but went along because of his interest and used the process to restructure and standardize the way by which classroom observations would be made. Input from teachers was solicited in the process.

At the same time one of the teachers who originally volunteered approached a student leadership class to do renewal. They agreed and did a survey of all the students. The survey indicated a need for more student-teacher responsiveness and a plan to form a voluntary course evaluation form was developed by the students. The students recruited eight individual teachers to help develop the form and presented their ideas at a faculty conference. As a result, 80 percent of the teachers volunteered to use the feedback.

During the second year of renewal in this school a small staff committee was formed. A staff diagnosis indicated that students were wandering in the halls, particularly during lunch periods, and student disruptions in the cafeteria as problems. The committee developed the idea of the staff offering voluntary clubs during the busiest lunch periods to reduce wandering and cafeteria problems. Sixteen staff members volunteered and offered clubs. The committee developed a student handbook for all students that is printed by the corporate representative and was first utilized during the fall of 1979.

The student group has continued and is now managing a lounge that they established during the lunch periods, which was furnished by their corporate representative. In this school, what is emerging as a potentially strong renewal program began as a result of a strongly committed principal, a group of eager students, and a single committed staff member (who later became the coordinator).

Department Renewal—Case 4: Developing Standards
When we heard that one of our strongest renewal coordinators became the chairperson of the English Department, we all waited eagerly to see if she could utilize the renewal process to improve her department. We did not have to wait for long. At one of her early meetings she presented the process to the more than forty members of her department many of whom had already been involved in school-wide renewal, and agreement was reached among the teachers to utilize the process to examine the shortcomings of their department, the largest in the school. A diagnosis by the teachers revealed the lack of standards in terms one to four, and the absence of standardized lessons for the first ten days of the term (when there are a great number of shifts among students from class to class due to program changes) as the two highest priorities.

Six task forces were created with each teacher choosing to volunteer to work on one. Teachers and task force leaders agreed to meet on their own time to work on these identified problem areas. Task force chairpersons coordinated the work of the task forces by meeting with each other and the department chairperson. Plans were made into action steps for the writing of new curriculum for the entire department. A small funding grant ($500.00) from the renewal program will provide for the writing of this new curriculum over the summer by a group of five teachers.

This same renewal process was used in the department simultaneously to produce a new writing curriculum, a book committee for systematically ordering texts based on teacher recommendations, and an inter-visitation program for observations among teachers highlighting effective practices. Finally, a student Renewal Leadership Class has been institutionalized as part of the English Department, Students in this class, among other things, will review the new curriculum.

Cabinet Renewal—Case 5: "Moving through the Continuum"
Renewal began in the cabinet of this school in 1976 at the request of the principal with some seminars on selected management topics, time management, delegation, and accountability. Finding these informative, the

cabinet, with very active support from the principal, chose to commit most of the time allocated by the contract for professional development training to the second model of cabinet renewal—working on administrative problems. The consultant spent the next year helping to facilitate work on a number of problems, such as supervision and preparing students for tests, using the steps of the renewal process. Having had a successful experience with this, the cabinet took a bolder step and agreed to examine its own functioning—the third method of cabinet renewal. Members filled out questionnaires and were interviewed by the consultant. The data was fed back in one session and another was devoted to planning for changes in the operations of the cabinet. A number of fundamental changes, particularly in an effort to strengthen accountability and the implementation system being used, were adopted. The cabinet is also committed to utilizing a number of new meeting procedures such as sharing in the preparation of the agenda and debriefing their meetings.

Feeling very positive about the steps taken so far, the cabinet has committed itself to move to the fourth model—feedback to supervisors. Throughout this two-year process, the renewal consultant has been able to develop a close relationship with the principal, which includes direct face-to-face feedback on his management style.

RESEARCH FINDINGS ON RENEWAL OUTCOMES

The renewal program contracted an assessment team in January 1977 to conduct an objective, external assessment of its work in the high schools. In addition, a formative assessment is conducted internally in an ongoing way by the renewal consultant team and the policy-making team (model team).

While the assessment team's report (Sole, 1977) is comprehensive, the most complete perspective on the dynamics of the renewal process, including benefits and constraints, would be a synthesis of the external assessment and the ongoing internal formative assessment. The following summarizes that synthesis in terms of the four levels of renewal.

1. *School-wide renewal*—a committee usually comprising teachers, administrators, and other staff

    Benefits: Most schools demonstrate that a new structural vehicle for participative planning is created with this school-wide committee.

    All schools report the discovery of previous untapped talent within the school community.

    Most schools report more open communication among all segments of the school community.

    Constraints: Time is short for adequate meeting and planning.

    The committee is under pressure to implement projects

within a short time frame in order to establish credibility.

Relations between the committee and the principal are sometimes strained either because the principal feels the committee is threatening his power or because the committee feels that the principal is not sufficiently supportive of agreed upon implementation.

As the committee attempts to implement change it often encounters resistance from other sectors of the school.

2. *Student renewal*—a committee of students usually organized as a subject class

Benefits: Students, in general, are highly motivated to improve their schools.

The success of students can motivate a hitherto demoralized faculty. For example, in one school the students initiated a course evaluation project for which 80 percent of the faculty volunteered.

Students often can work faster than faculty since they have fewer time constraints.

Constraints: It is difficult to organize a student committee that represents a cross-section of students.

Students tend to have low credibility with the faculty.

Student committees change from year to year.

3. *Department renewal*—a committee within an academic department

Benefits: Improvements have resulted in both the process and content aspects of department functioning.

Process improvements:
improved leadership style of chairpersons through feedback from staff
improved departmental meetings
increased use of other departments as resources

Content improvements:
Curricula

Constraints: Structurally, it is difficult to organize department renewal, since departments meet once a month for forty minutes and the teachers rarely have a common free period when they can meet.

The consultant working with the school is limited by time so that it becomes difficult to serve more than two or three renewal levels in a school simultaneously. Since department renewal is rarely attempted until renewal is already operational on some levels, it automatically becomes difficult for the consultant to initiate.

Because of these constraints this variety of renewal has been the rarest to occur. Of the thirty participating schools, each with six to nine departments, there are only two to three departments in toto utilizing renewal.

4. *Administrative team renewal*—cabinet renewal, the administrative team working on improving its own management effectiveness

Benefits: Fast results in improving school-wide processes such as programming or security have been possible by working with the ultimate decision makers.

The functioning of the administrative team has been improved in areas such as meetings, decision making, planning, and implementation.

Constraints: The time limitations of the assistant principals have been severe, especially during recent years when the schools have suffered extreme budget cuts and the assistant principals (including chairpersons) have had to pick up responsibilities previously covered by teachers.

Improving the functioning of any administrative team can be a threatening process. Principals and assistant principals often are reluctant to engage in the necessary self-examination.

Findings Concerning Renewal Products The renewal planning processes in the participating thirty-one schools have produced literally scores of educational improvements affecting thousands of students. Nonetheless, not all the schools are innovating at the same rate. One-third of the renewal projects, by the appraisals of the renewal participants themselves, are having a minimal impact in their schools. One-third of the schools are in the middle ground of effectiveness. While they have implemented some important projects, the committee members feel that the projects are either too few, or have been very difficult to implement. The latter third of the sample of schools have succeeded in implementing effective projects in an ongoing manner and simultaneously with several subsystems in the school. These successful renewal schools are the models for the others.

Since the external assessment team did not rigorously evaluate the projects and since the total number of projects is so numerous, instead of attempting to capture the entire array, examples of the projects will be presented briefly. The renewal products can best be summarized in three categories: *structural changes* within the school organization such as changing the format of monthly faculty meetings from large to small group discussions focussing on problem solving, creating new roles in the school such as proposal writer or ombudsman, establishing mini-schools, and creating student and teacher leagues; *programmatic improvements or additions* such as career resource centers and programs, new curricula, particularly in basic skill areas, and new teaching innovations such as peer-mediated instruction; and *modifications* in administrative processes such as improved security systems, improved programming procedures, and better communication systems. While none of these projects necessarily are new or dazzling, taken together they are demonstrative of a positive cycle of improvement in schools that often have had histories of just the opposite, a cycle of deterioration and despair.

LIMITATIONS ASSOCIATED WITH THE IMPLEMENTATION OF THE RENEWAL PROCESS IN INNER-CITY SCHOOLS

Creating a process such as renewal, whose aim is to help school people improve their schools more effectively and frequently than before, presents the same difficulties that make any attempt to improve schools difficult. The following are some of the more significant limitations of the renewal process in the face of these difficulties. Some are a function of the context of working in inner-city schools today and some are inherent in the process of change.

Renewal rarely persuades the majority of a faculty that significant positive change can occur and/or has begun. In spite of its positive track record in many schools, faculty often feel that while the individual accomplishments are helpful, the problems of the schools are so immense that much more is necessary than an approach from within. This pessimism is the consequence of experiences many have had with the failed programs of the sixties and the school budget cuts of the seventies. As a consequence, morale has been hurt; in the last ten years many teachers have been laid off and those remaining have been required to work more and at virtually frozen salary levels.

These kinds of working conditions are a severe burden for the participants in renewal as well. Since they are overworked to begin with, the time they can contribute to renewal is limited, at least until they immerse themselves in projects of their own creation.

The renewal participants have other difficulties to overcome, but these are limitations inherent in the process of change itself. First, they must be able to sustain their renewal project even though it does not develop in a consistent manner over time. There are failures to contend with, political obstacles to negotiate, and lack of cooperation from others in the school to attempt to turn around. That is, they must have the will and ability to maintain their efforts in the face of inevitable conflict. Perhaps the most difficult point of conflict, and unfortunately not uncommon, concerns the relationship of the renewal committee and the principal.

The principal of an inner-city school has an overwhelming job. A recent article in *Newsweek* magazine (March 1978) reported that even the most effective principals retire, or "burn out," within five to eight years on the job. The educational, political, organizational, and financial problems connected with running an inner-city school are staggering. Even when they take these conditions into consideration, principals and renewal committees sometimes still fail to establish an effective working relationship. Principals sometimes feel that the committees are encroaching on their locus of authority, while committees feel that principals are defensive and not facilitative enough of the process of implementing renewal projects. To deal with the problem renewal is currently developing a fifth level, a data-based method for providing direct feedback to principals. This will enable them to be more aware of the impact of their behavior on renewal and other aspects of the school.

LEARNINGS: MAJOR FACTORS FACILITATING CHANGE IN SCHOOLS

The problem-solving processes of the renewal model have been found to be effective in helping large, inner-city schools improve themselves. There are five areas of practice that have been instrumental to this success and fall in the category of "what works." Each has been presented already; the discussion here will attempt to answer the question, "Why do they work?"

1. *The model as a guide*—the utilization of a clear, detailed, pragmatic and evolving *model* of problem solving, the renewal model

The renewal model contributes to the successful process of school improvement primarily because the latter is so complex and involves so many people and political forces that the only way the interventionist (consultant) can make order of the complexity is with a conceptual map that serves as a guide to action. The conceptual map must have several characteristics. It must be clear enough so that the clients can readily understand its steps, because they must learn to employ it. It must be sufficiently detailed and flexible to account for the complexity of the system. It must be pragmatic enough so that, when followed, demonstrable outcomes of school improvement are effected. It must evolve so that it may reflect the learnings of past practices and keep pace with new levels (subsystems) that develop readiness for renewal. Finally, it must exemplify the philosophy it imparts to schools: feedback and learning lead to improved practice.

2. *The outside catalyst*—enlightened self-interest: Intervention in the school system and in the individual school by an outside catalyst

The business community (the Economic Development Council of New York City), functioning as an outside catalyst, has been effective in developing a long-term working relationship with the schools that contributes to school improvement. Perhaps the most important reason for this is the foundation of the relationship: the two institutions—business and the schools—necessarily are mutually dependent. Simply put, business needs educated employeees and schools need psychological, financial, and expert support from an outside catalyst so they may overcome their sense of isolation and their role as society's whipping boy. That foundation makes possible the development of a symbiotic relationship in which the two can accept and work with each other. The business community can work with schools not to impart educational answers but to serve as a catalyst so school people may find their own answers. Within this context business can give psychological, financial, and expert support to the schools.

3. *Entry, "starting on the right foot"*—careful attention to the initial steps between the consultant and the client and in organizing the problem-solving processes in the school

Research has shown that the implementation of school improvements relies on various variables, among them the following: support from the principal, ownership by the implementers for the implementation through voluntarism, and the execution of a planned process of change (Greenwood, Mann, and McLaughlin, 1975). The renewal model specifies that its first step, entry, is the time to assure the presence of each of these variables. For this reason, the careful employment of entry activities contributes significantly to later implementation. If entry is incompletely carried out, implementation is invariably problematic later on.

4. *Ability to adapt to the political climate of the school*—a contingency strategy for managing political conflict in the school by seeking and working with those levels most "ready"

Various taxonomies of conflict management methods exist (Deutsch, 1973; Walton, 1969). They range on the continuum of competitive to cooperative strategies. The renewal model advocates the more cooperative strategies and employes them wherever necessary. However, it also holds that if the conflict management methods are not successful in permitting renewal to be effective in the face of conflict, then there is an alternative. Renewal must disengage from the level (subsystem), i.e., client group (be it faculty, students, cabinet, or department) at which it is operating and link itself to another level. The new level may be more ready for renewal in terms of being able to sustain the three elements of entry (principal support, ownership, and the adherence to the planned process). The new level, if it achieves success with renewal, can then be the basis for reentry to the level where renewal was stymied. The demonstrated success serves as a motivation to people of the stymied level to develop the three elements of entry. This dynamic has been amply documented by renewal experiences.

5. *Implementation, the bottom line for improving schools*— utilization of effective processes to assure implementation of plans

The processes of implementation lead directly to school improvements. For this to occur the elements established in entry must be sustained: principal support, ownership, and the execution of a planned process. This requires effective management in the form of various support activities: organization, accountability, time management, group decision making and communications, management of political conflict, and maintenance of the relationship with the business community. The coordinator of renewal and the principal are responsible for carrying these out. It is the responsibility of the consultant to help both parties learn to more effectively execute these activities. If either the effective management practices or any of the basic elements of entry are absent, then implementation for school improvement will often not occur effectively.

The renewal model is an effective tool for improving schools. It has demonstrated its replicability in thirty-one New York City schools. Thus, the evidence is in—school people can significantly improve their own schools, even large, inner-city schools.

REFERENCES

Burnt-out principals. *Newsweek*, March 13, 1978.
Deutsch, Morton. *Resolution of conflict*. New Haven, Conn.: Yale University Press, 1973.
Ebel, Robert. The case for minimum competency testing. *Phi Delta Kappan*, April 1978, pp. 546–549.
Friedlander, F., & Brown, C. P. Organization development. *Annual Review of Psychology*, 1974, *25*, 313–341.

Greenwood, P. W., Mann, D., & McLaughlin, M. W. *Federal programs supporting educational change*. Vol. III: *The process of change* (R-1589/3—HEW). Santa Monica, Calif.: Rand Corp., April 1975.

Kaplan, Robert E. Stages in developing a consulting relation: a case study of a long beginning. *Jabs*. (*Journal of Applied Behavioral Sciences*), 1978, *14* (1), 43–61.

National Institute of Education. *Program plan: school capacity for problem solving*. Washington, D.C.: Author, 1974.

Phi Delta Kappan. A Special Issue: Violence and discipline problems in the school. January 1978.

Schmuck, Richard A., et al., *Handbook of organization development in schools*. Palo Alto, Calif.: National Press Books, 1972.

Simmelkjaer, Robert. Evaluation of an urban educational reform. *Educational Reform*, May 1979, *43*(4), 461–483.

Sole, Kenneth. School self-renewal assessment survey report. Fall 1977. Unpublished study, AERA presentation, Toronto, 1978.

Walton, Richard. *Interpersonal peacemaking: confrontation and third-party consultation*. Reading, Mass.: Addison-Wesley, 1969.

CHAPTER 8

Problems in Evaluating Planned Change Efforts in Schools

TERRY ANN SCHWARTZ

THE NOTION OF EVALUATING has been with us for thousands of years: cave dwellers probably "evaluated" which bear within a pack would be the best one to kill. However, evaluation has been pursued systematically as a field of knowledge and inquiry for only forty-five years (Guttentag and Saar, 1977). Since that time, people working in the field have proffered at least a dozen definitions and upwards of sixty models.[1] The greatest proliferation has occurred within the last twenty years, and, rather than clarify, has confused this arena for evaluators as well as their clients.

During the same time period as the model explosion in evaluation, notions of change underwent a considerable metamorphosis. Beginning in the 1930s, applications in organizations started; the systematic development of models and strategies for change began. It was about this time, too, when distinctions between change, planned change, and innovation were made. The focus of this chapter is on the evaluation of planned change efforts, where planned change is seen as a dynamic, deliberate, and organized effort to implement a program that has the potential for effecting modification in the tasks, structures, technologies, or people within a social system.[2] Planned change is set in an organizational context, not an individual one; e.g., the implementation of a counseling program for individuals is not viewed as a planned change effort, even if it occurs within a social system, whereas an organization development program is seen as such an effort.

No conceptual definition of evaluation seems to be agreed upon.

Writers speak of evaluation and research synonymously (Schmuck, 1973), and they speak of distinctions between evaluation and research (Ingle, 1976). There is now, even, a definition of "evaluative research." For the sake of clarity, the use of the term evaluation is meant to indicate a problem-solving process through which information about a program is collected, analyzed, and reported to decision makers responsible for or involved in the program being evaluated.

This chapter will present generic models of planned change and evaluation and explore various problems that arise in the evaluation of planned change efforts from both the change agent's perspective and the evaluator's perspective. In addition, implications drawn from these analyses will be used to make recommendations for the future conduct of both evaluation and planned change activities.

THE SOCIAL CONTEXT

As if the theoretical knowledge explosion isn't enough to grapple with, the changing social context of schools in which both the field of evaluation and the field of planned change exist is creating considerable difficulties for change consultants, clients, and evaluators. Schools can be viewed as the formal mechanisms through which notions about change and society are transmitted to school-age children. With the expansion of adult education programs, then, some of these notions are being transmitted to older members of the population, too. The norms of society that are evident today revolve around notions of rapid change and acceleration (Huse, 1975), change for change's sake (Bell, 1973), and confrontation politics.

Schools have been viewed as complex, turbulent, rapidly changing organizations whose external relationship to their environment and internal relationship among personnel within can be seen as adversarial. Such manifestations of conflict or confrontation are evidenced by teacher strikes, union-management collective bargaining processes, and community *demands* for participation in the decision-making activities within the system. These adversarial relations (Milstein, 1978) may characterize a shift from industrial society to postindustrial society, since the imbalance in this kind of society is "between those who have powers of decision and those who have not." (Bell, 1973, p. 119). In many ways, it seems as if this strong push for participation in decision-making processes by the patrons of schools, funding agencies allocating money for the development and implementation of programs, and governments is a result of the increased professionalization and specialization of the field of education. Additionally, the breadth of information now available to citizens about their schools, through various media, has only provoked people's desire for more. These reasons are probably just the tip of the iceberg. The impact of such actions in the context in which schools operate is being felt like earthquakes, from the demands for teacher centers and collective bargaining and binding arbitration to the demands for accountability.

Planned change efforts in schools, therefore, interface well with the societal and school context in which they exist. The need for evaluation of such programs meshes well, too. It is no longer only a matter of furthering knowledge about planned change through evaluations of its implementation but also a matter of satisfying cries for accountability of resources—time, money, and effort. Increasingly, then, planned change consultants or change agents will have to incorporate reliable and valid evaluation plans into their work. And these must be reliable and valid not only to the "experts," but also to the patrons and/or funding agencies of such programs.

GENERIC MODELS OF PLANNED CHANGE AND EVALUATION

It is necessary to present a generic model for both planned change and evaluation before the problems or pitfalls in evaluating planned change efforts can be discussed. The model presented for each area has been extrapolated from the dozens that exist in the literature. Although not all planned change or evaluation models will fit precisely into those proffered here, almost any planned change or evaluation effort would manifest most of the characteristics.

Since "evaluation" is the standard by which planned change efforts are judged, the model for evaluation presented serves as that standard. There are standards for evaluation studies, however. Thus, the description of the generic model for evaluation contains not only the stages of evaluation but also the standards for judging evaluations.

Planned Change Regardless of the number of models and orientations of planned change efforts in the literature (Human Interaction Research Institute, 1976; Greenwood et al., 1975; Zaltman et al. 1977) five stages for such a model emerge:

• Initiation—diagnosis and entry
• Implementation—design and intervention
• Evaluation—monitoring and examination
• Dissemination—diffusion
• Internalization—institutionalization or incorporation

Each of these stages occurs in most planned efforts, some occurring more formally than others.

The *initiation* stage deals with both entry and diagnosis. At the beginning stage of diagnosis a need is felt, manifested, or assessed. Someone in the social system is aroused by certain pressures; a problem is sensed within the organization. Early on, this need-sensing process is rather informal, usually felt internally in the organization, but sometimes observed externally; formal mechanisms for assessing needs usually follow. It is somewhere around the time of the informal need-sensing process that a consultant is called. When the consultant enters the scene, another dynamic is set up by that person's need to achieve successful entry. Knowledge is power, in this case, and a balance of power and trust is established between the client and the consultant, if successful entry is achieved. But this knowledge or power balance leads both the client and the planned change consultant into a more formalized diagnosis phase; the power balance and trust come from a sharing of expertise—the client about his situation, the consultant about his expertise. As diagnosis continues with the client and the consultant, transition to the second stage, *implementation*, is made.

By this time, the consultant and the client are working together. The implementation stage represents the time during which the planned change program is designed and implemented. As part of the design, the client and consultant may decide to do a more comprehensive diagnosis of the problem; or they may decide that the problem has been identified sufficiently and choosing between available interventions becomes appropriate. It is during this stage that attitudes toward the program are formed, where resistance of hostility is felt, and where people may feel uncomfortable because of the changing tasks, structure, or technology in which they are involved.

In most instances, stages three and four—evaluation and dissemination—either are dealt with as part of the design of the planned change program or are "patched into" the program plan after intervention has started. The *evaluation* stage involves processes of monitoring, usually done by a person within the system, and examination, usually done to assess the success of the program by an outsider. The *dissemination* phase of the effort may be an ongoing process of diffusing information to the rest of the system as the program progresses or an ex post facto process of sharing results, either behaviorally or verbally.

Finally, the fifth stage, *internalization*, is seen as the integration of the goals, values, and behaviors of the planned change effort into the system. Where the program initially stood out within the organization, it is now a part of the system. The behavior change among people involved in the program has become the norm for the system. Hopefully, the system as a whole had become a self-renewing organism.

Evaluation Those who write in the field of evaluation tend to dichotomize concepts as a means of clarifying models of evaluation: formative vs. summative; process vs. product; goal-based vs. goal-free; subjective vs. objective; and, systems oriented vs. decision oriented. Similar concepts are falsely dichotomized as they apply to evaluation strategies: subjective vs. objective; qualitative vs. quantitative; and, naturalistic observation vs. experimentation. Choosing one of the two alternatives places evaluators in a rather perplexing situation. Neither one alternative nor the other, alone, facilitates the comprehensive assessment of a program.

Two components comprise the generic model of evaluation presented—stages and standards. Both of the components are broad enough to cover most of the conceptual dichotomies and the models presented in the literature. The stages of a generic model include:

- Conducting a needs assessment
- Developing the program and understanding its intent
- Determining program goals and objectives and postulating intended and unintended outcomes
- Developing instrumentation, including procedures for its administration
- Collecting data and analyzing it
- Reporting results

The first and second stages may have been completed by the client before the evaluator appears on the scene. If possible, however, these activities should include the evaluator. If not, part of the evaluator's role should include an assessment of the accuracy of the definition of need and a desire to understand fully the complexities of the program, including its intent.

Conducting a needs assessment refers to the formal process of assessing discrepancies between what exists in the social system and the way it ought to be. A cooperative venture between an evaluator and client can save time, energy, and money at this stage.

From the results of the needs assessment, a *program* is *developed* (for a planned change effort, in our case). Through its development, an understanding of the why, who, and wherefore for the program become evident. Thus, its intent is made known to all involved.

Determining goals and objectives for the program as well as *specify-*

ing intended and unintended outcomes (or their impact on the structure, tasks, technology, or people) in the social system should flow from the program's intent. It is at this stage that the expertise of the evaluator and the expertise of the client must interface. Goals, objectives, and outcomes specified must be useful to all involved in the effort, and, thus, a meeting of the minds is necessary.

By this time, the specifics of the program have been dealt with and a *plan for the operation of the program* can be drawn. Here, relationships between various programmatic parts are necessary; i.e., selection of participants, administration of the program, and intervention strategies. This specification should make most of the design of the evaluation a fait accompli, since the evaluation design and the needs and activities of the program and its personnel should be congruent. In this phase, concerns about sampling, internal and external validity, and balance between what should be done optimally and what can be done realistically arise.

Developing instrumentation and procedures for its use establishes the collection procedure for information specified in the goals and objectives, and identifies the specific kind of information to be collected. Instrumentation should be relevant to the specific program and its context. Although adaptations of standardized or already developed tests are frequently made at this point, the information that is collected through the use of these instruments is only as accurate, valid, and useful as the instrumentation applied; i.e., garbage in, garbage out. Here, concerns of evaluators and clients focus on questions of reliability and validity. The procedures that guide the testing phase should be assessed according to their feasibility and appropriateness.

The sixth stage, *collecting the data and analyzing it*, should be called the "secret" phase. Clients generally have no idea what happens when those data leave the program setting and appear as numbers on a final report. At this time, the balance of power shifts to the evaluator. It is also the time when instruments are scored and tallied. It is this process that needs to be verified. But, most often, such concerns cannot be attended to by project personnel.

Finally, the findings or results of the evaluation are to be reported. The *reporting of results* can be in oral or written form, but must serve many masters. Agencies have different needs when it comes to the findings. Varied audiences may be looking for different things: perceptions of participants in the program; assessment of the worth of the program; degree to which the program has an impact on the system; and so on. Basically, though, goals and objectives are assessed, as well as intended and unintended outcomes.

The second component of the generic model of evaluation is composed of four standards by which people can judge an evaluation: accuracy, utility, propriety, and feasibility. These standards, and their thirty-four defining characteristics, are being developed by persons representing eleven professional organizations (Joint Committee on Standards for Educational Evaluation, 1977). Accuracy guides the production of reliable and trustworthy information about the entire program. Evaluations must be useful to their clients, so the utility standard establishes a guide to the production of "informative, balanced, timely, and influential" (p. 14) evaluations. The third standard, propriety, reflects concerns related to the ethical, moral, and legal impact of conducting evaluations with human subjects. And, as a group, the feasibility standard and its defining characteristics "call for evaluations to be realistic, prudent, diplomatic, and frugal" (p. 15). These four standards and their defining characteristics are portrayed in table 8.1

INTERFACING THE TWO MODELS OPERATIONALLY

Problems begin to surface, however, as soon as one tries to interface the two models operationally. Planned change consultants seem to find it difficult to deal with evaluators of their programs, and evaluators seem to find evaluating planned change efforts a difficult task. By hypothetically taking two people's perspectives—one a planned change consultant and the other an evaluator of a planned change

Table 8-1
Standards for Educational Evaluation and Their Defining Characteristics

Accuracy	Utility	Propriety	Feasibility
Defined object	Evaluator credibility	Formal obligation	Realistic design
Defined setting	Audience identification	Conflict of interest	Political viability
Replicable setting	Audience accommodation	Full and open	Evaluator diplom
Representative setting	Information scope	disclosure	Cost effectivenes
Well-defined sample	Information selection	Public's right to	
Stable sample	Information balance	know	
Validity evidence	Report timeliness	Rights of human	
Reliable measurement	Report dissemination	subjects	
Systematic data control	Evaluation impact	Human interactions	
Appropriate analysis		Fiscal responsibility	
Credible conclusions			
Objective reporting			
Clear reporting			
Premature summative evaluation			

program—descriptions of some of the problems they encounter are given in the next two sections.

Reality I: Problems from the Planned Change Consultant's Perspective

In the current state of affairs, a planned change consultant may experience a diversity of emotion, ranging from elation to disgust, at the thought of having someone evaluate the program effort. Either way, the consultant may have problems with the process of evaluation or the evaluator, and specific problems usually manifest themselves at each of the five planned change stages.

During the initiation stage, the beginning of the planned change effort, several concerns arise from the consultant's perspective. These center on the inclusion of various representatives from adversarial groups, the degree of commitment of the evaluator to the underlying values of the program, and the knowledge that the evaluator seems to possess about the program.

Dealing with the adversarial groups not only is a political and public relations necessity for the planned change but is also crucial to the comprehensive specification of information needs. People representing diverse interests in the program need to be included in the goal-setting and objective-setting activities; their views should help shape the specifics, according to consultants (Guttentag, 1977; Rovner and Pieczenik, 1977). Their involvement at the beginning stage might make all the difference in the world to the credibility and acceptability of the evaluation information collected. Evaluators often don't agree that their delineating activities should be a cooperative effort. In some instances, an evaluator would balk at the notion of defining or clarifying needs cooperatively with even the planned change consultant. What a problem this causes for the consultant!

It has been shown (Whitehead and Adams, 1977) that evaluators differentially assess the same program depending on their acceptance, neutrality, or rejection of the values inherent in the program to be evaluated. Planned change consultants, therefore, are rightfully concerned about the level of commitment the evaluator has to a program's values. Freeman (1977) concludes that evaluators ''are either proponents or protagonists of particular value positions and social action philosophies'' (p. 29.) It is this notion of the evaluator as an outsider that contributes to a lack of trust by the client system. Planned change consultants understand this problem, since they have had to establish trust with the client system before successful entry into the system could be realized.

As outsiders, evaluators do not possess the same breadth or depth of information about the program that the clients or consultants do. This problem is only exacerbated as the stages of change occur. As evaluators conduct their investigation, an initial lack of knowledge about the program effort progresses and creates a knowledge gap that cannot be closed. Clients and their consultants often feel that evaluators do not *want* to know, in a comprehensive fashion, about their program. Some clients and consultants feel that evaluators put up a screen to protect their professional "objectivity." Others feel that evaluators may desire only the money and/or the availability of research subjects. Such evaluators can be seen performing "quick and dirty" evaluations, where evaluation models are laid on client systems without any knowledge of the program entering into consideration. Thus, planned change consultants see problems with evaluation at the initiation stage.

At the implementation stage, problems that arise during the first stage still create concern among all involved in the planned change effort; and others come to the forefront. Since this stage covers the time period when the planned change program is designed and implemented, problems with the evaluation center on its design and implementation.

Change consultants see evaluators as negotiating for the implementation of an experimental or quasiexperimental design, where participants in the change effort can be randomly selected and assigned to treatment and nontreatment groups; they view evaluators as outsiders who desire to remain in that position. For example, in an ex post facto evaluation of twenty-six organization development studies performed over a sixteen-year period, Morrison (1978) found only three that met all quasiexperimental validity criteria (Campbell and Stanley, 1963). Speaking from the evaluator's perspective, Morrison views the validity criteria as "legitimate for determining the validity of all evaluation (p. 65)." "Hogwash!" says the consultant. By this time, the client system may be viewing the evaluator as a necessary evil. Human judgment, a variety of methodologies, and a developmental evaluation design are necessary. The specific problems at this stage, seen from the consultant's perspective, revolve around issues of flexibility of the design; ability of the design to foster the collection of information congruent with the complexities of the planned change effort; and the need to have the evaluation effort be inconspicuous and expeditious. And the gap between the evaluator and the consultant and the client system widens.

Evaluation incorporates notions of internal monitoring and external examinations of the success of the change effort. Planned change con-with the development and use of in-house forms and checksheets, and not concerned about helping them understand the kinds of monitoring, models for monitoring, and least disruptive and time-consuming strategies for monitoring. In effect, they see the evaluator as self-serving. Through examination, program personnel often express the desire to have the program assessed in terms of its larger situational impact, in terms of the utility of the numerous program components, and in terms of their own perceptions of the effort. Evaluators, on the other hand, may see this phase of evaluation as examining the attainment of objectives and goals, or the results of the specific program, or the degree to which the statistical significance of changes between need identification and program implementation is achieved. Planned change consultants view their efforts as being of a developmental nature. Changes in attitudes or behavior may take time to assess; likewise, time is needed to evaluate the use of statistics for the purpose of numerically demonstrating which components of a program work best and under what conditions. As said by an evaluator, "statistical significance is not at the heart of the inference process in evaluative research. The notion of policy significance . . . must guide the thinking of evaluation researchers" (Freeman, 1977, p. 41).

Once the evaluation stage of the planned change effort is completed, the evaluator usually leaves the scene by handing in a final report and possibly reporting the findings of the evaluation to the client. At the dissemination stage, though, planned change consultants would probably appreciate the services of an evaluator who would hold feedback sessions centering on the evaluation information. These sessions could include representatives of the various audiences for the information and participants at all levels in the planned change effort. The problem with evaluation, here, as seen by the change consultant, is a "sin of omission" rather than a "sin of commission."

Similarly, evaluators are potentially useful to their clients at the internalization stage. Without an evaluation, how could the extent of internalization be assessed systematically? Cooperating with an evaluator at this level could aid planned change consultants and their clients assimilate information into practice, and aid in the recycling process of the change effort. The degree to which the integration of the goals, values, and behaviors of the change effort have been internalized in the system represents the degree to which new norms have been created and the life-cycle of a renewing organization begun.

Reality II: Problems from the Evaluator's Perspective The stages of the generic model of planned change and the stages of the generic model of evaluation interface quite well, as may be concluded from the above analysis. Problems emanating from an evaluation of a planned change effort, therefore, are due not to a misalignment of the stages, according to the perspective voiced by the hypothetical planned change consultant, but to a need to adhere to certain evaluation standards.

Each of the four standards by which evaluations should be judged—accuracy, utility, propriety, feasibility—have been described in detail by from four to fourteen specific characteristics. It is each of these thirty-four characteristics that evaluators attempt to satisfy. Each characteristic, though, seems more appropriate as a concern during certain stages of the planned change effort than others; each one across the stages can be of primary, secondary, or no concern to evaluators. These relationships are demonstrated in table 8.2.

Evaluators view their problems with evaluating planned change efforts as emanating from three areas: the developmental nature of the program being designed and implemented; the resistance and hostility of the consultant and the client system to the notion of evaluation; and, the lack of flexibility of the program designers. These areas frustrate the evaluator in attempting to use the four standards as a guide for the production of a "good" evaluation.

At the initiation stage, five of the fourteen *accuracy* characteristics are of primary concern, although only three of them—defined object, replicable setting, and well-defined sample—are problematic. The developmental nature of a planned change effort precludes a thorough description of the program at its inception, since one aspect is built on the reactions and results of the first. Replicable setting, as a characteristic, demands that specific situational conditions of the program be controlled or well described. The program designers, however, are inflexible in providing for the control necessary at the evaluation level, and the developmental nature of the effort precludes sufficient documentation of the situation for practical reasons. Most times, planned change efforts do not involve the participation of a systematically drawn sample from a defined population; change efforts draw volunteer samples, because of the nature of the beast and the ensuing resistance and hostility of nonvolunteer participants.

Only one of the four characteristics of the utility standard, which have been seen as of primary concern, is a problem for the evaluator to attain—information selection. In this instance, the developmental nature of the program hinders the evaluator in attempting to adequately specify the crucial information needs of the various audiences. None of the characteristics of the propriety standard are particularly problematic.

Of the two characteristics of primary concern to evaluators in terms of the feasibility standard, both political viability and evaluator diplomacy do not interface well with the planned change effort. The developmental nature of the program, the resistance and hostility of the people involved, and the inflexibility of the program designers effect the satisfactory attainment of this standard. Many times, change agents bow to the sociopolitical pressures made by an adversarial group, and thus attempt to influence evaluators into making politically derived modifications in their plans of actions. In addition, political pressure can come directly to evaluators from individuals or groups. Confronted with program participant hostility and resistance, it is sometimes difficult for an evaluator to promote feelings of trust. Obviously, the longer the time that such a situation exists, the greater the chance that the evaluator will fail to meet this characteristic.

A consideration of the problems that evaluators have evaluating planned change programs must be considered in the context of the implementation stage, too. Here, five of the fourteen characteristics that define the accuracy standard are of primary concern, but only one—validity evidence—cause problems with the interface between program and evaluation. One major pitfall for evaluators regarding this characteristic is the "failure to identify and define relevant criteria clearly" (Joint Committee on Standards for Educational Evaluation, 1977, p. 36). Because of the developmental nature of planned change efforts, clear and comprehensive criteria are difficult to describe. In addition, if a successful entry is not obtained by the evaluator, the hostility and resistance of program participants and the planned change consultant might make the successful meeting of this characteristic quite difficult.

Three characteristics of the utility standard are of primary concern to evaluators during this implementation stage. All three can give headaches to an evaluator. If insufficient information is collected, and the evaluator cannot provide findings relative to different groups' questions, this characteristic will not be met successfully; if the evaluator is not provided an opportunity to meet with the adversarial groups to determine their information needs, the information selection characteristic will not be attained at an adequate level; and, if project designers see no rationale for allowing or agreeing to an evaluator's collection of empirical data on a before-after comparison basis, information balance is not fully achieved. As a group, the satisfaction of three characteristics can be influenced by the nature of planned change effort and possible resistance or hostility on the part of the program participants and the consultant.

Table 8-2
Evaluation Standards Which Concern Evaluators during Stages of Planned Change Efforts

+ = Primary Concern
- = Secondary Concern
0 = No Concern

Evaluation Standards	Planned Change Stages				
	Initiation	Implementation	Evaluation*	Dissemination	Internalization
Accuracy					
Defined object	+	-	+	-	0
Defined setting	+	-	+	-	0
Replicable setting	+	+	+	+	0
Representative setting	-	-	-	+	0
Well-defined sample	+	-	+	+	-
Stable sample	+	-	+	-	+
Validity evidence	-	+	+	-	0
Reliable measurement	0	+	+	-	0
Systematic data control	0	-	+	-	0
Appropriate analysis	0	+	+	-	0
Credible conclusions	0	0	+	+	-
Objective reporting	0	0	+	+	-
Clear reporting	0	0	+	+	-
Premature summative evaluation	-	+	+	-	-
Utility					
Evaluator credibility	+	-	+	+	-
Audience identification	+	0	+	+	0

Evaluation Standards

	Planned Change Stages				
	Initiation	Implementation	Evaluation*	Dissemination	Internalization
Audience accommodation	–	–	+	+	–
Information scope	+	+	+	–	0
Information selection	+	+	+	+	0
Information balance	–	+	+	+	0
Report timeliness	0	0	+	+	0
Report dissemination	0	0	+	+	–
Evaluation impact	–	0	+	+	+
Propriety					
Formal obligation	+	–	+	–	0
Conflict of interest	+	–	+	+	0
Full & open disclosure	–	–	+	+	–
Public right to know	–	–	+	+	0
Rights of human subjects	+	+	+	+	+
Human interactions	+	+	+	+	+
Fiscal responsibility	–	–	+	–	–
Feasibility					
Realistic design	–	+	+	–	0
Political viability	+	–	+	+	–
Evaluator diplomacy	+	–	+	–	0
Cost effectiveness	–	–	+	–	–

*Although one might expect each standard to be of primary concern during the evaluation stage of a planned change effort, the standard not marked as such in this column applies more as a standard for evaluative research than for program evaluation.

The evaluator's situation can be a perplexing one. A professional in a field whose work can be judged according to a set of criteria is pushed and pulled between such standards and the realities of the situations in which evaluations occur. The three other stages of planned change are not part of this perspective on evaluation problems. The evaluation stage is the one planned change stage where every defining characteristic (except one—representative setting) of every standard is of primary concern.

The purpose of this part of the section was not to detail possible problems in evaluating planned change efforts, but to give the reader a perspective on possible problems from the point of view of an evaluator. Neither did an analysis of the fourth and fifth stages of a planned change effort—dissemination and internalization—seem appropriate on which to base an evaluator's perspective, since evaluators do not often continue their relationships with programs through these phases. But if one takes into account the consultant's perspective, more evaluators might find themselves performing a useful function by becoming involved in these stages.

COPING WITH THE PROBLEMS, OR, TOWARD THE FUTURE

Viewing the problems that can be associated with evaluating planned change efforts in schools, it can be seen that persons occupying different roles have different perspectives on similar issues. In terms of their perspectives, both a hypothetical evaluator and a hypothetical planned change consultant see the problems as centering on these issues: conceptualization, design, analysis of data, and statistical analysis of data. The perspectives differ, however, in terms of the underlying framework of each of the fields in which these "persons" work.

The planned change consultant perceived problems related to the process arena; the evaluator perceived problems related to the product arena. It is a movement toward an integration of process concerns with product concerns that can be seen as the movement toward the future.

Attempting to cope with this broad-based, integrating paradigm shift within the social context of adversarial relations is not easy. To help simplify, modifications in the areas of central concern need to be considered separately.

Changes in the conceptualizations of evaluation need to be made. Guttentag (1977) discusses the current paradigm shift in the field of evaluation and proffers a decision-theoretic approach as a potentially new way to think about evaluation. By aggregating inferences rather than data and through the use of Bayesian statistics rather than classical statistics, evaluators and planned change consultants and client systems come together on more similar ground through the representation of adversarial points of view and the use of a feedback information system. Similarly, Deal and Huguenin (1975) conceptualize formative evaluation as a survey-data-feedback technique, where adversarial points of view focusing on organizational subsystems are put into operation by policy, peer, and advisory groups that form a temporary problem-solving structure. Schmuck (1973) and Conway (1978), in addition, see the value of using an action research model as a formative evaluation model. Thus, the separate conceptualizations from the fields of evaluation and planned change may be moving, hopefully, to common ground.

With evaluation beginning to be seen as a potential intervention strategy for planned change, what becomes crucial is to view the evaluator and the planned change consultant as occupying a "linker" role to each other and each to the client system. Seen as an intervention strategy, evaluation needs to have someone talk and understand the language, values, and bases on which planned change depends; and the field of planned change needs that same kind of person. A new synthesis, incorporating notions of evaluation with the values and processes of planned change, however, needs design or methodological innovations to make it operational. Dependence on or loyalty to the experimental model is no longer appropriate.

A number of authors have generated and "experimented" with adversarial models for evaluation, also called judicial models (Datta, 1976; Levine, 1974; Rovner and Pieczenik, 1977; Wolf, 1975). These models create a process for evaluation analagous to that found in legal proceedings. The collection of data is determined by a number of people representing various audiences involved in or responsible for the program effort and by the format of a legal brief. Given the findings, members of the groups are chosen to present them, each group from their own perspective, and a consensual process ensues. Although the data are analyzed in a classical fashion, a strong participative and consensus-seeking orientation pervades this model.

The introduction of evaluator subjectivity as a methodological innovation has made some impact. As the naturalistic inquiry method becomes as reputable as the scientific method, and as subjectivity reaches that stage, as compared to objectivity, the use of multiple methodologies to assess the same program aspects will multiply.

Even the use of innovative statistics with which to analyze data, and the heretical raising-of-questions about the meaningfulness of statistical significance have been dealt with in this new context (Guttentag,

1977; Freeman, 1977; Rovner and Pieczenik, 1977). This new synthesis, then, runs the gamut from conceptual innovations to statistical analysis innovations.

Both evaluators and planned change consultants are reactive to the complex school environments in which they work. The wave of the future, though, is potentially a surge of proactivity. As evaluators and planned change consultants establish linkages between themselves and their fields, and as a new synthesis or integration of thought on the matter of evaluating planned change efforts in schools is manifested, client-centered, collaborative evaluation may become a reality.

NOTES

1. Readers interested in a comprehensive treatment of the various definitions and models should consult Steele (1973) and Gasneder (1978).
2. Although a similar definition exists as "organizational change" (Owens and Steinhoff, 1976), the use of the notions of "dynamic" and "organized" are more consistent with the other literature using the term "planned change."

REFERENCES

Bell, D. *The coming of post-industrial society*. New York: Basic Books, 1973.

Campbell, D. T., & Stanley, J. C. *Experimental and quasi-experimental designs for research*. Chicago: Rand McNally, 1963.

Conway, J. A. *Perspectives on evaluating a team intervention unit*. Paper presented at the meeting of the American Educational Research Association. Toronto, March 1978.

Datta, L-E. Does it work when it has been tried? And half full or half empty? *Journal of Career Education*, 1976, 2(3), 38–55.

Deal, T. E., & Huguenin, K. M. *Water and the duck's back: the use of formative evaluation in schools* (Occasional Paper No. 5). Stanford, Calif.: Stanford Center for Research and Development in Teaching, August 1975.

Freeman, H. E. The present status of evaluation research. In M. Guttentag, S. Saar (Eds.), *Evaluation studies review annual* (Vol. 2). Beverly Hills: Sage, 1977.

Gansneder, B. M. Program evaluation. In H. J. Burbach & L. E. Decker (Eds.), *Planning and assessment in community education*. Midland, Mich.: Pendell, 1978.

Greenwood, P. W., Mann, D., & McLaughlin, M. W. *Federal programs supporting educational change. Vol. III: The process of change* (R-1589/3-HEW). Santa Monica, Calif.: Rand Corp., April 1975.

Guttentag, M. Evaluation and society. In M. Guttentag, & S. Saar (Eds.), *Evaluation studies review annual* (Vol. 2). Beverly Hills: Sage, 1977.

Guttentag, M., & Saar, S. (Eds.). *Evaluation studies review annual* (Vol. 2). Beverly Hills, Calif.: Sage, 1977.

Human Interaction Research Institute, in collaboration with the National Institute of Mental Health. *Putting knowledge to use: a distillation of the literature regarding knowledge transfer and change.* Author, 1976.

Huse, E. F. *Organization development and change.* New York: West, 1975.

Ingle, R. B. Evaluation parameters: as a class of activities; as applied to programs. *CEDR Quarterly*, 1976, *9*(3), 7–10.

Joint Committee on Standards for Educational Evaluation. *Standards for educational evaluation.* Mimeographed. Washington, D.C.: American Educational Research Association, July 1977. (Draft)

Levine, M. Scientific method and the adversary mode. *American Psychologist*, 1974, *29*, 661–677.

Milstein, M. M. Analyzing the impact of adversarial relations on the management of educational systems. In E. K. Mosher & J. L. Wagoner, Jr. (Eds.), *The changing politics of education: Prospects for the 1980's.* Berkeley, Calif.: McCutchan, 1978.

Morrison, P. Evaluation in OD: a review and an assessment. *Group & Organization Studies*, 1978, *3*, 42–69.

Owens, R. G., & Steinhoff, C. R. *Administering change in schools.* Englewood Cliffs, N.J.: Prentice-Hall, 1976.

Rovner-Pieczenik, R. Pretrial intervention program decision-makers indicate need for policy-relevant evaluations. *Evaluation*, 1977, *4*, 71–74.

Schmuck, R. *Some uses of research methods in organization development projects.* Paper presented at a research conference on Diffusion and Adoption of Educational Innovation. Bloomington, Indiana, July 1973.

Steele, S. M. *Contemporary approaches to program evaluation: implications for evaluating programs for disadvantaged adults.* Syracuse, N.Y.: ERIC Clearing House on Adult Education, 1973.

Whitehead, L. E., & Adams, P. R. The program evaluator's value orientation as a variable. *CEDR Quarterly*, 1977, *10*(3), 14–15, 21, 23.

Wolf, R. L. Trial by jury: A new evaluation method. I. The process. *Phi Delta Kappan*, 1975, *57*(3), 185–187.

Zaltman, G., Florio, D., & Sikorski, L. *Dynamic educational change.* New York: Free Press, 1977.

The View from the Superintendency

IN THIS PART we continue the exploration of efforts to change schools, but from a different vantage point. Whereas Part Two explored change from the perspective of outsiders, Part Three presents the reader with the perspective of those at the center of the action: school superintendents. Five superintendents, whose experiences vary from rural to suburban to urban, and from the Northeast to the Midwest, to the Intermountain states, and to the West Coast, share the rich experiences and insights they have gained while attempting to change schools. This is a relatively rare opportunity for many readers because much of the literature about educational change is written by outsiders who, though trained in observation, cannot possibly experience the same intensity of the dynamics of change as does the practitioner.

The school administrator's role today is fraught with uncertainty. Negotiated contracts limit freedom of movement at the same time that demand for results *now* leaves precious little time to prepare systems to make necessary administrative and programmatic adaptations.

Within these narrowing parameters of freedom superintendents must operate as consumate politicians as well as educational leaders. They must have hides that are sufficiently thick to field the criticism that will inevitably come their way. At the same time they must be supportive of others who are not as likely to be able to stand up to such abuse. They must sense emerging demands and be aware of where responses can be found. They must prod resistant, and increasingly senior, teachers to adapt rather than resist. And on and on. Not surprisingly the longevity of superintendents has declined dramatically.

As Harry Truman might have counseled, school administrators are realizing that "if you can't stand the heat, get out of the kitchen." (He also was fond of his desk plaque: "The Buck Stops Here!") Many have felt the heat and left, but others have viewed the situation as a challenge. There are even a relative few who appear to thrive on uncertainty and are rushing to the fore while others retreat.

The issue is, Can school people lead under such circumstances? Some have concluded that it is impossible and are merely going through the motions. Others have decided that it is possible to lead and reform schools under rapidly changing conditions. The debate is likely to continue for some time.

In this part, five superintendents who have chosen the side of leadership and reform and, in the process, have led educational settings to adopt significant changes share their perspectives with the readers. Their message is clear; times of major ferment *demand* consummate leadership from our schools' administrators. Each defines these qualities in his own way, but there is a common thread that winds throughout: change can be accomplished, but the role of the superintendent in introducing and implementing change is critical.

Bishop (superintendent, Brea-Olinda Unified School District, California) sets the scene by reviewing why it is so difficult to administer and then explores implications for administrative preparation and role taking. He believes that we have no other choice than to respond because the cost of not responding, which may in effect result in inadequate preparation for our youth to cope in a changing society, is unthinkable. Given this value orientation, he argues that today's educational leader must be "eclectic, gleaning from all of the humanities, business, and any other discipline that is useful," rather than pursue a traditional administrative preparation that will probably "guarantee under-proficiency." In this view educational managers should admit to their limitations and stop making pretenses that they can supervise daily classroom activity. Rather, he thinks this is better left to others and the administrator can then be freed up to do what he should do: manage the enterprise.

As to the administrator's role in "managing the enterprise" Crocoll (superintendent, Board of Cooperative Educational Services, Erie #2, New York) identifies two particularly difficult aspects that impinge upon educational reform: governance and management. He argues that the historical effort to isolate schools from the "perceived evils inherent in the highly political governance of schools" at the turn of the century has resulted in a closed system of governance in education. This has been compounded by a more recent phenomenon—the negotiated teachers' contract that specifies who can do what and when.

Neither, he argues, do many school districts have comprehensive, long-range plans to guide program development and administrative reforms. He concludes that we will not be jogged out of our present do-nothing approach unless the governance of schools is opened up and management is viewed as being centrally concerned with planning. Without these changes he perceives that we will continue to attack reform piecemeal. He suggests that institutionalization of community boards may be a way of unfreezing the governance and management dilemmas.

Bernardo (superintendent, Montgomery County, Maryland) focuses on powerful groups with whom the superintendent must interact if he expects to initiate changes. These groups include the school board, the municipal government, employee organizations, the school system's bureaucracy, organized parent groups, and the media. Bernardo explores major change efforts in two settings—Providence, Rhode Island and Montgomery County, Maryland—and the dynamics he encountered with these groups. His contribution and the variations he identifies across the two settings underscore the necessity of superintendents being intimately familiar with the particular dynamics of specific communities. Equally important, it underscores the central role of the superintendent in orchestrating the inputs and interactions of these powerful groups, a leadership function that cannot be shunted aside or assigned to a subordinate.

Looking back upon one of the most turbulent decades in America's history, Drachler (former superintendent, Detroit, Michigan) looks at the 1960s and the attempts to change schools, particularly Detroit's public schools. His conclusion is that there were monumental efforts but relatively little to show for them. He posits several reasons for this: previous experience was insufficient to meet the needs of the times; administrators' preparation was inadequate; there was insufficient information available; schoolmen lacked the skill required to rally others around the meager information that did exist; we were naive in our faith that goodwill would overcome the devastating problems associated with lack of funds, political interference, and social inequities; and the schools' organizational structures were usually more closely attuned to maintenance than change. Drachler, on a positive note, points to a variety of outcomes that were attained *in spite of* the obstacles to change. Most imporant, if we are to avoid repeating this history, his conclusions call for improving our preparation programs, sharing experiences (failures as well as successes), better collection and dissemination of data, and stepped-up efforts to modify school district structures and processes.

The last reading in the section takes an upbeat position. Bailey (superintendent, School District Number 12, Colorado) argues that change can be achieved, but that we often go about it in the wrong manner. Rather than narrowly and immediately focusing on a specific change program, he argues that administrators must first establish a positive environment, or as he refers to it, a "healthy organization." Once a conducive environment is established, *then* it is possible to introduce and implement changes. He offers some very specific advice for superintendents that is based upon his own experience. First, if possible, choose a community that shows potential for movement and which matches your own interactive style. Second, focus on the development of goals that are clear, attractive, and achievable. Third, help principals prepare to lead their faculties toward changes by providing training to upgrade their skills. Fourth, rather than force changes, offer inducements and opportunities. Finally, avoid "strangling change with participation." Participation is vital to get impressions, but not everybody can or should be in on all decisions.

CHAPTER 9

Change and the Management of the Educational Enterprise

C. GORDON BISHOP

TEACHER UNIONS, parent pressure groups, student activists, state and federal policy makers, in concert with the judiciary, have made the management of today's public schools a job requiring a new array of sophisticated skills relatively unheard of a decade ago. These same forces have eroded such traditional properties of the educational management function as instructional leadership, paternalistic problem solving, classroom visibility, and guaranteed community esteem.

The school administrator's ability to discover an institutional deficiency and quickly dispatch an appropriate remedy is a simplistic paradigm of yesteryear. The flow of activities from identification of needs to ultimate solution has been overlayed with a variety of obligatory checkpoints. For example, the political climate, legislative mandates, union contracts, categorical grants compliance demands, and parent advisory groups are ever present to temper and, possibly, redirect workable solution strategies. In short, the shifting winds of the environment make it ever more difficult for the educational manager to lead the organization through needed changes. Some of the more germane questions that ought to be weighed by those of us "on the line" are briefly explored in this chapter.

WHO IS IN CONTROL?

Education has always been everybody's business. During the agrarian era in the United States the stereotypical farmer would get off of his tractor to go down to the schoolhouse and quickly dispatch with the affairs of the school. The president of the football boosters always had a voice in the decision-making process. Interested parents have always had the potential to meet, discuss, and lobby for their points of view. The distinctive difference in the educational milieu of the 1970s is that no one appears to be in control of the situation. Certainly the once powerful superintendent of schools is not, in most cases, running things with the same authority that his counterparts were able to draw upon in the past. For that matter, neither are most boards of education.

Over time we have come to accept a notion of pluralistic management of the educational enterprise. Every interested group appears to have a trump card, so progress through change can usually only be accomplished if all relevant parties in the power structure are consulted and can agree on educational purposes *and* processes. For example, the United States can go to war with a 50 percent plus vote by Congress, but many school districts can't even buy a new bus without concurrence from the voters in their communities! Strangely, the democracy of American education seems to have evolved into a stalemate posture analogous to the Security Council of the United Nation; i.e., the power to veto, or say no, becomes the dominant means of participation. It seems fair to conclude that without the development of a responsive, accountable rudder system, the enterprise of public education may soon be so multidirected that it will be reduced to a state of irreparable nonaction, suggesting the end of public schools, at least as they have historically been known.

CAN SCHOOLS RESPOND TO THE INCREASING LEVEL OF CHANGE?

In a society geometrically exploding with change, education can hardly afford the luxury of educating the young of the culture on the trailing edge of that reality. When even the most somber conservatives admit that jobs for most children presently in school have yet to be invented, it makes a "business as usual" approach difficult at best in establishing the priorities of education. When coping, thinking, and problem-solving skills are the required tools to meet the future, isn't it obscene to even suggest that a child should have less than a functional laboratory for training in these processes? When in half a life span the planet has become so fragile that it is possible that all life could cease, shouldn't the curriculum of the public schools deal with related issues? In a time when the technology of man could end all life, should children be forced into the trade-off of a regimented set of mechanistic skills in lieu of training in human understanding? In reality we can no longer afford the luxury of asking "can" the schools respond; rather, we must turn to the question of "how" we can respond.

WHAT ARE THE IMPLICATIONS FOR ADMINISTRATIVE PREPARATION?

To be a successful change agent within our educational institution a set of skills that is paternalistic and omniscient will prove to be obsolete. Education has evolved into a unique entity with many of the managerial prerequisites long associated with the private sector, but with the added complication of accountability demands that have never before been called for, either in their diversity or in their intensity. This demand for accountability is directly related to the fact that parents, children, and government policy makers no longer view public education as an "untouchable."

Clearly, the attributes of would-be educational managers have changed. An ex-teacher, needing to progress because of family fiscal demands, can no longer be allowed to "shadow box" her or his way into management. The "Peter Principle" has never come to bear on the situation more profoundly. The dissimilarity between teaching children and the management of education is significant; more than a modicum of additional expertise acquisition is required. The management of education requires pre- and in-service exposure to training heretofore found cloistered in the disciplines of psychology, anthropology, sociology, and business. Many training programs for educational managers appear to guarantee under-proficiency in these areas. Given adequate aptitude, training, and in-services, challenges still exist.

WHAT MUST BE CONSIDERED IF THE CHALLENGE IS TO BE MET?

Since yesterday's game plan is but a sterile set of diagrams, historical perspectives and past logistical truths have become nearly counterproductive. Many sound strategies that ended in fruition ten years ago have been rendered inoperative. The clients, environment, and rationale for existence have been drastically altered.

New leadership does seem to be emerging. There are a group of people in educational management who have seen the need to "tool up" to meet the diverse challenges of the day. They've gained the ability to conduct a sound needs assessment based upon the multiplicity of factors pervading the work place. In some quarters carefully laid goals and objectives have been spawned in such a way that the whim of the perennial pressure groups remain outside of the protective net of what is to be. Staffs, students, and communities are being skillfully moved into the cohesive unit that is necessary for the occurrence of a needed educational change.

There appear to be at least several considerations for educational managers who hope to survive during this time of conflict and change.

First, there must be a thorough eclectic gleaning from all of the humanities, business, and any other discipline that is useful. For example, a rigorous legal training is necessary on a day-to-day basis and when confronting the complexities of legislative decisions and executive actions.

Second, there must be admission of human frailty; i.e., of not knowing all that goes on inside the enterprise, even with exhaustive skill development. Certainly a hospital administrator does not second guess the surgeon in the delicacy of penetrating the prefrontal lobe. He should, however, be in charge when it comes to the efficiency of the organization. Both have their jobs to perform and both require autonomy to succeed. Modern school administrators should take a hint from hospital administrators and concentrate more on managing the organization than on critiquing the operation. Whether proper or not, unions, tenure, and stature have brought the manager of education to the position of making little forceful difference in what happens in the classroom.*

The manager's relevance lies in his ability to provide an environment in which teachers can teach and youngsters can learn and then leave the institutional captivity as productive, energized citizens full of dreams, skills, and visions of the future. This simply cannot be done by a profession of union-clad technicians managed by a supervisorial staff of ill-trained, liberated, ex-blackboard jockeys. If you have been a pipe fitter, this might be an asset in the supervision of pipe fitters. It may or may not be an asset to have been a teacher in order to manage in education. A principal who taught sixth grade ten years previously is hardly able to judge the efficiency of a teacher doing that job now. If he is able, he may be keeping current in the wrong direction.

Third, principals, directors, and superintendents of schools should spend more time and energy in the management of the human and material resources of the organization without obsession for entry into the arena of the teaching and learning act. A well-directed plan to steer corporate energies into the voids of the times is not an extra-added attraction but the very marrow of the job. Study after study tell us that peer interaction is highly valued, so why not leave evaluation for improvement of instruction in the hands of the teacher? This makes sense

*We are dealing here with the role of the administrator. But it seems appropriate to not that the role of the teacher must also be given consideration. If teachers expect to find themselves at a professional level (with or without unions), they must begin the arduous task of self-policing. In most states the possession of triple job protection is no longer a benign issue. State sanctity, union protection, and contract guarantees are more professional protection than teachers should require to practice their trade.

and, more important, such an approach would allow principals, directors, and superintendents of schools to give more attention to managing the intricate and delicate *system* of education. If this division of labor can be established, the children-clients of the system will probably be better served. Managers need to focus on the "what ought to be" concept rather than getting caught up in the specifics of pedagogy.

ISN'T THIS A DRASTIC REDEFINITION OF THE ROLE OF THE ADMINISTRATOR?

At first blush this might appear to be a "bail-out" act. On the contrary, the improvement of instruction by personal intervention of managers (e.g., evaluation, in-service, coersion) is only a part of the possibilities that can be devoted to upgrading the state of the classroom art. Many educational managers do only what they already feel competent in doing; i.e., they were teachers so they like to spend their time in the supervision of teachers. That is no longer a viable role in the management of learning. The managerial environment is satiated with problems of a political nature. Whereas educators have traditionally responded to policial problems with benign neglect, the manager of today must be a highly skilled political animal and should not enter the classroom without wanting to learn. He should not be wasting energy hoping to revolutionize the educational world by his instructional expertise and grace. It may have worked in the past, but it won't any longer.

Although at one time education in America enjoyed a position that placed it above excessive societal demands and pressures, it has now become a prime target for growing social expectations. Feeling the brunt of this intense accountability are the schools' administrators. They will have to learn to cope with their own changing role as manager and executive and also learn to coordinate, to be a go-between for the other emerging and changing roles within the educational environment. In general the success of the administrator's attempt to cope will reflect the overall success of our educational system. In short, education's new leaders will have to be aware that change must be made and be secure in the fact that the change should be initiated by themselves.

CHAPTER 10

Governance, Management, and Change

WILLIAM T. CROCOLL

IN LOOKING BACK over almost two decades of my own efforts to influence changes in school systems from the position of chief school officer, I am discouraged that so few succeeded and that so many failed. This disproportionate number of failures also seems to characterize efforts in other school districts I have come to know fairly intimately. I am left with the haunting question, "Where have we gone wrong?"

In retrospect, I feel that in some cases there was a lack of thorough preparation of staff, board, community, and yes, students. In other cases changes initiated from the top never took hold because chief school officers did not stay in communities long enough to guide follow-through activities. In still other cases we focused our attention on specific change efforts and lost sight of the need to create a climate in which change could occur.

But I suspect that what is most damaging to change efforts is our lack of attention to *participative governance* and *management* of our institutions. Participative governance is here taken to mean the way in which community members can have an effective impact on their schools while management is used in Webster's terms, as "the judicious use of means to accomplish an end."

PARTICIPATIVE GOVERNANCE

In order to be effective, changes in education must be based upon the felt needs and aspirations of clients. Most especially in these times of diminishing resources, there must be "ownership" of educational aims and programs by a significant portion of the communities served.

Ownership by communities has diminished over time. A prime reason is that since the turn of the century we have witnessed an increasing professionalization of public education. This was largely in response to perceived evils inherent in the highly political governance of schools of that era. There is little doubt about the benefits that have accrued to educational systems and the children they serve as a result of this professionalism. However, the price paid for these benefits may be higher than necessary. That price is the development of school systems that are professionally dominated and highly resistant to community input.

This rigidity and the diminution of community control over educational programs has been reinforced by the advent of collective bargaining in public education. For day-to-day operations, the negotiated contract has become the educational manager's basic reference tool. A review of contract language reveals teacher unions' overriding concerns for job security. This is understandable, particularly in these times of declining enrollment. However, this concern, as ultimately expressed in contract language, results in our institutions becoming more rigid and more resistant to change. In the interest of job security, contract language has been devised that results in freezing *existing* practice. Within the collective bargaining process there is little concern that any of the frozen practices ought to be modified or scrapped in the name of better learning situations for youngsters or that a different utilization of resources might bring about better results than are now achieved. Job security is the order of the day. Any educational change is viewed with suspicion and, in some cases, is even barred by contract language.

Collective bargaining poses an even more ominous threat to participation and involvement in change. In many contracts we find language that maintains the closed nature of our school system. There are provisions that severely limit contact between parents and teachers and others that limit the role of parents in decision making on aspects of their children's school programs. There is language stating that the nature and quality of educational programs in districts is reserved as a responsibility of only boards of education and teachers' unions.

Provisions such as these not only place limitations on system changes in response to client demands but also raise the question of ultimate control of public education. Historically, there is a belief in this country that governments exist to provide services to their citizenry. There is a further belief that the nature and scope of these services should be determined by the electorate. Collective bargaining in public education, at least as it seems to emerging over the past decade, runs counter to this basic notion.

MANAGEMENT

Recent surveys have shown that relatively few school districts have developed comprehensive management systems that include intermediate and long-range planning components. Lacking a comprehensive management system, many districts have engaged in change efforts that are short lived. A number of change efforts have taken on a bandwagon aspect. Witness the proliferation of open classroom programs and, more recently, programs for the "gifted." Other change efforts have produced programs that are "lay-ons" and not integral parts of the basic school program.

Seduced by federal and state categorical funds, as well as monies from other grant agencies, districts have undertaken change efforts that are often more directed toward meeting the grantor's objectives than district needs. This has led to a proliferation of oft-times unrelated projects that quietly disappear with the withdrawal of outside funds.

What is needed is for districts to develop a comprehensive management and planning process in which change is a consequence of the process. The major elements of such a process should include the development of a mission statement; the extraction of goals and objectives from that statement; the priorities given to the objectives; the design of tasks to meet the objectives; the allocation of resources; and, finally, the provision of feedback through the evaluation of results. As I see it, the need for change would be highlighted by the evaluation. The nature of the change would be determined by a reexamination of purposes, objectives, task definitions, and resource allocation.

The relatively short tenure of chief school officers is related to the lack of a comprehensive management and planning model. The result of this is that there is not sufficient time to prepare staff and community for change. There is simply not enough time to develop and set a management system in place. Several chief school officers have told me that they estimate a three- to five-year period to install a comprehensive management system.

While it is true that some of the short tenures of chief school officers results from dismissals, it is equally true that there exists a model of a career ladder that calls for moves to districts of ever-increasing size every few years. This can result in a new set of directions for a district every three or four years. It can also result in change efforts that are rather superficial.

There is another problem with superintendent mobility. While it is commonplace to recognize risk taking as an inherent aspect of a chief school officer's job, I am not sure that we recognize that staff members and others who embrace our change efforts are also taking risks. For example, I recall a discussion on a new program proposal with a teacher in one district in which I worked. He said, "I would like to buy this idea but you're the fourth superintendent I've worked with in the eleven years I've been with this district. How much support will I have when you leave?"

A POSSIBLE RESPONSE: COMMUNITY BOARDS

Effective change requires the development of a system that not only permits but encourages more than episodic involvement of a substantial segment of the school community. In recent years there have been a number of attempts to give lay people a greater voice in school affairs. A few school districts have developed alternative schools in which parents can make programmatic choices for their children. The several voucher plans in existence also speak to this question. Some districts have increased parent participation by establishing advisory committees for each school.

I had occasion to work with the staff, board, and lay people in a school district in an effort to develop one possible response to the problem of developing effective change. This response was aimed at increasing lay involvement while at the same time incorporating a management plan with a built-in "change" capacity.

A key feature of the plan was an elected community board for each school unit. Each board was clothed with decision-making powers operative within defined parameters. Two-thirds of the membership of the community board was to be made up of parents of children attending that unit, with the remaining seats to be held by members of the school district at large. Open enrollment was to be established so that each school unit's community might become a community of interest rather than a geographic community.

The community board would have these major functions: management, advocacy, and liaison. The management function was viewed as the primary decision-making area of the community board. Working with the administrative head of the unit, the community board would be responsible for program development aimed at the needs of its constituency, selection and retention of staff, the allocation of resources relating to the instructional program, developing criteria for program evaluation, and, finally, accountability to the school district's board of education. The decision making would be carried out within the parameters of legislation and state education department regulations; a district-wide statement of direction; board of education policies/ central administration regulations; and fiscal constraints, i.e., the district budget.

The district's central office would directly administer support programs such as cafeteria, transportation, and maintenance. Each community board would submit an annual program report to the board of education that would include objectives for the year, together with a proposed resource allocation plan to meet those objectives. At the conclusion of each year, a program evaluation would be submitted to the board of education. The major management elements noted above would then be addressed.

A second role for community boards was to be one of advocacy. It was expected that these boards would represent the interests of their constituency before the board of education. For example, they might advocate changes in the district's goal statement because they found it too restrictive as they attempted to plan programs for their youngsters. They might advocate changes in board of education policy affecting their units or changes in dollar allocations per pupil in their budgets. The board of education would still make the final decisions on any of these matters, but the dialogue and, yes, the potential conflict, would be beneficial to the district at large, for it is through dialogue and conflict that change occurs.

The final function of community boards was viewed to be one of liaison, that process of bridging the gap between the several subcommunities and the board of education. The process was seen as one of interpretation that included assisting the constituency of the community board to understand what the board of education was attempting to do, as well as helping the board of education understand how its several communities were responding to its actions. It was felt that the community boards would provide an immediate vehicle for the board of education to consult with a fairly broad segment of the school district community on matters of new policy or program thrusts. Inasmuch as collective bargaining agreements have an impact on staffing and programming, it was anticipated that community boards would consult with the board of education on current contractual constraints and would provide input on the parameters to be established for the next round of negotiations.

The community board plan addresses the two major blocks to effective change identified previously. It provides for the involvement of lay people and for significant decisions to be made by communities. Further, it provides for systematic change through the insistence that programs evolve from goal statements and that programmatic decisions be evaluated annually. It is this evaluation phase that leads to program modification and change.

Resistance to the implementation of such a program comes from several quarters. Some of the established centers of community power will be fearful that they cannot exert control over so many decision-making bodies. Building administrators accustomed to working with other professionals in the central office will be apprehensive about working directly with a lay board. Board of education members will see an erosion of their control over the district's educational enterprise. Unions will be threatened by the number of decisions being made in this decentralized situation. The chief school officer may also feel that his authority is diminished and his role changed. As a matter of fact, one of his prime roles may become that of an orchestrator of conflict.

If we are to see successful change efforts in our schools, we must deal with resistance and develop the kind of governance structure in which citizens can make significant decisions about their schools. This governance structure would incorporate basic management notions such as setting directions for the institution, selecting short- and long-range objectives, identifying appropriate strategies for reaching those objectives, allocating resources, and evaluating results. I feel that the community board concept is one way of achieving lasting change.

CHAPTER 11

The Management of Instructional and Administrative Changes in Large School Districts

CHARLES M. BERNARDO

EXPERIENCE has taught us that change programs in schools are as significantly affected by the interplay of relevant power groups in specific communities as they are by the substance of the innovation. Over time school people have come to realize that their role entails the skillful management of this interplay, perhaps more so than does their knowledge about and commitment to the substance of the innovations. This is particularly true when the situation is marked by major conflicts.

The purpose of this chapter is to explore learnings I have derived from managing administrative and instructional change efforts in conflict situations. The key power groups to be examined are the school board, the municipal government, the employee organizations, the school system bureaucracy, the organized parent groups, and the media. Though the substantive content of two specific innovations in two school systems will be identified, the major focus will be upon my best judgment of why things seem to work or not work in such major innovative efforts.

Definitions and contextual descriptions are essential at the onset. My perspective is that of the public school superintendent. The two school systems are Providence, Rhode Island, and Montgomery County, Maryland. The two innovative efforts fostered in each of the two school jurisdictions were a learner-centered management support system in basic skills instruction (hereafter referred to as "instructional systems") and administrative reorganization. The former involved implementation of an objectives-based K-8 curriculum supported by criterion referenced tests, intensive staff development, a five-year plan, program budgeting, and computer monitoring of student progress. The latter involved major redesign of two rather traditional school bureaucracies so as to emphasize centralized planning, decentralized program and policy implementation, and independent program monitoring and evaluation.

As with any change effort, it is important that one understands the major characteristics of the environment. Providence, the capital city of a very small and somewhat insulated state, is one of a few middle-size urban communities in southeastern New England. The population of 158,000 represents a dramatic reduction over three decades due to out-migration and demographic shifts characteristic of central cities across the nation. The public school system serves a student population of approximately 30,000 students, one-quarter black and about one-third minority. The depression mentality associated with the great cities of America, particularly with respect to general student and staff performance, clearly characterized the Department of Public Schools in the city of Providence. The school system operated as a fiscally dependent unit of city government with a mayor-appointed board and line item budgetary veto power vested in the city's chief executive. School affairs in general and labor-management relations in particular were extremely politicized.

Montgomery County, Maryland, a growing, increasingly urbanized region outside of Washington, D.C., has a general population of 584,000 and is one of the nation's largest school districts serving in excess of 100,000 students. The rapid growth of the school-aged population characterizing the past two decades has been supplanted by declining and shifting enrollment as well as a more diverse population. The public school system is approximately 17.2 percent minority and 9.9 percent black. Montgomery County citizens long have appreciated the importance of education. Their high expectations of the public schools over the years have been reflected by exemplary programs for a broad, although not complete, spectrum of the student population. The board of education is both elected and fiscally dependent. Though there is a county executive, the county council plays the more dominant role in the fiscal affairs of the school system. The council has been generally supportive. The intensity of political pressures is primarily felt through the normal involvement of the citizenry in educational decision making as opposed to monolithic partisan control. Perhaps the only peculiarity in labor-management relations is representation of a large number of administrative and supervisory personnel by the teacher-dominated education association.

With the context set, I will now explore the roles of the several power groups identified earlier. I will first look at the instructional systems innovation and then turn to the administrative reorganization effort as they were responded to in each setting.

INSTRUCTIONAL SYSTEMS APPROACH

The instructional systems and accountability-oriented approach to delivering basic skills instruction was limited to reading in Providence. In Montgomery County the approach encompassed pre-algebra math, reading and language arts, pre-high school science, and pre-high school social social studies. The narrower effort took three years for complete diffusion in Providence while completion of the much broader approach is anticipated within five or six years in Montgomery County.

The School Board The Providence School Committee evidenced a strong and sincere desire to reverse the worsening situation in reading, especially at the elementary level. The committee supported efforts to move to the instructional systems though it was severely constrained fiscally. Therefore, staff relied heavily upon federal funds especially in the early years. These supported projects were so designed that external contracting was frequently used for design and development. The largest component was funded under the Emergency School Aid Act and lodged the responsibility for program implementation with two external contractors. Eventually, the responsibilities of design, development, implementation, and monitoring and evaluation were "turnkeyed" to the school system to conduct with local resources. This was the major concern of the committee. They could hardly turn down federal money that was resulting in better student mastery as reflected by a turnaround in test scores. Their level of confidence was raised by our demonstrating long-range budgets that restricted the large start-up costs to the supported grants.

The instructional systems approach was introduced to the Montgomery County Board of Education through presentation of two policy statements asking for their commitment to comprehensive planning and objectives-based elementary curriculum. These policy recommendations were accompanied by a five-year implementation plan. Reliance on external sources of funds was extremely minimal. The major issues raised by a minority of the members were individual school autonomy and the cost-effectiveness of the use of computer terminals for individual student and program monitoring. By ensuring good evaluation, the latter issue was minimized. The question of school autonomy was dealt with by stressing the wholeness of the county system while accommodating as much descretion as possible by the school principal and staff. A minor yet sensitive issue concerning the humaneness of the computer as an instructional device arose at the board level. These concerns were markedly reduced when board members were able to see children and staff work successfully with the project.

The Municipal Government   The Department of Public Schools in Providence functioned in many respects as a city department. In addition to the exercise of line item veto power over the school budget, all substantial internal transfers were subject to approval by city hall. Further, a city board of contract and supply chaired by the mayor reviewed and approved all procurement. The success of the instructional systems approach was heavily dependent upon some measure of fiscal flexibility and timely and favorable contract awards. The incumbent mayor, though a rigorous fiscal administrator in terms of "bottom line," became increasingly supportive of the unorthodox educational management required by the new approach to teaching students to read. He was open to being briefed on our short- and long-range plans and school officials of my choice worked with him frequently. Another positive strategy was integrating the funding packages for the instructional systems with other efforts the mayor was planning with federal funds coming to the city. Thus, the mayor sanctioned the use of model cities funds for the initial costs of the instructional systems in the target schools of the model area. A succeeding mayor was not supportive of my choices for service contracts for the effort resulted in some serious delays and, ultimately, serious harm to the project.

Though fiscally dependent upon the county executive and council for educational appropriations, Maryland school law provides for a significantly greater measure of fiscal authority in the board of education and the superintendent. Contracting is solely a board function and the superintendent is afforded discretion below certain prudential limits. Additionally, the strength of the county council has traditionally presented school officials with a coequal or better status in relation to the executive branch itself. The instructional systems approach required particularly effective communications to the seven member council during budget deliberations. Also critical was that the bottom line budget for the entire school system be within previously defined fiscal levels.

The Employee Organizations

Of the two school department employee unions, the Providence Teachers Union is the relevant organization to any discussion of the implementation of the instructional systems. The local leadership of this unit took a dim view of any major curricular effort that they perceived as threatening to their hold over the faculty of a school. Thus, they endeavored to turn a diagnostic and prescriptive approach to reading into a plan for teacher evaluation. They personalized their opposition to the superintendent and ultimately withdrew their political support from the supportive mayor. In addition to dealing with the union leadership directly, the school system's objectives for students was conveyed to parents and the general public at every opportunity. The teachers union also identified strong and skillful administrators to manage the effort. They, in turn, selectively employed or deployed teacher leaders in the project who were supportive of the effort and yet seen as loyal to the union. The union then wanted the project to be negotiated as a "term or condition of employment." I adamantly opposed this successfully through my tenure there.

In Montgomery County, the education association represents certain administrative and supervisory personnel as well as teachers. The Council of Supporting Services Employees represents the typical supporting categories, but also teacher aides, computer personnel, and some fairly high-level noncertificated administrators. The association and the council have traditionally felt compelled to posture a proeducation and innovation stance and thus took no adverse action to impede the diffusion of the instructional systems. The two most often discussed concerns at our monthly meeting with association leaders were teacher evaluation and increased paperwork. Verbal assurances backed up by the absence of administrative abuse seemed to suffice in the personnel evaluation issue. The gradual introduction of computer terminals and support personnel to handle the logistics of individual and group student monitoring moderated the latter concern. It is important to note that this innovation served as the catalyst for latent fears in both units over increased centralization of power over the two hundred schools by the superintendent. It will be seen that this latent tendency escalated significantly during administrative reorganization.

The School System Bureaucracy

Since administrative reorganization took place in the Providence School Department concurrent to the development of the instructional systems, there was little resistance at the central and administrative area levels. The principals' resistance came more in the form of bewilderment reflecting their general lack of confidence to carry out the change. Strong supervision and heavy in-service, coupled with accelerated turnover of principals, aided in the success of the instructional systems. Active Title I parental involvement, supplemented by a strong advisory mechanism under the Emergency School Aid Act, put the burden of proving the innovation defective upon the opposition.

While the central planning and staff development units in Montgomery County supported the instructional systems splendidly, elementary principals, as a group, were sometimes vocal in their opposition to the approach. Capitalizing upon the lack of a crisis in test scores (although they were sliding in the early 1970s), they sometimes gave tacit support to the fear of dehumanization emanating from certain quarters. Continued support from the board of education and the central and area offices caused the instructional systems to spread and show results. The administrative reorganization coming three years after the introduction of the instructional systems confirmed the new direction. Record high test scores generally and a reducing gap between black and white student performance contrasted with the experiences of neighboring jurisdictions. These trends neutralized much of the latent opposition within the school bureaucracy.

The Organized Parent Groups The councils of parents and teachers in both Providence and Montgomery County were and continue to be led by persons with a genuine interest in forwarding the cause of education. Their historic efforts to remain independent from school administration have cast them more in the role of mediator between administration and teachers than an advocate for the administration. Thus, in both communities PTA leadership took a relatively neutral stance regarding the instructional systems. In Providence, PTA leaders were preoccupied with reducing the tendency for long strikes of school employees. In Montgomery, the major mission seems to be strengthening the local school parent organization and supporting the system in its effort to obtain adequate funding. In Providence the parent groups, with a penchant to support the instructional systems, were social activists in their orientation: Title I, Head Start and follow-through parents, community action councils, and groups such as Rhode Island Fair Welfare or People Acting Through Community Effort (PACE). School officials sought support for the innovation from these and not PTA. In Montgomery, school officials concentrated more on supporting PTA initiatives than on seeking explicit organizational support for their efforts.

The Media The major distinguishing factor between the press in the two communities is the competition between a series of smaller weeklies in Montgomery County. With a combined readership slightly in excess of 100,000, the focus of reporting was more on internal controversy and less on the substantive merits of the instructional systems. The *Washington Post* and *Providence Journal*, on the other hand, were more inclined to look at pupil mastery as an issue. Editorial support for such efforts came from the *Providence Journal Company* without personal contact by the superintendent. In Montgomery, annual meetings with every editor are imperative. With respect to radio and television, the effort was more widely broadcast in Providence, primarily because there was less competition for time from national and international news.

ADMINISTRATIVE REORGANIZATION

As previously referenced, the administrative reorganization efforts in both Providence and Montgomery County were common in their generic design and in their impact upon the system. Each school system bureaucracy behaved as though each administrator exercised major responsibility over the administrative functions of planning, organizing, reporting, staffing, directing, coordinating, and budgeting. This traditional approach vests more program autonomy with the administrator while promoting reduced integrated effort and accountability. The new designs, though adapted to the nuances of each school system, encompassed more program interdependence and accountability by emphasizing coordinated planning and program development, clear lines of authority for implementation, and an independent program monitoring and evaluation system.

The School Board The major impetus for administrative reorganization in Montgomery County came from the superintendent and board of education as a team. Together they decided on mutual goals and the responsibility of the superintendent to propose a design for which he later would be held accountable for implementing. This is an unusual policy decision for a major restructuring effort in that boards and superintendents more generally favor assigning major design responsibility to outside consultants. Obviously, "ownership" was assumed in this case. This atmosphere fostered success throughout the many battles the board and superintendent were to encounter in carrying through this effort that affected some four hundred employees. Though laudable from the management perspective, we did not launch this effort in the beginning of my tenure when restructuring generally augurs the achievement of its objectives best. This delay can be accounted for by the deliberative nature of the board itself, the lack of certainty over the need for the innovation, and my need to do a comprehensive needs assessment as the designer while managing the many other demands upon my time. The presence of a fiscal crisis served as a catalyst and receptivity for the change was heightened.

Critical among the strategies in working with the board were: insistence on a public directive from the board, a board-adopted set of goals for reorganization, a clearly delineated process announced by the superintendent, and reasonable assurances of employment and maintenance of salary of those to be adversely affected. Numerous options were presented and the board was heavily involved in the structural decisions.

In Providence, the major impetus for reorganization came from the superintendent and the mayor. I was interested in ensuring a functional and supportive school bureaucracy for the educational reforms to follow. The mayor was interested in reducing administrative overhead in the school system. A vocal minority on the school committee maintained its independence from the entire planning process resulting in the superintendent's single design being presented to the appointed school committee in the presence of the mayor. Those who supported the superintendent carried the vote with the mayor's support being clearly enunciated within the context of a cut in positions and a closer control mechanism to the business management functions of the school system. There were no job or salary guarantees. The majority of the board remained resolute after its decision successfully challenging a lawsuit from the school principals' union that was then affiliated with the Teamsters' Union.

The Municipal Government It should be clear to the reader that administrative reorganization was but another example of the mayor's intuitive sense of the commonality between the goals of his administration and the efforts of the then new school superintendent.

In terms of the government in Montgomery County, suffice it to say that the county executive and the county council fully recognized that administrative reorganization was exclusively within the province of the elected board of education. They restricted their level of involvement to that of being certain that they understood the budgetary implications.

Such groups by definition advocate the cause of their members. Thus, it is not surprising that the Providence Teachers' Union (PTU), which then excluded administrators, took an officially neutral posture on administrative reorganization and their counterpart custodial union was virtually disinterested. Compare this PTU stance with their mili-

tant opposition to the instructional systems approach. Ideologically regarding administration as the "enemy," they were as disdainful of the
"old" administration as they proved to be to the "new," with some
noticeable increase in the tension level of teacher union leaders as
more "outsiders" were introduced into the school department hierarchy.

The organized principals' group, on the other hand, strongly challenged the reorganization in court and lost. The single most important
administrative strategy in this ultimate vindication was the involvement of the legal counsel to the superintendent and school committee
in the design stages of the reorganization at the onset. His intimate
knowledge of detail equipped him to be a most effective advocate of the
school department's position on this matter to the courts, the mayor,
and the school committee during a period of eleven days in the next
fiscal year when the court ordered both administrations to be retained
on the payroll.

In Montgomery County, the teacher-administrator educational association and the supporting services employee organization adamantly opposed the administrative reorganization as it affected their
members. Assiduously avoiding the criticism of virtually any of the
substantive merits of the proposed structure, they focused rather on
the relatively closed planning process that the board and the superintendent deemed necessary. The personal rancor of the educational
association against the board and superintendent, but particularly the
latter, in some ways eclipsed the personal tactics employed by their
counterpart union in Providence. A precipitating factor was concurrent
consideration of the superintendent's contract renewal.

Essential to the ultimate success of the reorganization and the
superintendent's reelection to a second term was the unswerving support of the board of education and the superintendent's broad-based
involvement of employees in committee work aimed at planning for the
implementation of the new order. No small factor either was the placing of an increasing number of committed administrators from within
and without the school system into new assignments.

The School System Bureaucracy There is only one significant distinguishing factor between the reaction of the school administrative bureaucracy to the advent of reorganization between Providence and Montgomery County. As would be expected, both groups
were deeply concerned over how the proposed change would affect
them and the operation of the system and the schools. But the matter
went to the courts in Providence. Clearly the Providence adminis-

trators had more to lose without job and salary assurances. It is also suggested here, though hardly a point that can be proven, that the administrators in Providence held the appointed school committee in lower esteem than their Montgomery County counterparts toward the authority of the elected board of education.

Perhaps worthy of mention in Montgomery County is the bureaucracy's reaction to the outsiders phenomenon. It was mentioned that tensions increased as non-Rhode Islanders were brought into the Providence school department. This became strident in Montgomery County only in staffing positions in the assistant, associate, and deputy superintendent levels.

Although a bureaucracy accustomed to outsiders in a highly cosmopolitan setting, it still felt more comfortable with known and meritorious administrators in the highest positions. Thus, the introduction of a few new faces at the highest levels sent disproportionate chills through the various spines that supported the system. Clearly these concerns were based on the realization that the superintendent was developing the capability to redirect the focus of the school system from that to which it had become accustomed under the stable and able leadership of his native son predecessor. Critical to the success of the staffing effort in reorganization was the superintendent's maintenance of balanced selections and broad-based involvement of constituency groups in the selection process.

The Organized Parent Groups The autonomy of the organized parent groups in the two school communities has been covered in the previous discussion of the instructional systems approach. Not surprising, therefore, was the strong personal support for the superintendent and for administrative reorganization exhibited by the non-PTA groups in Providence. In many instances they saw reorganization as their only shot at obtaining a more sensitive and responsive school bureaucracy in relation to their need. A similar phenomenon occurred in Montgomery County with organizations representing minorities. The city- and county-wide PTAs in both communities retained their traditional posture of neutrality. The most effective strategy in these cases was to maintain open communication and cooperation with these groups throughout the period of crisis and beyond.

The Media Again, the nature of the media in both communities has been previously discussed. As would be expected, major bureaucratic redesign and its attendant controversy captured the attention of the media to a much greater extent than substantive instructional change.

The focus of the smaller newspapers in Montgomery County seemed to be less on the reorganization activity itself and more on the personal conflicts that ensued. In contrast, the larger newspapers were more prone to analysis of the potential benefits. As with the instructional systems in Montgomery County, direct contact with the editors appeared to be important. In Providence, being a smaller operation, the media source of information was more often the superintendent. Montgomery County, being vastly more complex, afforded many more opportunities for alternative sources of information. In one sense the reorganization tampered with traditional pipelines to the press. Another assist in this regard was the willingness of members of the board of education to be openly critical of the press when they felt that local reporting was inaccurate or ineffectual.

Two large school districts were compared concerning the specific innovations of instructional systems and administrative reorganization. The analysis, constructed from the superintendent's perspective, shows that characteristics of the school district were at times very different and, consequently, necessitated different strategies to attain change objectives. Reaction in the form of support or nonsupport from the power groups involved establishing the initial decisional parameters that had to be followed in order to avoid further conflict and to continue needed support. The importance of power groups within the educational system played an integral role in the decision process but "outside" forces were significant factors in the change process. The chief school administrator's role in any conflict-related change effort must be viewed as the management of the interplay of these internal and external power groups.

It is is hoped that this chapter has clearly identified learnings I have derived from managing administrative and instructional change efforts in conflictual situations. Without focusing too heavily upon the substantive content of the two innovations treated within the context of two school systems, I have attempted to reveal my best judgment why things seemed to work or not work in such major innovative efforts. At best, they reflect my natural biases as advocate. It goes without saying in this highly politicized field of educational leadership that one's definition of success is his adversary's definition of failure. Nevertheless, aspiring chief school administrators cannot be unmindful of the dynamics of the process. It is hoped that in some small way this exposition will be helpful to those who follow.

CHAPTER 12

Educational Change in
a Decade of Conflict

NORMAN DRACHLER

It's easier to deplore the fate than to describe the actual condition of Corsica.—Edward Gibbon, *The Decline and Fall of the Roman Empire*

FROM 1960 THROUGH JULY 1971 I was an assistant superintendent and superintendent of the public schools in Detroit, Michigan. During this period, large cities probably experienced the most turbulent decade in American educational history. It was the era of the civil rights revolution, a period when the black and poor would no longer tolerate the educational inequities of the past, and when parents, students, and teachers demanded a more effective voice in school decision making. An age when courts and legislatures ordered the rectifying of educational injustices inherited from previous decades and changed the rules and regulations under which schools had functioned in previous years. And it was also a time when children witnessed riots and burnings in their streets. It is little wonder why William L. O'Neill, author of an informal history of the 1960s, entitled his book, *Coming Apart*.

During these years educators were challenged to reexamine their goals and procedures; to revise their textbooks; and to alter their pupil and personnel practices. As the decade drew to a close, it became increasingly clear that a revolution in educational thinking had taken place. A child's failure in school was no longer the sole burden of the student and home but also a professional responsibility. Although this latter development was not new, there never previously had been a period when professional competence was questioned with as much vigor and persistence.

WHAT DID WE WANT TO CHANGE?

Detroit entered the 1960s with a set of recommendations made by a citizens committee, appointed by the board in 1957. In 1963 the board received a report with recommendations from the second appointed group, the Committee on Equal Educational Opportunity, and by 1967, the third committee, the High School Study Commission, presented its recommendations. The first two committees included citizens and some staff and the third had only citizens and some high school students. The first committee "thanked" the board of education for involving citizens, the second debated with the staff about the placement practices for minority teachers, and the third warned that it will monitor closely the implementation of its recommendations!

Several organizational changes were proposed by the committees: The first strongly advocated the establishment of a School Community Relations Division, a 6–3–3 organization (kindergarten to sixth grade, seventh to ninth, and tenth to twelfth) for the total school system, and the establishment of a primary unit in the elementary schools instead of grades 1, 2, and 3; the second committee was concerned with all aspects of integration and called for a new assignment and transfer policy to achieve a balanced staff; and the third, chiefly concerned with quality education in inner-city high schools, recommended a second reorganization that would bring the ninth grade back into the senior high school. There were, of course, many other recommendations but primarily their intent was that we do better in existing programs.

The board of education and the central administration generally attempted to fulfill the recommendations as they were approved or amended. A number of experimental projects followed: the evaluation of five different methods in the teaching of reading; the development and publication of our own urban readers, involving staff and a parent committee of inner-city parents; the introduction of the primary unit, first in ten schools, and then throughout the city; the Great City Project for disadvantaged children in a number of schools, etc. Our research department, which at the beginning of the decade reported fifty-seven studies, was engaged in over two hundred studies by 1966. Probably our most intensive change effort came after the riots of 1967 when, with the aid of federal funds, we attempted more basic changes in five schools.

These changes of the sixties were generally of a secondary nature, but they were not lacking in conflict. We were taken to court by the teachers for attempting, between contracts, to introduce a new teacher evaluation plan; there was controversy over the introduction of new materials; our efforts to integrate the staff led to the ignoring of seniority and another court battle; and, last but not least, the four board members who had voted for the integration plan for students were recalled.

We and the nation floundered—first the "culturally deprived" and later the "culturally different." We invested in cultural enrichment, special programs for the disadvantaged, paraprofessionals, and technology while seeking to establish a climate conducive to evaluation and change. Our new policies called for sound attitudes and practices, involvement of teachers and parents in decision making, and the intensification of staff development programs. We recognized the significance of institutional change and we also knew that it was needed *before* 1960. But because of the size of the system and the pressures all about us, we turned to incremental changes since these held some promise for immediate implementation—they were affordable and probably safer. More intensive efforts were reserved for a number of experimental schools.

In 1967, after the riots, we convinced the federal government to designate funds for a more intensive effort in five elementary schools within the riot-stricken area. We involved staff and community in the planning and transferred from these schools some principals and teachers that were judged to be unsuitable for the new program.

From the time the grant was approved until the funds arrived took nearly a year. And then we had to spend nearly six to eight months while staff, community, and federal representatives defined the project. Despite efforts by leaders of the community, only a small portion of the community participated in selecting a governing board, though the election was held on a pleasant Sunday. Nevertheless, we proceeded. We convinced Ralph Tyler, a nationally eminent educator, to serve as a consultant to the staff, and he met with them periodically throughout the year. His wisdom, patience, and skill in working with people were most valuable in defining the program. There, in that isolated situation, a more intensive plan for a new program was initiated. But, how often does one obtain funds to enable extensive planning?—and, How many Ralph Tylers are there to guide a staff in developing basic changes? Let us now turn to the city and its people.

A City in Transition As Malcolm W. Bingay said in *Detroit Is My Own Hometown* in 1946—

> The fluidity of life, this refusal to "jell" or ever to grow old, helps to explain why everything that is right or wrong which happens to our nation seems to break here first.

The demographic changes in Detroit during the sixties were so vast that they almost seem a rationale for the problems encountered by the schools. In one sense change was more difficult. But the more significant factor was that these *new conditions made change imperative*. They were the raison d'etre for new concepts, methods, and strategies.

During this turbulent era school administrators did not have a monopoly on failure. Other agencies both in government and higher education were equally in trouble. What made our shortcomings so glaring and urgent was that elementary and secondary education were compulsory and that so many millions of students and parents were dependent on us.

POPULATION. Detroit's total population dropped from 1,670,000 in 1960 to 1,511,000 by 1970. Whereas minorities comprised 29 percent of the total population in 1960, the percentage rose to 46 by 1970, of whom 98 percent were black. During this period the proportion of aged and poor increased. In 1960 Detroit school officials estimated that three out of ten children enrolled in public schools came from depressed areas. By 1970 the count was six out of ten. In 1950 the estimate was one out of ten.

SCHOOL ENROLLMENT. While the city's population declined, public school enrollment increased from 285,000 in 1960 to 290,000 students by 1970. The proportion of minority students rose from 40 percent in 1960 to 65 percent by 1970.

SCHOOL STAFF. Detroit began a concerted effort to hire black teachers in the early 1960s. In 1961 we conducted our first racial count of the instructional staff—black educators comprised 21.6 percent and other minority groups 0.3 percent. By 1970 blacks were 41.22 percent and others 0.8 percent. We also shortened the number of years of experience formerly required for administrative positions, enabling personnel to compete earlier, so that by 1970 31.6 percent of school and central administrators were black.

These changes in population, school enrollment, and school staff influenced our directions and affected our program.

Today, as I ponder upon the sixties, the extent of our undertaking, and the prevailing limitations, our shortcomings seem more distinct— yet I find more positive elements than I recognized earlier. The following premises seem worthy of exploration.

1. Neither our professional education nor our school practices had prepared us for the social-educational issues of the 1960s.
2. We lacked the research, data, and skills necessary to convince staff and public on the changes we proposed.
3. We did not comprehend our limitations within the community and the school system.

4. The traditional school structure and organization was inadequate to promote change in a time of crisis.
5. Despite the above problems, schools accomplished more than was recognized during the heat of the confrontations.

Let's examine these premises one by one.

WE WERE UNPREPARED FOR THE UPHEAVALS OF THE 1960s

For many years Detroit public schools had a Division for Improvement of Instruction, which was regarded as one of the better large-city agencies concerned with educational change. During the 1940s this division added two departments, one for parent-teacher activities and the other for human relations. Each had one staff member who served as an advocate of better school community relationships. These officials disseminated literature and convened seminars to further the system's goals.

In 1957 after a new superintendent and a new breed of board members came into power, Detroit appointed its first major citizens committee to review school needs for the coming decade. It is noteworthy that along with recommendations for curriculum, personnel, housing, and finance, the committee also developed special recommendations for school-community relations. The committee called upon the board of education to establish a separate division on school-community relations with an adequate staff and an assistant superintendent to direct it. They also asked the board to appoint a separate committee to develop recommendations on equal educational opportunities. The request for an assistant superintendent for school-community relations was based on the belief that this would demonstrate to staff and public the high priority of school-community relations in the school system.

In addition to the many changes influenced by this committee, a most significant by-product was the new experience for board and staff to work with citizens on a sustained basis. It was a harbinger of events to come. We gained some insights into the new school-community climate that was developing in the nation, particularly in large cities.

Our experiences with citizen committees caused some uneasiness on the part of some staff members. Citizen participation in school decision-making was new. Most principals were former teachers, who like the teachers in *their* building, had been left alone with a classroom of children, with little opportunity for sharing or working with other adults. Those who succeeded in establishing good relations with staff and community, and there were many, did so because of personal skills and attitudes they possessed or developed rather than through administrative or university training.

The isolation of teachers within classrooms has, in my opinion, contributed to the difficulties encountered when change was proposed. Teachers often said that changes were requested by administrators who had been out of the classroom for many years or advocated by others who had no elementary teaching experience. On occasions teachers pointed to earlier changes that were discarded later. Some teachers, aware of the growing emphasis upon test scores, hesitated to embark upon projects that were unpredictable. And there were those who preferred to continue in an atmosphere that was familiar to them—and which they regarded as effective.

Central office and principal leadership were, of course, vital in the development of change. Vision and unique skills were necessary to influence staff to venture forth in new directions that often called for new concepts and new classroom habits. John Dewey is credited with saying that "the trouble with supervision was that there was too much 'super' and not enough 'vision.' " Some of us who could develop excellent teaching materials were not the best promoters of new ideas.

During one year we asked the teachers' union and the central staff to nominate a group of outstanding teachers in reading and math. This group was relieved from classroom responsibility and designated to assist teachers who needed or wanted help. It was understood that there would be no reporting to administration by these helping teachers. Their sole responsibility was to help. They would observe for a day or two and then demonstrate or suggest new approaches. We were convinced that this procedure was beneficial to teacher and children and more effective in promoting change.

A very serious failing was our collective insensitivity to the omissions and, on occasion, degrading writing and illustrations in our textbooks concerning minorities. Publishers, authors, and consultants from schools and universities produced textbooks as if there had not been a civil rights revolution. The books reflected the deep-seated bias or insensitivity in our society. What concerned us most was that *parents* and not supervisors or teachers reported these deficits to us.

We found that bringing about changes in textbooks was no easy task. In 1969, frustrated over the slow pace of change, we recommended to the board of education not to purchase new books for that year. This measure did cause some of the publishers to ask for suggestions.

Yet, as one looks back at these changes, they were superficial. We lacked a theoretical basis for change. Blacks complained, so materials affecting blacks were improved. Then the Hispanics and later women made similar complaints, and these were dealt with. The principles that liberty is indivisible and that each group in our heterogeneous society deserves fair and dignified treatment were a problem then and now.

Toward the close of the sixties it became apparent that in our anxiety to correct the historic inequities to blacks we had failed to sense the *real* or *imagined* concerns of the white ethnic groups. An incident in 1971 may illustrate my point best. A group of leaders in Detroit's Slavic community visited one day and informed me that only one high school still had between 20 and 30 percent Slavic students. Then they pointed out that despite the presence of Slavic administrators in the system, this particular school had none. Their concluding remark was posed as a question: "Don't our students need models too?" Embarrassed by their report, I told the group that what bothered me most was that we had not sensed this concern. These insensitivities applied not only to personnel practices but to curriculum content as well.

WE LACKED EDUCATIONAL DATA AND SKILLS FOR PROPOSED CHANGES

Among Detroit's major concerns were integration of students and staff, collective bargaining, decentralization of school authority, and low achievement scores on national testing programs. Let us review these briefly.

Integration of students and staff Detroit's 1970 plan to integrate students was very modest. It involved only high schools and did not include bussing since the schools paired were adjacent to each other. This plan began with the tenth grade, so that enrolled students would be able to complete their education in the school where they had started. The plan also enabled students to enroll in the school where an older brother or sister was attending. The one unique aspect about the plan was that no longer were only blacks asked to change for integration—whites had to do the same.

The plan was not approved by all board members: four voted yes, two voted no, and the fifth yes voter was very ill and could not vote unless present. In our discussions with board members we lacked adequate data to convince the dissenting members on the educational values concerning integration. An overwhelming number of speakers at the board meeting opposed the plan—only the NAACP, the State Civil Rights Commission, the Civil Liberties Union, and several individuals spoke in support.

The year 1970 was an election year for the state legislature. So, within three days after the plan was approved, one house of the state legislature passed a bill to stop the integration move, and within three months both houses approved a joint bill to stop the plan in September. During this time literature appeared throughout the city opposing bussing and carrying photographs of black youth attacking white girls on buses. The Mayor too came out against bussing, and when reminded on the next day that the Detroit plan did not provide for bussing, he replied that he was referring to a bussing plan that was proposed for Los Angeles! And within a month after the above bill was passed by both houses and signed by the governor, the four board members who voted yes were recalled.

During the integration debate, Dr. James Allen, U.S. commissioner of education, Father Theodore M. Hesburgh, chairman of the U.S. Civil Rights Commission, and Professor James Coleman issued statements supporting the plan. The press gave little space to their statements and had no editorial comment but published letters chastising the above for their stand. It was an issue on which the public did not trust experts. (One bit of advice that I can offer to those planning major changes in education is—don't try it in an election year!)

On the integration of staff, we were more successful but not without problems. Many teachers were disturbed about being transferred. The teacher group that won the right to represent the staff in collective bargaining agreed to our new transfer policy, so the losing group took us to court for disregarding seniority.

Collective Bargaining When collective bargaining came to Detroit in 1965–66, there was a great deal of learning to be done by both teachers and administration. Teachers were to elect building representatives in each of our over three hundred buildings. The teacher elected was both a guardian of the conditions of the contract and, in a sense, a defender of good teaching. A case could be made that next to the children, other teachers in the building suffered most from an incompetent teacher. The same applied to principals. In both instances, preparation and educational literature were needed to educate the staff. The legal profession was prepared. We were inundated with literature about the legal aspects of collective bargaining, but the negotiators and staff needed to observe *educational* as well as *legal* principles. Unfortunately many educators were busy writing how unionism would destroy educational quality (as if up until collective bargaining only quality education had prevailed).

Decentralization Much was written in the early 1960s about the bigness of large-city school systems and the importance of decision making closer to the local school. I accepted this thinking, hoping for greater parental involvement and more judicious planning at the local level. In the early stages of decentralization planning the literature was generally written either by advocates or opponents of decentralization. There was little objective research to aid us in developing plans for the approach of decentralization. With more data the current controversies over decentralization in Detroit and New York might have been reduced and educational services improved.

National Tests and Low Achievement Scores I was among the first to publicize test scores, school by school. Now—I believe it was a mistake. Individual profiles for each child, sent home to the parent, would have served much better.

The norm-referenced test is misunderstood by the press and the public. The misleading headlines upset parents and staff. A test in which half of the participants *must* fall below the norm is difficult to comprehend and to accept. It is like saying that half of the people must be poor—it is un-American! Americans evidently want a test where *everyone* will be above the norm.

This national misunderstanding of the norm-referenced test is both a reflection of the school's poor teaching of math and a failure on the part of measurement experts to educate the public on the content, intent, and significance of the test.

The above problems, the lack of data and research, and the limited expertise of educators on these issues affected the relationships between board members and staff. The position of board member was no longer an honorary post, where the staff recommended and the board approved. Now, citizens called board members, protested at meetings, and threatened defeat at the polls. It is remarkable that so few board members used the position as a platform for another, more rewarding public office. Here and there an office-seeker did appear whose primary occupation was to serve as an adversary to the board and the superintendent. This condition flourished primarily because of the controversial nature of the issues and the lack of knowledge of more satisfactory solutions.

WE DID NOT COMPREHEND OUR LIMITATIONS

School administrators in the early sixties, like many Americans, had almost a naive faith in the potential of the schools. As in the past, Americans assumed that most of our social problems could be cured, e.g., by adding another course to the high school curriculum.—And school administrators did little to disclaim this belief. Thus, when deaths on highways increased, schools were asked to teach driver training. Or, when the divorce rate became a national concern, home and family living courses became part of the curriculum. In the 1960s we were deluged with demands that we do "something" about drug abuse. Few questioned whether teachers were prepared to deal with so complex a problem as drugs. I feared that with the staff unprepared, a crash program on drug abuse would probably aggravate rather than ease the problem. Then there were new economic, social, and political problems that placed limitations on the school, which made educational change more essential and yet more difficult.

Economic   In the early 1960s Dr. James Conant proposed that sixty professionals per thousand pupils was a desirable ratio for quality education, a figure that prevailed in several suburbs adjacent to Detroit. Our ratio was forty-seven per thousand. If, in 1968, Detroit had aspired to an average class size equal to the rest of the State of Michigan, we would have required an additional twelve hundred teachers, about 10 percent of our existing staff. To fulfill Dr. Conant's goal an additional $70 million was necessary in 1970–71 beyond our budget of $264 million.

Obviously money was not our sole deterrent to educational change, but it certainly was an obstacle. Fund shortages decreased research and staff development, prevented additional auxiliary staff to stimulate change, and drained a major portion of our energies. Though I stress funding, I must add that in 1967, two years after federal funds were made available, we recognized that in addition to acquiring funds we also had to establish wise choices and priorities for these funds. Yet without adequate funding, options for change become more limited.

Social Problems   The population changes of the sixties caused a great deal of ferment in the city. Neighborhoods changed within a period of months, often shifting the ratio of black students in a school from 30 percent in June to 70 percent by September of the same year.

Under the term *mobility*, we included all children who registered three weeks or more after school began, who moved during the school year, or who left Detroit three weeks before school ended. For the system as a whole, our mobility rate was over 40 percent annually. One inner-city school had about 85 percent white Southern Appalachian children with an annual mobility rate of over 100 percent! Each Monday morning the office in that school resembled a railroad station, with twenty to thirty new students enrolling and an equal number leaving. We altered our practice of semiannual promotions to an annual plan, and we informed parents who moved that if they wished, their child could continue in the former school, but the problem remained. Our Attendance Department annually made some 130,000 home calls, of which only about 12 percent dealt with truancy, the rest were illness, lack of clothing, helping parents, poverty, "could not locate," etc. As one read some of the reports, one just wondered how some of the children survived.

During these hectic years, the city was not a community with common goals, but a geographic area with groups of citizens having contrasting sets of values: the rich and the poor, the white and the black, and the young and the aged. Whenever the board of education made an important decision the only thing certain was that at least a quarter of a million people would disagree.

Then, beginning with 1963, probably the peak of the civil rights protest movement, the white population generally voted against additional school funds, whereas the black voters, still a minority in the sixties, continued to support the schools.

Political   In the early 1960s the city's political influence began to decline. The one-man, one-vote principle, while democratic, shifted the balance of political power to the suburbs. The city's representation in the state legislature and Congress declined and gradually legislation, both at the federal and state levels, began to favor rural and suburban areas. The Detroit public schools were fiscally independent from city government. They had no ties with any political machine. The division within the city also weakened our influence within the state legislature.

These economic, social, and political problems affected the city and its institutions.

The aged, most of them white, were captives of the city. The availability of public transportation, nearby medical and shopping services, and, particularly, the higher property costs in the suburbs, caused the aged to remain. Within the city, they had few ties with the schools because their grandchildren were generally in suburban schools. The schools, in turn, did little to involve senior citizens. A few did invite them to serve as tutors while others converted an empty classroom into a reading center for senior citizens in the neighborhood, but the impact was small. The aged in Detroit generally continued to oppose higher taxes.

In the past, schools have generally assumed the entire credit for a child's success in school. The ferment of the sixties has convinced this author that, in addition to school input, community and family stability are more important factors to a child's education than we had assumed in the past.

SCHOOL STRUCTURE AND ORGANIZATION WERE INADEQUATE TO PROMOTE CHANGE

The two divisions primarily concerned with change in the schools were the Division for the Improvement of Instruction and the School Community Relations Division. But the power to implement change was in the Administrative Division. The former divisions were primarily auxiliary services; the latter had line authority. The Administrative Division was not opposed to change but it had problems in the implementation of its own directives and programs as well as concerns with community unrest, vandalism, discipline in the schools, etc.

Of the two auxiliary services, the curriculum division had a longer history in the system and was probably more acceptable to the staff. Many, however, looked with skepticism on efforts to improve human relations. The staff members of the Human Relations Division were often regarded as "do-gooders" rather than "practical" members of the system.

An example of the above attitude was noted during our Human Relations Institutes, to which each school was asked to send a representative. Principals either asked for volunteers or sent the newest assigned teacher and, in a few instances, they delegated a teacher having difficulties and needing "therapy." As I observed these gatherings, I found a larger proportion of minority and beginning teachers than our staff distribution warranted. The influential teachers, those who could upon returning to their buildings influence change, were not represented in sufficient numbers.

The above situation led us to increase our efforts in gaining prestige and power for the Division of School Community Relations. Our first step was to decide that all textbooks and instructional materials to be purchased must have the approval of both the Division for Instruction and the Human Relations Department. Then we established a separate department to review all bids made by the Business Office and the Housing Division for compliance with our Affirmative Action Policy. We placed this new office within the School Community Relations Division. Probably our most effective measure was to include representatives from the Human Relations Division on all promotion committees of the system.

Though our primary motive for each of the above measures was to improve the educational program, indirectly we sought to elevate the prestige and influence of the School Community Relations Division. To some extent we were successful.

BUT SCHOOLS STILL ACCOMPLISHED
MORE THAN WAS RECOGNIZED

How does one arrive at the last premise after the previous analysis? Aside from the fact that institutional change is not a short-term process, let us note the differences between the sixties and the earlier criticisms of American education.

During the 1890s Dr. Joseph M. Rice, not a professional educator, attracted national attention with a series of articles expressing great dismay about the condition of teaching in several large cities. In 1909 Leonard P. Ayres published his study, *Laggards in Our Schools*, which pointed out that in large cities all children attended through the fifth grade, one half finished the eighth grade, and only one in ten graduated from high school. Rice was attacked by the profession and Ayres was not heeded. The rationale then and during the 1920s was to attribute school retardation to "undesireable" immigrants and their children. Detroit, too, carried out a study in the early 1920s on school retardation, based on the nationality of the children's parents, and concluded that the *least* retardation was found among children of Scotch, English, and Canadian immigrants.

By 1960, however, the political climate and conditions were different. And the reaction of the profession, though on occasions defensive, was more positive. After all, educators had been sufficiently exposed to the writings of John Dewey for several decades, to the publications of the Educational Policies Commission during the thirties and forties, and to the growing educational research in American universities to cause them to rethink their programs and practices.

The 1950s witnessed the era of Sputnik and its critics of American education. Thus, when the sixties arrived, though institutional change was still distant, the readiness for change was more positive. Let us now review some of these changes.

1. Citizen advisory committees became an accepted practice.
2. Efforts to revise instructional materials with concern for our pluralistic society came into being.
3. The "equal educational opportunity principle," which meant that some children require additional services, became an accepted policy.
4. Prior to 1960, educational innovation occurred primarily in wealthy suburbs. Federal funding brought educational innovation to the inner-city schools.

5. New behavior codes for students and faculty were formulated. A high school student, expelled from school in Detroit, could appear alone, with a parent, or an attorney before a central appeal commission and challenge the expulsion. There were instances where a principal's decision was reversed.
6. Shortcomings of the educational profession were widely publicized. Though some of the charges were inaccurate and the expectations unrealistic, the public dialogue was beneficial to children and the profession.
7. Schools no longer continued the former apathy about children who failed or dropped out. The situation was greatly improved.
8. School budgets reflected higher proportions for educational research.
9. Continuing education for staff became an accepted program.
10. By the close of the decade, schools and universities accepted the need for joint efforts to identify needs and to develop programs.

The above list does not lessen some of the criticisms directed at schools. Much more should have been accomplished. Achievement was small because the need was so great and the expectations so high. Schools in the 1960s were asked not merely to make up for their own shortcomings, but also those of society as well. I believe that when the educational historians in the coming years will examine the challenges and efforts of the sixties, they will record this decade as an important turning point in American education.

CHAPTER 13

Management and Change

GEORGE W. BAILEY

The expected often does not occur, whereas the unexpected does.—Disraeli

EDUCATIONAL INSTITUTIONS must constantly look to the future if for no other reason than to avoid being its victim. As Cribbin (1972, p. 238) said, "Three things are certain about the future: it will be radically different from the past; it will be somewhat different from the present; and it will be rather different from what we expect it to be." Society is dynamic rather than static. As the world around the schools changes rapidly, it is ever more important that education must change also. It is obvious that the process of change in education is necessary in order for schools to remain tributaries to society rather than disassociated parts of it, or even refugees from it. It it equally obvious that just any change may be more disastrous than no change. Change must be planned, requiring managerial leadership of a special order to introduce, implement, and maintain the positive effect of the change and thereby assure that schools continue to function as tributaries to society.

Some people believe that school organizations are generally inflexible and incapable of changing themselves significantly. Change is possible in any organization, given commitment and perseverance by those trying to bring it about. People make up organizations and people will change (1) if they understand what it is that needs changing and why, (2) if they understand their role in the organization, and (3) if they are provided with the training necessary to develop the skill required for the new activity. These things do not just happen; they must be planned and made to happen. Let us turn our attention to the options available to make them happen.

THE OPTIONS: ORGANIZATIONAL HEALTH OR CHANGE STRATEGIES

I do not believe in change strategies as the best solution for implementing change over the long haul. Rather, I believe strongly in development strategies, both individual and organizational, as a better and more lasting approach for implementing change. Specific change strategies should be used after the personnel are ready to accept change and able to cope adequately with change requirements.

One reason that I have little faith in targeting change strategies for a specific proposed change is the tendency to place change itself as the priority or the goal. Change, which is actually a means or a process for attaining goals, often becomes the focus of attention rather than what the change is really designed to accomplish. Such focus will never attain more than short-term gains. Goals are derived from a purpose that in turn originates from needs. Change is of no useful purpose unless it contributes in some way to fulfilling the organization's purpose and attaining its goals.

Moreover, a school system's purpose must relate directly to students' learning; if it doesn't, there is little need for educators to be involved in the process. Successful change depends upon a clear and agreed-upon set of goals; we must define the outcomes we expect. Change will not be a success unless its outcomes are defined in terms of the learner's skills, attitudes, and knowledge. The importance of this principle has become more meaningful over the past several years.

School District no. 12, Adams County, Northglen, Colorado has identified ten district priorities or goals for the next three years, each with an accompanying set of measurable standards. Eight of the ten goals relate directly to the learner; each of these defines the changes expected in the student in terms of achievement. Although a few members of the organization have questioned the source of either the goals or the standards, none has indicated serious concern about their validity or attainability. Such a statement could not have been made a few short years ago.

Following careful development and statement of clear, measurable goals based solidly upon the organization's purpose, how can one be assured of their successful attainment? How does one manage in order to accomplish change and success? We believe the only two options open to the manager are (1) to deal directly with each proposed change through strategies aimed to implement that change or (2) to focus on the dynamics of the organization, building a climate in which changing one's behavior in order to accomplish goals is relatively common practice.

Any planned change effort is deeply conditioned by the state of the system in which it takes place (Miles, 1969, p. 375). For the greatest amount of change to occur with the least amount of agony, organizational dynamics should be the focus of attention rather than change strategies. This is not a chicken or egg situation; rather, it is the chicken (the organization) that must first receive the attention if it is to produce the egg (change). Planned change efforts should be focused on the organization's health rather than the structure of the curriculum or the teaching process. Changes in the latter areas will occur after health factors have been improved and the proper climate exists.

Many purveyors of change have the correct aim in mind—producing change in people—but often emphasize the wrong things to bring it about. Too often they religiously follow the advice of the recognized authorities in change and concentrate their efforts on the early adopters, the middle adopters, and the laggards. They carefully plan for the preparation stage, the adoption process, and the diffusion process. Rather than all this, it is probable that both the rate and the amount of change in the target group would be greater if the strategy were that of developing a condition within the organization which causes people to accept change. This can be accomplished only through careful attention to the health factors of the organization.

How is a healthy organization to be recognized? Since organizations are composed of individuals, it is appropriate to look first at the healthy organization member before considering the organization.

Recognizing a Healthy Individual What is a healthy member of a social system? Social psychologists refer to the healthy individual as one who is functioning effectively and efficiently. This person sees himself or herself in essentially positive ways. He feels good about himself or herself and others. On the other hand, an unhealthy individual is one who thinks about many things in negative ways and is generally less effective and hence less efficient than the healthy person.

Are there ways to recognize a healthy member of an organization in her or his day-to-day job? If one can accept the innovator as being healthy, the following traits, revealed in an individual's daily routine, tend to distinguish the innovator or the healthy individual (Cribbin, 1972, pp. 243–244).

Is intellectually inquisitive

Is constructively critical

Does not relate easily to authority but accepts it

Is zealous about his ideas and programs

Seeks to improve things
Has firm convictions
Is somewhat unconcerned about protocol
Carries on in spite of opposition
Pushes ideas to completion
Is not bothered by disagreement

Prefers complexity
Deviates only when necessary
Is willing to persevere for lasting results
Listens to ideas of others
Is genuinely interested in the success of the organization

Recognizing a Healthy Organization

This returns us to the organization. The healthy organization is one able to cope adequately with its environment over a long period of time in an effective and efficient manner. Effectiveness is the extent to which goals are achieved. Efficiency is the achievement of outcomes with the least possible expenditure of time, resources, and personnel to be effective. A healthy school system is one that accomplishes its goal in an effective and efficient manner with the product being well-educated, self-sufficient, decision-making, relatively happy, and productive students.

A healthy organization can be identified by looking at those factors of group dynamics that behavioral scientists and organizational psychologists have found to affect organizations in positive ways, making them more able to accomplish identified goals. Miles (1969, p. 378) provides ten dimensions of organizational health that have to do with the organization's continuing ability to cope with its environment and to achieve its goals. None is mutually exclusive and may actively relate to the others, particularly in healthy organizations. The ten are goal focus, communication adequacy, optimal power distribution, resource utilization, cohesiveness, morale, innovativeness, autonomy, adaptation, and problem-solving adequacy.

Although all ten dimensions relate to or affect an organization's ability and willingness to change, we operationalize only the first four hoping to develop the other six in the process. These four dimensions or factors affect all aspects of the organizations through structure—committees and councils; role and task—position descriptions and performance agreements; and process—relational skill development and functional skill training. Miles (1969, p. 380) describes the four factors as follows:

1. *Goal focus*. The goals of the organization are relatively clear, reasonably well accepted, achievable in light of available resources, and appropriate.
2. *Communication adequacy*. Communication channels are relatively distortion-free, flowing vertically and horizontally. People are able

to get the information they need with little effort. They do not have to depend on gossip to get information.

3. *Optimal power equalization.* There is a relatively equitable distribution of influence. Subordinates can influence upward and they know that their boss can also. Influence rests primarily on the competence of the influencer.

4. *Resource utilization.* People are neither overloaded nor idled. They may be working hard, but they feel that they are learning and growing in their contribution to the organization. They feel good in their jobs.

As stated above, these dimensions of organizational health are operationalized in all aspects of the organization in order to reach or build the other factors. Stated simply, organizational health can be developed through good management. Such development is based on a growing body of knowledge relating to ways organizations can best adapt to the changes in society. Bennis (1969, p. 1) describes it as—

> . . . a response to change, a complex educational strategy intended to change the beliefs, attitudes, values, and structure of organizations so that they can better adapt to new technologies, markets, and challenges, and the dizzying rate of change itself.

Change itself is a means or a process for the organization to attain goals related to the organization's purpose. It is important to recognize that organizational health is likewise a means or a process for the attainment of a desired state within the organization. It is equally important to identify the desired state before the processes for reaching it are identified and sequenced. As Kaufman et al. (1974, p. 3–10), state, "showing *WHAT IS TO BE DONE* permits us to begin to make sensible decisions on *HOW* to do them." They add, "We should choose our processes (health factors) in terms of the product we want to achieve" (p. 6–1). The following is identified as the desired state of performance and relationships—the product sought in organizational health—in a school system:

1. Higher productivity
2. Increased employee satisfaction
3. Better quality of work
4. Greater teamwork
5. Less resistance to change
6. Reduced turnover and absenteeism
7. Deeper sense of responsibility in individuals and groups

Notice number five—less resistance to change! This does not mean developing a strategy for dealing with resistance but rather managing and working with people in such a way so as to increase their acceptance of change.

All components of the desired state can and should be measured from time to time. Information derived from all evaluation is "not for punishment and affixing blame—but for providing the necessary information for self-renewal (Kaufman et al., 1974, p. 6–9).

Change is of no useful purpose unless it contributes to fulfilling the organization's purpose and to attaining its goals. The purpose of an educational organization is to produce students who can function effectively in a life role situation. The two goals contributing to this purpose include (1) improving the conditions so that more learning can take place and (2) increasing students' achievement in all areas at all levels. The degree to which these goals can be realized determines the success of the organization and, of course, the success of any change efforts designed to accomplish them. Change can succeed only as well as its expected outcomes are defined. The value of the change will depend upon the expected outcomes' relationship to learners' skills, attitudes, and knowledge.

Although presented in reverse order, thus far our premise has been:

1. If change is to be truly successful, its expected outcomes must be defined in terms of the organization's purpose and goals.
2. The healthy organization can attain goals efficiently and effectively over a sustained period of time.
3. The healthy organization's expected outcomes must be defined in terms of a desired state of performance and relationships.
4. The development of certain dimensions of organizational health serves as processes to reach the desired state of the organization that in turn will produce change to attain the organization's goals and purpose.

We will now focus on pragmatic methods and approaches for generating and expanding a climate for change.

SUGGESTIONS FOR THE SUPERINTENDENT

There are a number of factors that can significantly affect a superintendent's ability to bring about change in a school system. Each of these factors, to a large extent, can be considered or ignored but they can be controlled by the superintendent. For as Carlson's studies on diffusion of innovations clearly indicate, the superintendent is neither a victim of the budget nor a powerless officeholder dominated by the school board (Woods, 1967, p. 41). The superintendent can (1) choose a school district in which to work that can be changed, (2) develop leadership in the management team first so that it can truly lead, (3) make the change goals clear, public, measurable, (4) use training as a change inducer, and (5) refrain from strangling change with participation.

Choose a District in Which Change Can Occur

There is considerable evidence that tells us that certain types of school districts are changeable while others are inert. A well-known law of physics that applies to these latter districts says, "A body at rest tends to remain at rest." The community in which a school district is located more often than not determines the potential, the desire, and the expectation for change. Elected boards of education generally reflect the expectations and desires of the community they represent. Some highly significant research on this topic by McCarty and Ramsey (1971, p. 17) is reported in *The School Managers*. Some of their findings are paraphrased below. The thoughts in brackets are mine.

1. *The dominated power structure*. This concept holds that the power structure in a community is pyramidal with a few people at the top making or substantially influencing most of the important decisions, including those affecting the schools. The school board generally reflects the wishes of the power group. FINDINGS: A dominated community power structure is most often accompanied by a dominated school board. Both in turn are most often accompanied by the superintendent playing the role of the functionary. [If the power structure is more interested in the status quo than in change, then little change will occur]
2. *The factious community power structure*. This type is found in communities that have at least two durable factions competing for control over important decisions. The elected school board is split between the factions and vote accordingly on most issues. FINDINGS: A factional community power structure is most often accompanied by a factional school board. Both in turn are most often accompanied by the superintendent playing the role of political strategist. [Suggesting change may endanger the political future of any board member and the superintendent may become expendable. Little change is likely to occur.]
3. *The inert power structure*. This type is generally found in rural communities but could exist anywhere. Power is latent and maintaining the status quo is reflected in most school board decisions. FINDINGS: An inert community power structure is most often accompanied by a sanctioning school board. Both are most often ac-

companied in turn by the superintendent playing the role of decision maker. [The community has little active interest in educational policies. If change is to occur, that decision will be made by the superintendent; the board's role will be one of sanctioning the change, not insisting that it take place. The superintendent's main problem is to raise the community's aspiration level so that it will desire change.]

4. *The pluralistic power structure.* This is one in which the decision-making power is dispersed or diffused among many individuals and groups, as found in many suburban communities. There is likely to be interest in education and people will probably be quite active in school affairs. FINDINGS: A pluralistic community power structure is most often accompanied by a status-congruent school board. Both in turn are most often accompanied by the superintendent playing the role of professional adviser. [The community and the board have high educational aspirations; the superintendent is expected to initiate the change necessary for the school system to meet or exceed expectations. The superintendent generally has stability in his position, allowing him to implement change as needed.]

I have worked in communities with pyramidal power structures, having boards of education that represent this power structure. I have also worked in rural, inert communities with sanctioning boards. By far, my most rewarding experience has been in two pluralistic communities. One had a factious board, but with a change in membership it became status congruent. The other community, my present job, is a model of pluralism represented by a status-congruent board. The degree of change possible in the latter two districts is almost without measure. As for possibilities for affecting change in the first two districts, the law of physics applies: "A body at rest tends to remain at rest."

All of this tells us that there can be a match, or a mismatch, between community expectations and the person hired to direct that community's school system. The school superintendent, who aspires to help the public school system respond positively to changes required in the 1980s, has no business accepting a leadership position in many of the country's provincial-type school districts. In many such situations, the relationship, and the superintendent's job, face almost certain disaster.

Significant changes in education take place in school systems that are open, located in pluralistic communities, have status congruent boards of education, which choose successful superintendents and expect them to lead—not dominate, but lead. As McCarty and Ramsey (1971, p. 144), state:

Successful superintendents make appraisals of community environments to find out if it is possible to build a school system which will have a reasonable chance of meeting public expectations before they accept a position . . . the school community for which the superintendent works is as responsible for his success or failure as the superintendent himself.

Make Goals Clear and Measurable

It has been suggested that an organization's effectiveness depends to a degree upon its ability to achieve goals. Therefore, the goals of the system need to be reasonably clear to the members and based upon the demands of the environment (Miles, 1969, p. 380). Without prior knowledge of the organization's goals, individuals do not have the necessary information to set personal objectives that tie into the organization's overall plans. In order for individuals to help achieve organization goals, the goals must be known and understood by these individuals. It is management's responsibility to see that the system's goals are established and communicated.

A goal is an end, a result, not simply an activity or a task to be carried out. It tells us where we want to go, when we should arrive, and what the conditions or situation will be when we get there. Too often in education today, there is lots of activity but little concern where it is taking us. For decades many educators have claimed that educational output cannot or should not be measured. It may be true that change in human behavior may be difficult to measure, but "part of this output measurement difficulty [among educators] seems to be a form of organization defense or protection against criticism from the surrounding environment" (Miles, 1969, p. 382). Although it may be difficult to do so, behavior can be measured.

Even though many teachers and teacher groups still defend the educational goal ambiguity point of view, there is a sizable number who now believe that student output can be measured. There are even some who feel that teacher performance can be measured by the achievement of their students—and are willing to be assessed on that basis, provided that student limitations are taken into account. The point here is that goals, standards, and goal setting are becoming important factors in the change process in healthy organizations. Let us consider why this is true.

School systems generally fail to take advantage of the opportunities goal setting affords as a change-inducing activity. Hughes (1965, pp. 26–27) makes a strong case for top-down goal setting as an aid to individual achievement and happiness. He states, "Participative management cannot be equated with the absence of top-down planning.

Further, bottom-up planning is not a sure way to achieve either employee participation in company objectives or employee happiness." If activity in support of organization goals will allow people to reach personal objectives, then we have a potentially healthy, happy, and satisfying environment along with the willingness to change.

Furthermore, school systems often ignore or fail to recognize the high expectation–high performance cycle as a possibility to improve organizational health and change receptivity. The "effectiveness" cycle, as it is called, is dynamic. High expectations result in higher performance that reinforces the high expectations and produces higher performance (Herser and Blanchard, 1972, p. 150). Expectations that come from the board of education in the form of expected standards accompanying identified goals have almost unlimited possibilities for organizational improvement and individual change. The problem has been that school district management has hesitated too long to state exactly what standards of achievement are expected.

Develop Managers First The development of leadership at the proper time is often overlooked. In many cases, the implementer of the change—the teacher—is the prime and first target. The manager of the change—the principal—is often left to his own devices or must receive training concurrently with the teacher. Such practice does not place the principal in a true position of leadership. Healthy organizations cannot develop at the lower levels unless each level is developed ahead of the next, beginning at the top. In the first place, the person with the greatest amount of credibility with the worker is the line manager (Frye, Seifert, & Vaney, 1977, p. 6). It follows that the principal should and could be most successful in introducing and implementing change with teachers. If the line administrator is to fill this role, the skills required to carry this out must be developed.

In the second place, it is through training that an individual can most often gain the skills and thereby build understanding and commitment to change. For instance, healthy organizations communicate adequately (Miles, 1969, p. 380). This implies that the movement of information is relatively distortion-free and that it moves both vertically and horizontally. For this to take place in a school building at an optimal level, the building principal quite often must have some special training himself in one-to-one communication skills. Such training provides a depth of understanding of not only how to communicate, but also of the value of good communication. Following mastery of these skills, the principal is then ready and able to transmit them to or use them with the teacher.

Use Training as a Change Inducer

Use Training as a Change Inducer The potential of personal development as a motivating device and a change inducer is almost unlimited but generally is ignored or overlooked. Most educators, even those who may be only lukewarm toward a proposed change, are desirous of gaining new skills that might make their efforts more effective or easier. It has been the writer's experience that training sessions related to a proposed change activity draws more "takers" than can be handled, provided that—

1. The training is provided on a voluntary basis; people are not coerced.
2. The training is carefully designed to develop skills required in the change effort.
3. It is generally offered in a block of time (one week) during the summer months (not after school).
4. There are no out-of-pocket costs to the participant except for college tuition.
5. The training is provided prior to the implementation of a planned change or prior to an individual's being required to employ skills required in the change.

The psychological effect of being prepared for a well-publicized change effort is tremendous. Simply feeling prepared not only improves morale but also reduces resistance to the planned change. It may be one of the more effective of the change strategies.

The type of persons used as trainers is crucial to the success of the change effort. Whenever possible, in-district people should be used as trainers. There is considerable evidence available that states that the immediate supervisor has the greatest degree of rapport, credibility, and communicability with the worker. It follows that the unit administrators might be the most effective trainers of other people.

The writer's strategy is to use external consultants and trainers only under the following guidelines:

1. Their skills or expertise must contribute directly to planned change.
2. Their primary role is to train key internal people who in turn will train others, generally their own subordinates.
3. When external consultants have imparted the required skills, their services are terminated; they have no role in implementing the change. (This is sometimes a blow to a consultant's ego.)

External consultants and trainers serve another useful purpose. The change effort can often receive a substantial boost by the outsiders' honest and candid statements about the state of the district's change activity. Provided that the outsiders have some national reputation for expertise, their stating that the district's efforts are not up to par with other districts attempting similar changes can serve as a stimulus for "getting with it." On the other hand, their saying that the district's efforts compare favorably or are above that of other districts can be a real morale builder.

Refrain from Strangling Change with Participation Many so-called leaders in education apparently do not understand and often misuse the participation principle. A common solution for dealing with acceptance of change is to get people to participate in making the change. There is considerable evidence that dealing with change in this manner is not always productive and it may even lead to resistance.

The purpose of participation is not to provide people opportunity to help *make* decisions. Rather its purpose is to provide people affected by decisions or opportunities to *influence* decisions. Influencing decisions about change does not necessarily mean helping decide whether the change will take place. If the decision to change were left to the entire organization, or to a group within the system, it is highly probable that very little, if any, change would ever occur. The decision to change is management's decision. Individuals are involved when their ideas and suggestions are gathered concerning how the change will be made.

I believe that more change will take place faster if personnel participate in change decision on the technical or "how" level. Participation or involvement in change decisions in our school district generally proceeds as follows: First, the decision to change is made by top management sometimes with but often without input from personnel who might be affected by the change. The decision is always based on (1) the organizations' goals, (2) the impact the change is expected to have in achieving these goals, and (3) the skills, understandings, or attitudes personnel must have to implement the change.

Next, to save time, the proposed change is reduced to writing. It is at this point that leadership is required and representative personnel who may be affected are invited—I emphasize "invited"—to participate in study sessions devoted to deciding how the proposed change will be implemented. Management must demonstrate that ideas and suggestions from the group will be followed, provided that there is a consensus on each point. Participants must be able to see that they are truly influencing the how decisions. All discussions in these sessions are predicated on a clear statement that the decision to change has already been made and that the role of the participants is to decide how the change should best be implemented. Requirements that the proposed change may generate, such as information needed by affected individuals, timing, training, personnel, processes, and approaches, are all legitimate areas for study by this group. At least 90 percent of all recommendations of the group are accepted; some must be modified because of money or time constraints. Very few are ever entirely rejected.

This procedure provides professionals with meaningful influence over important decisions but keeps the decision to change or not to change in the hands of those who have the necessary perspective to make it. This approach to participation or involvement in decision making has had support in the literature for over twenty years.

Participation sometimes helps build acceptance of change, but not for the reason that people simply participated. Hughes (1965, pp. 26, 28) debunks the notion that mere participation increases productivity:

> Participation is not, any more than profit, an end in itself, although management may never recover from the lingering myths arising from the Hawthorne studies to the effect that participation leads to happiness which leads to productivity. . . . Management must realize that it cannot "participate" an employee into producing.

Neither will participation necessarily reduce resistance to change. "As a practical matter, 'participation' as a device (for dealing with resistance to change) is not a good way for management to think about the problem. In fact, it may lead to trouble" (Laurence, pp. 145, 152).

Participation is a feeling on the part of people, not just the mechanical act of being called in to take part in discussions. Participation will not reduce resistance to change if it is treated as a way to get somebody to do what someone else wants him to. Participation is not successful unless it is built on respect; the respect people feel when their ideas and suggestions are honestly sought to avoid unnecessary mistakes. To me, this type of participation reflects and produces healthy organizations.

Leading people to change, attitudinally and behaviorally, requires adherence to three general principles of leadership. First, organizational goals and individual objectives, as well as performance criteria, must be developed and made clear and measurable. Second, this must be accomplished through a process of participation. The main criterion of such participation is that people will attempt to arrive at explicit objectives and standards of performance and will accept responsibility for helping themselves and others achieve them. Finally, the entire process must be based upon value of individual and organizational development. In other words, change must be a humane process, operating from a solid base of knowledge of what it is the organization is attempting to accomplish by the change and how the individual can contribute to its attainment.

The manager will find gimmicks far less useful in developing change than a climate that stimulates people to think in new ways about old procedures and practices. Strategies for specific change targets are used, but they should be employed after the organization's health has been developed to a state which is conducive to accepting change as little more than a natural course. Such a climate is produced and developed by good management.

REFERENCES

Bennis, Warren G. *Organization development: its nature, origins, and prospects*. Reading, Mass.: Addison-Wesley, 1969.

Cribbin, James J. *Effective managerial leadership*. American Management Association, 1972.

Frye, Nelson, Seifert, George, & Yaney, Joseph. *Organizational change through feedback and organizational efforts*. Presented at the Annual Conference of the National Society for Performance and Instruction. Chicago, April 16, 1977.

Greiner, Larry E. Patterns of organizational change. *Developing an effective organization*. Harvard Business Review reprint, Harvard Business School, no. 21072.

Harrison, Roger. Understanding your organization's character. *Developing an effective organization*. Harvard Business Review reprint, Harvard Business School, no. 21072.

Hersey, Paul, & Blanchard, Kenneth E. *Management of organizational behavior*. Englewood Cliffs, N.J.: Prentice-Hall, 1972.

Hughes, Charles L. *Goal setting: key to individual and organizational effectiveness*. American Management Association, 1965.

Kaufman, Roger A., Feldman, David, Snyder, Edward, & Coffey, Warren C. *Role behavior for success*. Research for Better Schools, 1974.

Laurence, Paul R. How to deal with resistance to change. *Developing an effective organization*. Harvard Business Review reprint, Harvard Business School, no. 21072.

Lawless, David J. *Effective management: social psychology approach*. Englewood Cliffs, N.J.: Prentice-Hall, 1972.

McCarty, Donald J., & Ramsey, Charles E. *The school managers*. Greenwood Publishing, 1971.

Miles, Matthew B. Planned change and organizational health: figure and ground. In Fred D. Carver & Thomas J. Sergiovanni (Eds.), *Organization and human behavior: focus on schools*. New York: McGraw-Hill, 1969.

Rogers, Everett M., & Svenning, Lynne. *Managing change*. San Mateo, Calif.: Operation PEP, San Mateo County Board of Education, 1969.

Woods, Thomas E. *The administration of educational innovations*. Bureau of Educational Research, University of Oregon, 1967.

Where Do We Go from Here: Emerging Approaches

THE BOOK has presented a variety of views about change as it is being carried out in schools. Change-related issues have been identified and a number of approaches to reforming schools have been suggested. While writing from different vantage points the contributors seem to share some conclusions about the art of changing schools. They tend to agree that the forces that are resistant to change are many and complex. As a result, change programs must also be complex. They also agree that changing schools is a high-risk venture, and that our experience thus far is that many change programs have been initiated but few have persisted. In spite of these limitations, they share the belief that there is potential for reforming schools. All identify leadership as a critical element in the process and most encourage diverse approaches to improve the probability of effectiveness. We are left with a feeling of hope, but a clear message that our efforts will have to be improved before we will have a lasting impact on school life.

What is keeping us from improving our efforts? In part, at least, our difficulty lies in the fact that much of what is being done in educational settings has been taken from other organizational sectors. This has created two major difficulties. First, change strategies are often adapted in their entirety rather than modified to meet the unique needs of the educational sector. The result is that a strategy may be viewed critically when, in reality, it is the *way* the strategy is applied that is the problem. For example, management by objectives is relatively easy to apply when one is measuring the production of widgets, but relatively difficult to apply when measuring preparation of our youth for citizenship. It took a period of time before we recognized this fact and began to make appropriate modifications. By the time we did, the process itself had become suspect. Once it falters, people become hesitant to commit themselves to such a process.

Second, there is often a time lag between the development of a strategy and its application to educational settings. For example, organization development (OD) is an outgrowth of the experiential learning notions developed by the National Training Laboratories and others in the late 1940s and early 1950s and soon modified and applied in business settings. It was not until twenty years after the initial exploration of these concepts that OD was finally, and tentatively, explored in a few school settings and ten more years before it became widely known. Often this lag in application to educational settings is critical because the conditions that lead to the development of a change strategy are modified over time. Therefore, what may have been appropriate at one time may not be appropriate at another time, or at least may require a major reorientation. To illustrate, OD strategies require at least a modicum of goodwill among the parties involved. This may have typified school settings in the 1950s, but today more typically those involved are diametrically opposed to each others' values, styles, or actions. OD strategists can no longer operate as though former conditions still prevail. If they do, they may well fall short of expectations. We are slowly beginning to realize that we will have to modify our strategies to meet changing conditions and shifting issues.

Part Four is devoted to this reality. The readings present and examine emerging change concepts. Based upon a recognition that we must adapt our approaches to meet changing conditions, they build on our learnings over the past several decades. Thus they represent both an analysis of our shortcomings and a reconceptualization of strategies to change schools.

To begin, Tye looks at OD as it is typically practiced and concludes that it often falls far short of expectations because its advocates have tried to operate outside of the political system. Rather than view OD as "apolitical" Tye feels that we must confront the political realities of schools directly. Teacher militancy, community interest groups, and the evolution of policy are the frameworks within which OD strategies will prosper or falter. If we do not take these realities into consideration and behave accordingly, Tye feels that OD will never be effective. For example, it is unlikely that attempts to equalize power will be accepted in a school when the teachers' union is urging its members to refrain from cooperating with the administration. Tye feels that OD technology includes the basic capacity to respond, but that a new mind-set will be required on the part of its advocates. They must be willing to expand into an area that has often been neglected or purposely avoided. Tye concludes by proposing that a new role be defined for OD specialists, a role he calls "political linkage agents." This is a controversial concept but one that deserves our attention given the prevailing conditions in school settings.

Lieberman next describes the emerging role of the linking agent, which seems to have gained wide recognition as a legitimate function in our efforts to introduce change in education. As she defines it, "the role of the linker is to stand between two organizations or groups of people and make connections." Examples of such role players include district-wide officers interacting with school personnel, teacher center staff members visiting rural schools, and university personnel bringing new approaches into schools. Such bridging roles are growing in importance as we recognize the need to support change programs as they are tested and institutionalized. The linker role is a difficult role because the linker, as an outsider, will probably be suspect from the start. To gain legitimacy and be effective, the linker, therefore, must model openness, risk taking, and creative problem solving. After pointing out traps that linkers must avoid if they hope to remain viable, Lieberman focuses on means of strengthening the role. She identifies skills required and provides ideas, out of her own and others' experiences, that can help linkers to build a support base. She also emphasizes the importance of knowing one's self and the realistic limitations of the role. Since many readers are probably presently in some sort of linkage role, these ideas and suggestions should be directly relevant.

Whereas the linker concept focuses upon "outsiders," team administration turns inward toward administrative role players who share the burden of managing a school system. Owens explores team administration, its growing popularity, its potentials, and conditions that must exist if it is to be an effective tool for improving schools. He stresses that team administration puts an "emphasis on team members participating *actively* in decision-making processes." This deviates from usual arrangements where the superintendent holds forth while subordinate administrators silently acquiesce and carry out assigned tasks. Owens believes that team administration, which has become popular at least in part because of the growing militancy of teachers and the subsequent strong sense of isolation on the part of the building administrators, holds much potential for improving the responsiveness of school districts to conflict and demands for change. To realize this potential, changing the form but retaining the substance will not suffice. He argues that we must give due consideration to *processes* such as team building, trust development, and shared inputs, but that we must also devise *structures* that can lead to the institutionalization of team administration. In short, Owens argues that since the context in which we run our schools has changed rapidly, it may be time to devise administration processes and structures that are more closely attuned to this reality.

The last two contributions in this part propose frameworks that view conflict management as residing somewhere along a continuum of possible responses. The first, by Derr, presents a contingency approach in which conflict managers are viewed as practicing collaboration, bargaining, or power. Collaboration stresses internal commitment while bargaining stresses legal commitments. Also, both assume open, face-to-face interactions. Power, on the contrary, stresses covert actions and a win-lose orientation, with the intended outcome being control of the other parties involved. Derr admits to a bias toward the collaborative approach because it "(1) promotes authentic interpersonal relations; (2) is a creative force for innovation and improvement; (3) enhances feedback and information flow, and (4) promotes openness, trust, risk-taking, and integrity within an organization." However, he cautions against taking a monolithic approach to conflict management and change. Rather, he argues, *effective* strategies are based upon the realities of place, time, issues, and personalities. He provides a typology to help the reader decide "when to use which" approach. If a situation calls for power, collaboration is inappropriate. Perhaps with time it will be possible to move the parties from power relations, to bargaining and, ultimately, to collaboration, but Derr stresses that we must start where the parties are. If there is lack of trust it is unrealistic to assume collaboration and maybe even bargaining.

Finally, Conway develops a "map" that should help school administrators recognize and respond to the connections between sources of conflict and strategies for responding to them. He begins by noting that the literature is replete with books that categorize strategies for responding to a conflict situation. Though useful, there are limitations to such schemes because they are generally associated with all forms of change but the administrator faces crises in rapid succession. What is required is a means of recognizing which strategies should be selected to respond to which conflicts. Conway focuses on the development of this important linkage. To make the tie-up he first focuses upon sources of conflict; they may come from inside the organization or from outside of it, and they may be discrete or continuing in nature. He then develops a framework that lines up the variety of possible strategies that could be considered against the various sources of conflict. Readers will probably find both Derr's and Conway's contributions useful as they seek to place the strategies explored throughout the book into a coherent framework for action.

CHAPTER 14

Politics and Organization Development

KENNETH A. TYE

ORGANIZATION DEVELOPMENT specialists have assumed that their roles are apolitical. Indeed, many of the most widely read books and articles having to do with planned organizational change, including change in schools, completely ignore the political context within which public organizations such as schools operate. Even when that context is acknowledged, it is frequently dismissed as being outside of the concern of organization development theory and practice. The theoretical assumption is that organization development is concerned with the health of the microsystem (the school) while politics occurs at the macro-level (government). This assumption has to be challenged given today's realities. Events of the recent past have more and more caused school affairs to become politicized.

This chapter will discuss the relationship between the politics of public schooling and organization development work at the school level. Out of the discussion, an attempt will be made to describe a more realistic role for the organization development specialist—one which will be more in line with the realities of an era in which public schooling has become highly politicized.

THE POLITICS OF SCHOOLING

Political scientists define politics as "the authoritative allocation of values for the society." Stated another way, politics is about who should set *policy* or make decisions. Until recently, the matter of policy setting for schools was fairly straightforward. Education was seen as a state function and the legal responsibility of the state was extended to the local school board. Within the broad guidelines established by the state, each local board of education set policy for the schools within its jurisdiction. In so doing, it determined values for those schools by selecting and assigning personnel, by allocating resources in various ways, and even by setting curriculum priorities. An increase in student health or counseling services, the promotion of interests having to do with patriotism, the reduction of class sizes, the employment of reading specialists, the increase of salaries and the purchase of athletic or band uniforms are all examples of rather common and usually noncontroversial board of education decisions that have expressed educational values for schools.

Such decisions are not made in a vacuum by boards of education. To begin with, boards operate as open political systems. That is, the various preferences, beliefs, ideologies, wants, and needs of the populace are brought together and articulated to the board by community groups or by individuals in the form of demands for change or as supports for the status quo. Historically, such demands and supports have been articulated by the better organized and more influential members or groups in a community. Likewise, board members themselves have tended to be members of those groups or at least to represent their interests. To a degree, this has caused a situation wherein values for schooling have been determined by the more conservative elites in communities throughout the nation, a situation that has seldom seemed to particularly concern the general populace.

In addition to interaction with the community, board members have traditionally taken much guidance from superintendents and other district administrators. In fact, the lines between policy making and administration have frequently been blurred. The result has been that the so-called professional administrators have both set policy and administered the schools. Infrequently, and more of late, the reverse has occurred. That is, in a growing number of cases, boards of education, rather than being rubber stamps, have sought to control administrative functions as well as those of policy making.

Either way, the situation has been such in education that at least until recently almost all policy at the local level has been formed, administered, and even enforced by the political subsystem made up of the board of education and the district administration.

The central function of politics is the formulation of policy. In order to set policy, individuals and groups must have *power*; and herein lies the new reality of public education. However one might judge the sixties, one thing is for certain. The congressional legislation of that decade put the federal government squarely in a position of power with regard to schools. Equality of educational opportunity and quality education for all was national policy. It still is. Title I of the Elementary and Secondary Education Act (ESEA), Head Start, bilingual education, migrant education, and mainstreaming are but a few examples of the direct federal policy role in education. Not only has the federal government passed legislation, but it has established guidelines to which schools and school districts must adhere if they are to get federal funds. Likewise, judicial decisions have been important in the formulation of educational policy. Of particular note has been the Supreme Court decision that declared segregation illegal and subsequent court decisions that have implemented and enforced desegregation.

The federal legislation of the sixties also strengthened the policy role and thus the power of the states vis-à-vis public education. Thus, today one finds far more direct relationship between local schools and state departments of education than ever before. Also, state legislatures are far more active with regard to educational policy formation. For example, most attempts at enforcing accountability and competency-based education have their genesis with state legislatures and state departments of education.

Even more subtly, the federal legislation of the sixties encouraged wide-scale community involvement in local government affairs, not the least of which were school affairs. Community power became a reality in many locales and is evidenced today in regional boards of education, school-site councils, and various school district and school advisory councils.

Finally, teacher organizations have become more militant as they, too, seek a share in the policy-setting process. At present, the focus is upon such matters as wages, benefits, and working conditions. If the experience of other Western nations holds true, it will only be a matter of time until organized teacher demands will also focus on curriculum issues.

In order to dictate policy, any group or individual must have power. However, those who already have power do not wish to nor will they hardly ever give it up voluntarily. The result more often than not is intense conflict—conflict over who shall have the power to set policy. Such conflict is continually going on in and around our schools and traditional coalitions seem to be breaking up. Whereas boards of education and administrators have typically worked together, one can see more and more instances of superintendent firings over issues of policy. Likewise, recalls of board of education members over value issues such as sex education, prayer in schools, the teaching of reading, and the teaching of Americanism are not uncommon. Certainly, teacher strikes are on the increase. Even the long-standing coalition of minorities, intellectuals, liberals, and the middle class that has supported free public education as a national institution is torn apart over the issue of school desegregation. Finally, one can see the federal government at odds with states and/or school districts over issues of noncompliance with federal regulations.

Schooling today exists in an environment of conflict—political conflict. No amount of wishing or ignoring the fact will make it go away. The microsystem of the school is in constant interaction with its environment and directly affected by it. Organization development workers not only must take this fact of life into account but they must also deal with it directly as they go about their work in schools.

Implications for Organization Development There are at least five implications of the politicization of education for organization development workers in the public schools. These are: (1) the need to press the case for OD in the political systems; (2) the need for OD workers to assess the political environment of the school or district as part of an initial assessment; (3) the need to focus upon clarification of the values of the organization vis-à-vis participatory decision making; (4) the need to develop power equalization strategies as part of OD work; and (5) the need for updated and politically realistic training for OD workers themselves.

PRESSING THE CASE FOR OD IN THE POLITICAL SYSTEM. It was not until 1968, nearly three years after the passage of ESEA, that those responsible for the implementation of Title III realized that schools and school districts that had federal grants for innovation needed to tend to the process of change as well as to its substance. Today, with reference to all Titles of ESEA and other categorical state and federal programs, the situation is even worse. To be sure, there are projects and programs, most notably sponsored by some regional laboratories and some research and development centers, which attend to how change takes place. However, we are definitely in an era wherein both the politicians and the federal and state education authorities are consumed with what has to be changed and not with how schools can become organizations wherein improvement can take place.

The systems planners, the accountability advocates, and even the evaluation advocates won the day with Title III and they still hold sway when it comes to state and federal education legislation. The advocates of organization development, organization problem solving, and even so-called linkage strategies are perhaps listened to. However, very little, if any, educational legislation is written that recommends, not to mention mandates, that organization development should be part of school improvement efforts.

Both research and experience tend to demonstrate that the applied principles of OD (i.e., goal clarification, open communication, group problem solving, participatory decision making, conflict resolution, and process evaluation) create environments wherein change can take place. That message has to be delivered to policy makers at all levels of the political system. This requires the lobbying of administrators and legislators at the federal, state, and local levels by advocates who serve on advisory panels or who make personal contacts. In the final analysis, it may require the formation of a national organization of OD specialists and associates that has such lobbying as one of its major functions. As much as OD people might perceive lobbying as distasteful, they must realize that in this day and age relying solely upon the merits of a theoretical or an applied idea is naive at best.

ASSESSING THE POLITICAL ENVIRONMENT. The beginning step in organization development work is diagnosis. Additionally, data collection and data analysis should occur throughout OD efforts. Beckhard (1969, p. 26) describes the typical scope of diagnostic activities as follows:

> The development of a strategy for systematic improvement of an organization demands an examination of the present state of things. Such an analysis usually looks at two broad areas. One is diagnosis of the various subsystems that make up the total organization. These subsystems may be natural "teams" such as top management, the production department, or a research group; or they may be levels such as top management, middle management, or the work force.
>
> The second area of diagnosis is the organization processes that are occurring. These include decision-making processes, communications patterns and styles, relationships between interfacing groups, the management of conflict, the setting of goals and planning methods.

Such diagnosis has become basic to organization development work. However, it does not go far enough with reference to schools that presently operate in a highly politicized environment. Additional diagnostic work must be done.

The mandates under which a school operates should be carefully examined. These include the guidelines of the various state and/or federal categorical programs and they include local board of education mandates. Knowing what those mandates are and what they require is important. Also, the degree to which the organization is in compliance is a measure of the consistency between the school program and the values of the body politic. Schools that are out of compliance will at one time or another most likely undergo conflict with that environment. Efforts at internal organization development can be significantly hampered if the school is engaged in such conflict. The resolution of conflict between the school and its environment, if it exists, is prerequisite to any internal organization development efforts.

The values of staff members must also be assessed since they may not be consistent with those expressed in program mandates. Teachers who believe in neighborhood schools may have difficulty working in schools where students are bused for desegregation purposes. Principals and teachers who are used to making most or all significant decisions may have difficulty working in situations wherein parents and/or students are expected to share in decision making. These are situations, dictated by the political system, wherein typical OD strategies can work. However, the subtle difference from the past is that there is a set of values to which staff members must learn to subscribe. It is not simply a matter of clarification of values. Additionally, it is a matter of the OD worker assisting staff members of the school to learn to behave in ways that are consistent with the values of the body politic as those values are expressed in policy. This is not an easy task. In such situations, these staff members might have to learn new skills (e.g., ways of grouping for instruction, language patterns, new methods of motivating students). Also, they might have to become aware of such things as their own nonverbal behavior and their own values as these are expressed in the giving of approval or disapproval to students.

Finally, the power relationships within an organization should be assessed. Questions of who holds what decision-making authority (power), what decisions they are willing to share and what decision-making authority other groups want are all questions which should be answered prior to organization development work. Such an assessment should include both the formal system of decision making and the informal system. In a school, for example, it would be important to know if there are individuals who influence decisions by virtue of tenure, perceived verbal ability, or any other reason. Likewise, one would want to know if there are parents or community members who influence school decisions disproportionately by virtue of their status, who they know, or how they behave.

CLARIFICATION OF VALUES VIS-À-VIS PARTICIPATORY DECISION MAKING. Several assumptions have tended to undergird organization development to date. In a highly politicized environment such as schools exist in today, some of these assumptions may need to be reexamined.

The first assumption is that people in an organization have drives

toward personal growth and development and that they want to become more capable of doing their job as well as contribute more to the
attainment of organizational goals. The assumption itself is not
questioned. However, if those who have power in an organization do
not operate with the assumption, then the odds are that organization
development efforts will either be very difficult or doomed to failure
from the beginning. The acceptance or rejection of this assumption will
affect the promotion of dependence or independence, the reward system of the organization, communication patterns, work norms, levels
of trust, motivation, and the like. It is the self-fulfilling prophecy that is
at work here, and it is imperative that the organization development
worker initially test the degree to which the assumption does or doesn't
exist in the school and district prior to any development efforts. If the
assumption is not or cannot be made to be operative, it may be unwise
to undertake OD efforts.

A second assumption is expressed by French and Bell (1973, p. 67)
as follows:

> For a group to optimize its effectiveness, the formal leader cannot per-
> form all the leadership amd maintenance functions in all circumstances at
> all times; hence group members must assist each other with effective
> leadership and member behavior. For many managers and groups, these
> are difficult patterns from which to extricate themselves and frequently
> require a change in perspective on the part of the manager and the total
> group.

If the OD worker sees such a pattern in a school, it is obvious that he
or she must confront it and work it through with the group. While the
principal of that school is most likely the critical person, the problem
can often go beyond the school itself. So many conflicting demands and
expectations are placed upon principals in today's climate that he or
she may be very reluctant to "share" leadership with staff members
when, in fact, he or she is ultimately accountable to the district administration and board of education, advisory groups, and even the state
and federal government and when, in many cases, he or she represents
"management" in collective bargaining with teachers and other employees.

Often what is clearly needed is clarification of staff and principal
roles in decision making. In working with groups the principal is well
advised to make clear the task of the group somewhat as follows:

1. The task of the group is to provide information or make recommendations for others to decide upon (e.g., evaluating the effectiveness of a particular board policy as it relates to the school).

2. The task of the group is to consider/suggest alternatives or recommendations for a decision the principal must make (e.g., preparing an overall school budget).
3. The task of the group is to make decisions (e.g., selecting personnel, assigning students, preparing an overall school budget).

Often, the locus of decision making can logically be in one place or another. For example, schools can function well if the staff advises and the principal makes the budget. It can also function well if budget decisions are made by the staff as a group. What is important is that the locus is clear and agreed upon by members of the group and the various superordinate systems.

Finally, an assumption usually attributed to organization development is that participatory decision making and the democratization of the organization are desired conditions. To date, organization development workers have not adequately addressed this assumption. They have decried being "power equalizers" while at the same time working to create conditions wherein organization members can make greater contributions toward organization goals. It can be hypothesized that the "hedging" on this one issue, a political issue, is at the root of most OD failures.

POWER EQUALIZATION STRATEGIES. Decentralized decision making and parent/community involvement are common terms in the literature of schooling. In the first case, decision making is supposed to be moved "downward" to the school level from the school district. This can take the form of regional or area structures within a district and/or more decisions to be made at the school itself. In the latter case, the notion is that parents and other members of the community should be directly involved in decisions at the local district and/or school level.

It is in such settings wherein organization development work would seem most applicable. As schools move toward more responsibility for decision making, the members of the staff and involved lay persons need to develop goal setting, communication, conflict resolution, and other OD skills. However, the reality of shared decision making is a political reality and OD efforts that deny this fact are unrealistic. A case study completed by this author provides an example. Because of strong leadership provided by a superintendent in a large school district, a plan of decentralizing decision making to the school level was implemented. It involved parents, teachers, the principal, and students. Everything went well for awhile, until those at the cabinet level of the district—the various assistant superintendents—began to realize that their roles had changed significantly. They were responsible for serving the needs of others rather than making decisions for others to carry out. At this point these "leaders" became the major stumbling block to change. Frankly, the decentralization effort never really materialized. While there was initial enthusiasm, a sense of being "manipulated" eventually set in at most schools.

In another case familiar to this author, a community advisory council was formed at a large urban junior high school as part of a district-wide plan of advisory councils for all schools. For two years the council involved itself in gathering needs data and goals data from students, teachers, and parents. It interviewed educational experts. Finally, it drafted a recommendation for an alternative school within a school. At that point, the principal found a variety of reasons why the program could *not* be implemented—budget, lack of staff skills, not enough study, a new principal, who was to be assigned and would have to be consulted. No alternative school within a school ever was developed.

The fact of the matter is that these are examples of political problems. In both cases, the setting of policy, the equalization of power, and ensuing conflict are involved. Strategically, OD workers must do three things when they are involved in a situation wherein participation in decision making is a purported goal:

1. They must demand clear guidelines as to what decisions are to be shared.
2. They must communicate these "rules of the game" to the client group so that they can agree initially to live by them, question them, or withdraw from the process.
3. They must monitor to see that initial agreements are kept, particularly when groups make decisions that are less than popular to superordinate levels in the system.

Only after such political matters are dealt with, can the OD worker proceed to assist people to become better problem solvers or decision makers. In an era of high politicization, the OD worker must be sure that the political realities are clearly understood. Without such understandings, it is questionable as to whether organization development work should even take place.

TRAINING OD WORKERS IN POLITICAL SKILLS. What has been stated thus far is based upon the assumption that, at the present time, power in school systems is controlled by systems superordinate to the local school (federal and state government, district administration, and boards of education). That is so because these superordinate systems make *policy*. Further, another assumption is that before significant change can occur in schools, this situation must change. *Power* to make decisions—set policy—must be equalized. A final assumption is that when efforts are made to redistribute power those who hold it will resist. *Conflict* will result.

The standard work of OD specialists within schools has been adequately defined by others. (See Havelock, 1970, Miles, 1970, and Schmuck et al., 1977.) However, these descriptions have avoided the problems involved in the politics that circumscribe OD work. An added role of the OD worker in the realities of today's school is that of "political linkage agent."*

What follows is a description of ways in which political linkage agents (PLAs) can be trained to perform their vital roles as change agents. Such training can be pre-service or in-service. Whichever, it has to be reality based.

The PLA will answer to a variety of groups that have power in the educational system as well as to groups that are powerless. In such a situation, the PLA will be vulnerable to being co-opted by the more powerful, particularly since those groups have the ability to give or withhold rewards. The PLA must be aware of such situations, and as part of the preparation for that role, must learn to make a complete commitment to participatory decision making and nonauthoritarian structures. The PLA must learn to make these commitments to all of those who would be potential clients. As part of this training, the PLA will also have to confront his or her own needs for personal power.

Basic to the training of all OD workers are both organizational theory and small group theory and application. A knowledge of the social psychology of organizations will serve as the basis for the PLA to appraise an organization's situation, strengths, and difficulties. Likewise, such knowledge will serve to provide the solutions and methodologies needed to move the organization forward. Small group theory and application will allow the PLA to understand and evaluate the interaction patterns of the members of the client system. Further, it will provide valuable insights into his or her own interactions with those clients.

Additionally, the specialized role of the PLA will require knowledge

*This term was originally put forth by this writer at a 1972 conference of individuals interested in change agentry. The conference was organized by Ronald G. Havelock, sponsored by the Institute for Social Research of the University of Michigan and funded by Title III of ESEA of the U.S. Office of Education. Results were subsequently reported in Havelock & Havelock (1973). Special thanks is expressed to Norman Hearn, the USOE representative who recognized the need for this conference and the need for alternative strategies to educational improvement.

of how political systems operate. The elite theory of C. Wright Mills (1956), pluralism as put forth by Robert Dahl (1961), and political systems analysis as discussed by Gabriel Almond and James Coleman (1966) and by David Easton (1965) are examples. An examination of the range of theory in this area will give the PLA a base upon which to construct new possibilities to fit the demands for power equalization, conflict resolution, and policy formation for the client system.

Often, we approach problems in education as if they exist only within the present. We tend to be ahistorical and aphilosophical. The reality is that most, if not all, of the proposals for change in schools are rooted in history, philosophy of education, and the overarching social and economic issues surrounding schooling. Thus, it seems important to suggest that the PLA be well versed in these foundation areas so that a truly systemic view of schooling can be brought to bear upon the problems of local schools.

No change agent, including the PLA, can provide all of the resources that may be needed by a school undergoing change. For this reason, the PLA will have to be familiar with as many as possible of those resources from which the client system may draw. This implies both knowledge of services available and a knowledge of the ability of individuals and agencies to provide those services. In the case of the PLA, the resources to be known are not only standard education ones, but they also include political groups and agencies, policy centers, and even politicians and government workers.

Finally, with the advent of collective bargaining, the PLA will have to have a knowledge of the procedures employed in negotiations and, more importantly, the impact of collective bargaining upon the school. Too often, collective bargaining has resulted in adversary relationships at the school level. It doesn't have to and it shouldn't. The sharing of information with union or association leaders, frank and open discussion of issues, humane implementation of the negotiated contract, and the allowance of dissent are all behaviors which must be learned by school staffs as collective bargaining becomes more and more prevalent.

The establishment of the PLA role will not be easy because of the need to have that role legitimatized by the political subsystem—the very group which will be distributing its power over a wider base. The degree to which such a role can be played successfully will depend upon how well a PLA is trained. Institutions of higher education might well consider a new type of advanced degree program based upon what has been set forth here. Details of such a program can be found in Havelock & Havelock (1973, pp. 143–150).

Organization development theorists and workers, for the most part, have tended to "hedge" on the political issues that surround public schooling. They have attempted to isolate themselves from those issues and suggest that their work is apolitical because it focuses on the ability of the microsystem (the organization) to deal with its internal functioning. At the same time, they acknowledge and even urge that microsystems should be viewed as open systems.

Organization development efforts in public schools have had less than optimum success in recent years. Some theorists and workers have attributed this to the "unique" nature of schools. This writer has even heard it suggested that the reason OD doesn't work in public schools is that schools are not organizations; but, rather, they are institutions. The truth of the matter is that they *are* organizations. And they are public. They are part and parcel of the political system and they must be treated as such.

Policy that guides action in schools is made at many levels of the political system. Schools must adhere to that policy since it is made to represent the values of the body politic. Likewise, all of the actors at the local level must have the opportunity to participate appropriately in the policy-making process. The critical task is to determine what those policy issues should be and how that involvement should occur. Unless these political issues are dealt with within the context of organization development, our schools will constantly find themselves in conflict with their environment.

One of the tenets of a pluralistic and democratic society is that power should be equalized across all groups and individuals. Organization development workers must make power equalization an avowed goal of their own work in public organizations such as schools. This means more than assisting others to clarify their values. It means *not* facilitating the development of organization functioning unless the organization is willing to commit to the equalization of power and behave as if it is possible and desirable.

Organization development is a new field. It is at a crossroad. To date, it has drawn heavily upon social psychology, itself an emerging field, for its theory and practice. It is time now for organization development to consider the addition of principles from other disciplines. One of those that is most appropriate in our present society is political science.

REFERENCES

Almond, Gabriel A., & Coleman, James S. (Eds.). *Comparative politics: a developmental approach*. Boston: Little Brown, 1966.

Beckhard, Richard. *Organization development: strategies and models*. Reading, Mass.: Addison-Wesley, 1969.

Dahl, Robert A. *Who governs?* New Haven, Conn.: Yale University Press, 1961.

Easton, David. *A systems analysis of political life*. New York: Wiley, 1965.

French, Wendell L., & Bell, Cecil H., Jr. *Organization development: behavioral science interventions for organization improvement*. Englewood Cliffs, N.J.: Prentice-Hall, 1973.

Havelock, Ronald G. *A guide to innovation in education*. Ann Arbor, Mich.: Center for Research on Utilization of Scientific Knowledge, Institute for Social Research, The University of Michigan, 1970.

Havelock, Ronald G., & Havelock, Mary C. *Training for change agents: a guide to the design of training program in education and other fields*. Ann Arbor, Mich.: Center for Research on Utilization of Scientific Knowledge, Institute for Social Research, The University of Michigan, 1973.

Miles, Matthew B. *Learning to work in groups*. New York: Teachers College Press, 1970.

Mills, C. Wright. *The power elite*. New York: Oxford University Press, 1956.

Schmuck, Richard A. et al. *The second handbook of organization development in schools*. Palo Alto, Calif.: Mayfield Publishing, 1977.

CHAPTER 15

Emerging Role of the Linking Agent: Some Problems and Prospects

ANN LIEBERMAN

> I feel I am a tightrope walker, a conduit between the staff and the principal. As a linker, there is constant pressure to gain legitimacy.
> (Linker, 1977)
> I think I can describe my role as a movement from no trust, to frenzy and fear, to trust and respect with much conflict in between.   (Linker, 1977)

EFFECTIVE SUPERINTENDENTS, district personnel, principals, and teachers have always played a role in opening people up to fresh ideas about the complicated work of educating. In addition, more project workers of all kinds have been working with schools during the last decade. Federal, state, and local initiatives have sent individuals into schools in an effort to link school people to ideas that will lead to school improvement (including teacher centers, universities, intermediate agencies, R&D centers, and the like.)[1]

The very nature of their task, i.e., linking two organizations or bringing information from one place to be used in another, is problematic. We now have some examples of such people and projects and can begin to talk about what they do, what they need to know and understand, and the conflicts and contradictions they face in their emerging roles.

The purpose of this chapter is to provide a better understanding of the linkage role as it relates to schools by discussing problems that arise as a result of linking people, ideas, and organizations together and some ways of thinking about and coping with these problems.[2] What follows is a view from linkers' perspectives as they attempt to do their work.

WHAT DO I DO FIRST?

When I entered the school, the principal had already talked to the teachers. They knew they would have a person to help in their ongoing work. There was a sense of ownership that linking to a university was a good thing. (Linker, 1977)

The superintendent controls everything. You can even feel it in the school. (Linker, 1977)

I spent hours with the principal. I wondered where the staff was. (Linker, 1968)

There was an announcement on the bulletin board that I would be at the next faculty meeting. The teachers had already voted *not* to be involved in the linkage project. (Linker, 1966)

Whether the linkage effort is a federal program to be conducted on a district-wide basis, a linkage between university and school(s), or district office personnel working to change the way teachers teach writing, one is initially faced with the problem of how one behaves when he or she first enters a school. Most often there is *no* preparation for bringing a new person into a school. Schools are busy places and outsiders are problems. Most people who play a linkage role see themselves as do-gooders. They are coming to help. "Why don't these people understand that?"

Who is she? What does she want? We all have masters degrees, write curriculum, and take courses. (Teacher, field notes, 1969)

Despite all the talk about schools being open systems, we recognize that, because of the way most teachers and principals have learned their job, there is a tremendous personal investment in the style that is developed. Most school people learn their role by doing it (Lieberman, 1977). New ideas threaten this personal style. Theoretically schools are open, but practically, "No one really understands my kids." Therefore, entry becomes a complicated process for the linker. Some diagnostic questions we developed attempt to deal with this initial conflict.[3]

1. What role does the *superintendent* or district personnel play vis-à-vis the school? (i.e., visible, supportive, centralized, cosmopolitan)

2. How does the *principal* understand the linker's role? How does the principal relate to the faculty? (Often this information is revealed in one meeting.)
3. Where is the *faculty* in terms of experience in improvement efforts? Are there any existing groups or committees?
4. Does the school have a history of dealing with new programs? Or, as in some schools, are there so many programs that the school lacks cohesiveness?
5. What understanding is there, if any, about the ideas or project that the linker represents?

Useful diagnosis can be developed by attempting to answer these questions. The following examples offer two differing scenarios and the linker's response to them.

School A
This linkage project involves connecting a group of schools to a university and to each other. The purpose is for the schools to eventually share resources by creating a network. Initially the linker works with individual schools, helping them define their own problem areas. This will then serve as the basis for linking the schools together.

The superintendent of School A is eager, open, and well connected to many cosmopolitan sources. He is supportive of all efforts at linking schools to outside resources. The principal is very pleasant but very ineffective (teacher reports). The teachers are very strong but do not have any existing groups organized to do anything other than the usual faculty meeting (principal report). The district is known for its "good schools." This school carries the district "halo." Teachers do not know why they are involved in this linkage project but are not generally opposed to it.

The linker can use this information to plan his or her initial relationship with this school. One can make several observations to start:

1. The district will support the effort.
2. The principal will probably feel threatened as it may look as if this new role should be part of what the principal should do.
3. Teachers probably hold high expectations for their performance. They may feel "schitzy" about their school; i.e., they may think they are very good, yet feel somewhat frustrated because they have no mechanisms to deal with their organizational problems.
4. There is probably a core of teachers who will support an external linker.

With this information, the linker must begin to work *with* the principal and the supportive core of teachers to focus on a theme, problem, project, or idea that is sufficiently compelling and important to them. The linker must understand that the principal is vulnerable in this situation and she or he may be substituted for the principal. This will make the linker feel good but will exacerbate an already troubled relationship. Building team responsibilities and aiding the principal in support activities might be a useful strategy.

School B The state has initiated the possibility of linking rural schools to a teacher center close by, thus attempting to relieve school and teacher isolation. Schools that can identify a problem in the basic skills area will get a linker, whose job it is to help the school obtain the resources to initiate and implement a tested program to meet its needs.

The superintendent is supportive of the whole idea and has suggested School B. The principal of School B has several programs going already and does *not* welcome another one. Principal and faculty relations are already strained. The school has a history of exploring innovative ideas. There is little understanding of this particular project. It is just "another project."

In this case, the linker has a different set of problems. Pressure is basically coming from the state. The superintendent is exerting additional pressure on the principal because there is support (money and people) available to improve a school. The principal feels she *must* participate in this project. Teachers will probably openly resist this "gift." Innovation overkill adds to the difficulties here.

The linker needs to do much of the actual work to involve this faculty. Both teachers and principal will resist this linkage. Clarity, simplicity, feasibility, and immediate results will have to be the guiding objectives here. The dice are loaded against the linker, but there is a small possibility that a concrete, small, powerful project might work.

THEY NEED ME OR HOW CAN I ACCOMMODATE?

In different projects, whenever we began to talk about what we thought about the schools we were working with, we uncovered a set of assumptions that appeared to dominate our thinking.

> I gave the principal a plan that described how to get teachers to individualize instruction. (Linker, 1966)
> I saw myself as facilitator, resource getter, information giver, educator. (Linker, 1977)
> I negotiate between teachers and principal. Then I do the same at the next level. (Linker, 1975)
> I felt pressure to gain *legitimacy*. (Linker, 1977)

On the one hand, we, as linkers, wanted very much to be accepted. We wanted to see our role as useful. When we were impatient, we were critical of the school people. This led us to want to tell, to push, to coerce. But when we realized we were involved in the process of brokering and matchmaking, we became aware that facilitation skills were not only more appropriate, but made us think differently about how we worked with the people in the schools. We realized we had more time to garner resources for them. We had connections to materials and people and were relatively free to come and go as we pleased. And we had more time to think about all the complexities we were seeing as outsiders. But this didn't take away that nagging feeling that we were constantly fighting to feel a part of the ongoing rhythm of the school.

WHAT MAKES ME FEEL LEGITIMATE?

"How did you do today?" "Oh! They loved me! They won't meet together unless I come to the school. And I am the focus of the meeting."
(Linker, 1969)
I think I raised expectations but then couldn't produce.   (Linker, 1977)

The role of the linker is to stand between two organizations or groups of people and make connections. That very description relates to a major problem for the linker; that is, she or he is peripheral to the major flow and life of a group. This often causes the linker to press hard to become part of the organization, sometimes usurping roles that are best assumed by insiders and making promises that *tell* the people you are worthwhile. This is especially so in the early part of a linkage relationship, when the linker legitimates the role by being a "gofer," i.e., a resource getter, collector of information, librarian. For many, these activities seem demeaning and peripheral. It is here that the linker must recognize the long-term development of his or her relationship with the staff. The excitement of the role is in building enthusiasm for fresh ideas that aid people in becoming more competent. This initial period is often followed by guided activities and other types of assistance. But, in a sense, though the linker may be the impetus for improvement, he or she is always on the outside.

GIVING HELP?

A consultant who has had rich and varied experience in an area where he will offer help does better to the degree that he can use this experience in ways other than talking about it   (Corey, 1963)

How to provide help is at the heart of the linkage role, yet it is the least understood and often gives the most trouble. Linkers are not therapists, yet many of our views of providing help have been formed by therapeutic models often blaming the victim, rather than dealing with the complexity of the social context. The role demands picking up cues, caring, and encouraging *at the right time*, being silent, sometimes talking, often feeling like an outsider, yet providing information as if you were an insider, often questioning others for purposes of clarification while questioning your own participation and behavior at a given meeting or exchange.

Much of the feel of when to give direct help, when to encourage, when to provide structure, when to question (like teaching) is learned on the job. But what about the substance involved with these processes?

WHAT DO I NEED TO KNOW?

I must sense the level of development of the principal and staff.

(Linker, 1977)

They wanted a written curriculum, and fortunately I know how to do that.   (Linker, 1977)

The staff is so socialized to do their own thing that the idea of group discussion is an innovation.   (Linker, 1977)

No matter what the linkage project, or its specificity, a linker is supposed to be a myriad number of people all in one. Crandall (1977) refers to a set of skill clusters that include:

• Problem solving
• Communication
• Resource utilization
• Planning
• Process helping
• Implementation
• Content/subject matter knowledge
• Evaluation/documentation
• Survival skills

Clearly, trying to be this superperson creates problems for the linker. We prefer to think about the linker's knowledge and skills as developmental. Few people are prepared to face the many-faceted role that Crandall describes but many could handle the possibility that one needs to know different kinds of things at different times in the life of a project. Perhaps the greatest strengths of an effective linker are to know where the resource people are, to either get what is needed or provide it oneself, and to recognize that as a group moves, it changes and will make different kinds of demands on the linker. Consider this vignette:

Case Notes (1975)

I was to be the person who would bring the knowledge of the university to this district that had just built an open-space school. This was part of a project with which I was working. Teachers were going to move into a new school and needed preparation for the move. I was to work with the teachers on how to get them to make use of open space and team teach where feasible and useful. I had met the director of curriculum. She had worked for eight years to get this school built. Meeting number one was arranged between me and the twenty-five teachers who had volunteered to go to the new school. They had never been together as a group. I did not know any of them. We were to work together as they moved into their new school.

How should I introduce myself? What should I say? How do I deal with an hour and a half meeting after school where teachers will be tired, confused, and probably uneasy? Where is the principal? All these questions ran through my head.

I assumed this was the beginning of this project and that most teachers probably didn't know what was going on. I also had heard that several district people had idealistic visions about what the school would look like and what the teachers would do with the children but that there had been little or no work with teachers.

Problem 1—There was a big gap between district expectations and teacher realities.

Problem 2—This first meeting had to deal with this gap and also deal with teachers' fears and concerns about the move.

Problem 3—The district had hired me. Whose interests was I to represent?

Problem 4—The principal was very congenial but had done nothing to get the group together and had no future plans.

Problem 5—This was a group of individual teachers but in no formal sense a group.

In order to deal with these problems, I decided to introduce myself, say as little as possible to legitimate my presence, then break the teachers into small groups representing grade levels. A task for the group was structured, but it was made clear that if the structure was binding, not to use it. The task was to talk about what the teachers were doing now that was successful and to explore some ways that working together might seem feasible. They were to jot down anything they needed, such as materials or assistance so that I could be a broker for them. It worked! They weren't being lectured at. I had provided the opportunity for people to engage at their own level. Indeed, they provided the agenda items for the next meeting. (Many teachers came to me at the end of the meeting to say it had clearly been worthwhile and they were looking forward to the next meeting where we could become more concrete.) But had I done what was necessary? Who was to support me, give me feedback, provide suggestions?

WHO SUPPORTS ME?

Few linkage projects provide the support necessary to help linkage agents grow or provide knowledge for a better understanding of the role.[4] One of the difficulties of linkage without a supportive group is that while much personal learning goes on, it remains just that—not being written about, shared, or conceptualized. Effective linkers are created, but we know little about how they work, think, and perform and even less about their effects on others. Most organizations do not provide group support, nurturance, or growth possibilities. But linkers, although they often act as individual consultants, have the possibility of gaining support from their own organizations, whether the linkage emanates from a university, teacher center, or intermediate agency. Without support, individuals may learn a great deal, but it will not add to our understanding of their role.

WHO AM I ANYWAY?

I always thought of myself as a nice, warm person, but the teachers said that anyone who drives 80 miles to see them must be an expert.

(Linker, 1967)

I need to know that I am accomplishing, that I can point to something definite at year's end. (Linker, 1977)

My very presence threatened the principal. (Linker, 1977)

My role is constantly changing. I used to do a lot of talking. Now I do a lot of behind the scenes work. (Linker, 1977)

I do everything! I negotiate with the university. I meet with district personnel. I write proposals. I go to school meetings to help them.

(Teacher Center Linker, 1976)

Most of us have grown up in schools where the model for learning was that one person had the knowledge and the rest of us could somehow absorb it. Those who take on a linkage role, which is essentially bringing new information or helping create supportive conditions for the sharing of resources, all quickly come to realize that the "telling model" has a place in a much larger, more complicated configuration of interaction. There is a time and place for telling, but there is so much more. We find that the complications of simply bringing ideas and having people use them causes us to suffer from what sociologists term role strain, conflict, and overload. We try to do everything to make the group work. Anything we think is needed we do, whether we should or not. This is what causes many linkers to become very uneasy about their role and unsure of themselves. For example:

Case Notes (1966–67)

In the school where I was working, the principal played an interesting role. He told me at our first meeting that he didn't really do much reading and wasn't very strong at conducting meetings where innovations were to be discussed. He said, "You handle the meetings and I'll run the school." Since I knew I had to work with him, I consented. I soon found myself planning the agenda, running to the library, Xeroxing everything in sight, and feeling like I was the principal. After he introduced me to the teachers, he never came to the meetings again. The teachers were delighted to have this extra resource. They were quite isolated from the city, and I felt I was connecting them to information that was interesting and useful to them. But I didn't know who I was and worried that somehow I had overstepped my bounds.

It has been suggested that one way to deal with the tremendous pressures of a linker's job is to take on responsibilities as they arise and recognize that as the group takes more responsibility, one changes from telling and providing to facilitating and arranging (Lieberman, 1977).

But this case reveals still another problem: linkage agents must be aware that in some situations they will be asked to do things they shouldn't do. In this case, if the principal couldn't take on responsibility for leading this group, the linker might have created a team that could share leadership responsibilities. One of the prime functions of linkage is to work oneself *out of a job*, not into one. There is always a great temptation to ease the pain of a weak leader by doing it oneself. While that may satisfy immediate needs and give the linker feelings of satisfaction, it may have nothing to do with the learning that needs to go on among the school people. The struggle to keep perspective and to deal with both one's own expectations and the school's is continuous.

FUTURE AGENDA ITEMS

Several agenda items emerge from both the linkage projects discussed here and the collective experiences of many of us involved in school improvement. They include:

Situational Demands Perhaps we ought to begin to amass a number of case studies that reveal the myriad types of situations in which linkers find themselves. Then we can begin to see what linkers do, given particular situations and particular project demands. It may be that some patterns will emerge. Instead of talking solely about the need for "interpersonal skills" or "subject matter competence," we may find out that there are commonalities among projects that make some strategies more useful than others. We are at the stage where personal learnings need to become the source for public discussion.

Understanding Developmental Phases Related to a better understanding of situational demands is a strong hunch of mine that understanding the developmental growth of linker-school relationships would help both the schools and those agencies responsible for improvement to deal better with the complexity of the job. One might speak about phases or stages that seem similar. It is clear that there is a lot of exploratory behavior in the beginning of a relationship. For example, both linker and group trade and negotiate different sets of expectations. Searching for a focus around which to organize activities is often stressful. Linkers who are impatient or uncomfortable with ambiguity often seek closure too soon. All these dynamics can be recognized, discussed, identified, and understood, but we need a body of information to guide such understanding.

Universities currently seeking better connections with the field are well suited to do this kind of data gathering and conceptualizing.

Individual to Organizational Growth Anyone who has ever worked in a school as an insider or an outsider knows that improvement efforts always start with individual teachers—even though people may talk about a "school project." The Rand Change Agent Study (Berman & McLaughlin, 1974) revealed the importance of a "critical mass" of teachers necessary to change the norms of a school. What we have then is the beginning of a way to think about how ideas get moved from individual teachers' classrooms to affect the school. To date we have no data for thinking about how to move from individual growth to organizational growth. We have theories about individual change and still others about organizational change. But how do individual teachers who develop affect their organization? Or do they? How do linkers move from working with individuals to working with the organization? Miller and Wolf (1978), in working on a long-term Teacher Corps project, describe a set of activities in which they engaged the teachers in a cycle that makes an attempt at moving from activity to conceptualization. They describe activities in the school that move in the following manner:

• Individual growth
• Individual action
• Dialogue about action
• Collaborative action
• Organizational change and support for change

This conceptualization grew out of their understanding of the activities they created as they moved from working with volunteers to involving a larger group of teachers. It also emerged from their (the linkers) use of existing conceptualization (in this case, Goodlad, 1975, and Hall & Rutherford, 1975). They identify what they call "systematic ad hocism"—a way of reacting to the individual and social conditions but thinking about them in a systematic way. This is the type of case description we need in order to better understand the dynamics of the actual work that linkers do in schools. It helps us to begin to think about the gap between working with individuals and working with groups.

These kinds of descriptions can only be written by people who have one foot in the action-oriented fieldwork of developers *and* one foot in an organization that supports conceptualization. The university supports the conceptualization but only recently the activities. However, research and development centers and teacher centers as well as school districts could support this kind of person and these functions.

Linker as Teacher
In describing the role of a linking agent, one becomes aware that many of the jobs these people do look very much like our descriptions of what effective teachers do. Their role is to open school people to fresh ideas, link them to knowledge, and help them use this knowledge. They need to know how to work with individuals and groups, be sensitive to individual differences, and understand the power relations that affect the people involved. They need to move the ideas through a process of awareness to actual use, being always aware of the concerns that stand in the way of movement (Hall & Rutherford, 1975). If a structure is needed to initiate or sustain a group, linkers invent it. Linkers who know themselves well have fewer obstacles to overcome as they work with an incredibly complicated dynamic.

There are differences between teachers and linkers, but there appears to be a common core of similarities. We need to better understand these general qualities through in-depth fieldwork by people observing the role and by case notes and insights by people doing the work. We have much folklore on the fact that "teaching is teaching," but we do not actually know whether adults do respond the same as children or whether teachers of children make good teachers of adults.

This chapter has attempted to discuss the problems that linking agents face as they work with people on the school level. The problems and the suggestions for the resolution of these problems were discussed from the vantage point of the linker. The day-to-day work was illustrated with field notes from school improvement projects. Problems include:

1. Entering a school as an outsider
   (What do I do first?)
2. Thinking about how one will work
   (They need me, or how can I accommodate?)

3. Marginality of the role
   (What makes me feel legitimate?)
4. Providing the impetus for improvement
   (Giving help?)
5. Substance of the linker
   (What do I need to know?)
6. Learning for the linker
   (Who supports me?)
7. Role conflict, overload, and the problem of identity for the linker
   (Who am I anyway?)

Several agenda items for the future were identified as a result of this exploration. They include such topics as the documentation of situational demands on the linker, the developmental approach to linkage, the problem of our lack of a way of thinking about individual and organizational improvement, and the possibility of the conceptualization of the linker as teacher.

NOTES

1. All quotes used in this chapter are taken from actual linkage projects (1966–78) where cases were written in field notes, people interviewed, or accounts of experience spoken about at meetings.
2. The discussion that follows is drawn from several sources:
   a. I was a linking agent in a long-term project whose purpose was to better understand how schools improve and have since been involved in many linkage projects as consultant, evaluator, and staff member.
   b. I worked with eleven linkers as part of the Metropolitan School Study Council (1978–79). Our purpose was to link fifteen schools to each other and to share resources. The first year was spent getting into the schools and beginning this effort.
   c. As part of an NIE team, I looked at linkage projects whose purpose was to create a linkage system.
   d. There is some literature on linkage (see References for annotated references).
3. The "we" refers to the collective knowledge of my work with other linkers over the past decade and a group of eleven linkers who worked for the Metropolitan School Study Council, 1977–78.
4. Notable exceptions are the /I/D/E/A/ project where we met regularly to try to understand what we were about. Also the *Network* in Andover where project workers (linkers) meet to provide continuity and learn more about the efficacy of their work. See David Crandall's chapter, "Needed Perspectives on Linking Agent Training and Support" in *Linking Processes in Educational Improvement* (1977).

REFERENCES (Annotated)

Bentzen, Mary M. *Changing schools: The magic feather principle.* New York: McGraw-Hill, 1974.

See Chapters 1 and 10. In these chapters, Bentzen discusses the process of dialog, decision making, action, and evaluation. This process was observed over a five-year period. This kind of conceptualization is a useful way of thinking for those in linkage roles.

Berman, Paul, & McLaughlin, M. Federal programs supporting educational change. Vol. I. *A model of educational change*. Santa Monica, Calif.: Rand Corp., 1974.

A different view of implementation is discussed as a result of data from a national study of federally initiated projects. Successful implementation took place when both the project participants and the project itself mutually adapted.

Butler, Matilda, & Paisley, William. Factors determining roles and functions of educational linking agents with implications for training and support systems. San Francisco, Calif.: Far West Laboratory, January 1978.

The authors discuss the historical context in which educational dissemination has evolved. They describe three modal roles of the linker as resource finder, process helper, and solution giver. The relationship of these roles and selected functions is described.

Corey, Stephen. *Helping other people change*. Columbus, Ohio: Ohio States University Press, 1963.

A classic in educational literature, Corey describes his conceptualization of the consultant role. He describes his own experiences and attempts to create generalizations from it. This type of conceptual work is what is needed in the linkage dissemination literature.

Crandall, David. Training and supportive linking agents. In N. Nash and J. Culbertson (Eds.). *Linking processes in educational improvement*. Columbus, Ohio: University Council for Educational Administration, 1977, pp. 189–274.

This is the most comprehensive written work on the complex world of the linkage agent. Crandall has created, as an independent agency, many linkage projects. The chapter is a compendium of both the literature on change processes *and* a framework for understanding the complex role of linkage.

Emrick, John, & Peterson, Susan. Synthesis of five recent studies of educational dissemination and change. San Francisco, Calif.: Far West Laboratory, January 1978.

This paper takes five major school improvement studies and extracts the implications of these studies. Included are such conclusions as:

a. Some form of personal intermediary or linkage is essential to the dissemination process.

b. A comprehensive yet flexible external support system is needed to provide materials and in-person assistance.

The findings from these studies aid in our understanding of the linkage process as the authors describe the importance of both the style of the interventionist and the local commitment of the schools.

Goodlad, John I. *Dynamics of educational change*. New York: McGraw-Hill, 1975.

A five-year project, which was a collaboration between a foundation, a university, and eighteen elementary schools, is described. But there is much more. Goodlad reflects on the state of research on schools, school improvement, and the complexity of support that the schools need to solve their own problems.

Hall, G., & Rutherford, W. Concerns of teachers about implementing the innovation of team teaching. Research and Development Center for Teacher Education, University of Texas at Austin, 1975.

Working with the innovation of team teaching, the authors document the phases teachers appear to go through as they deal with concerns that range from personal to organizational. This typology has been empirically tested with other innovations.

Havelock, Ronald G. *Planning for innovation through dissemination and utilization*. Ann Arbor, Mich.: Institute for Social Research, Center for Research on Utilization of Scientific Knowledge, University of Michigan, 1969.

This was the first discussion of linkage roles and the problems of linkers. Drawn from a massive literature review, Havelock describes the roles and functions of linkers in different institutional settings.

Lieberman, Ann. Linking processes in educational change. In N. Nash and J. Culbertson (Eds.), *Linking processes in educational improvement*. Columbus, Ohio: University Council for Educational Administration, 1977.

This article focuses on the basic understandings linkers need as they work with schools. A view of the school as a social system with its unique effects on teachers and principals serves as the basis for the chapter. Also included are emergent generalizations about linkage drawn from several long-term studies.

Miller, Lynne, & Wolf, Thomas. Staff development for school change: theory and practice, *Teachers College Record*, September 1978.

This article focuses on a three-year Teacher Corps Project in which the authors attempted to understand and conceptualize their behavior as linkers and the types of activities created with the teachers. Especially noteworthy is the discussion about how the linkers moved from involvement with a few volunteer teachers to a large group of teachers.

Temkin, Sanford. *School improvement processes and external agency roles*. Research for Better Schools, April 1, 1978.

Comprehensive literature review of the phases of development schools go through as they improve. Major focus is on mobilization and implementation.

CHAPTER 16

Team Administration as Contingency Management of Conflict

ROBERT G. OWENS

ONE UNANTICIPATED CONSEQUENCE of the rise of collective negotiations in American education was the impact upon what may be described as the middle management group—the principals and key central office administrators—in local school districts. As teachers and superintendents became accustomed to confronting each other as adversaries over the bargaining table, lesser characters in the scene were largely ignored. Increasingly, boards of education and the superintendents looked to principals to be their loyal and trusted agents in the schools in the new adversarial relationships with teachers. Organized teachers tended to view their school principals as, in fact, being in such a role. This has wrought major changes in the relationships between teachers and principals that are difficult to soften and blur even by principals who emphasize collegiality, comaraderie, and interpersonal warmth to maintain harmonious relationships with their subordinates.

Ignored when they felt that they had much to contribute, "used" by management when it was convenient to share responsibility for unpopular actions, but having little input to policy development, principals across the country have protested their concerns. To the dismay of school boards and superintendents, they have, with increasing frequency, sought to establish their own collective bargaining units as a way of gaining power to deal with their developing plight. Alarmed superintendents and school boards have reacted by encouraging the development of administrative teams designed to include principals and other middle managers in an effort to manage the conflict between the realities of adversary relationships in collective bargaining and the legitimate need of principals to have a clearer role in school district management.

A survey of American and Canadian schools reported in 1976 that "vast numbers of the 92,000 principals in the United States—and many of Canada's 10,000 as well—are providing ominous indications that they are perilously close to rebellion against the top management in their school districts" ("The Brewing—and, Perhaps, Still Preventable—Revolt of the School Principals," 1976; "It's Late, but There's Still Time to Give Your Principals a Real Say in Management," 1976). Half of the school principals surveyed see themselves as being seriously in conflict with their superintendents and/or school boards either regularly or on occasion, and they feel that their prerogatives have been eroded in the collective bargaining between teachers and top management. The principals felt that they were consulted very little: chiefly in times of crisis or when top management wanted to spread the onus of unpopular decisions. While 30 percent of the principals reported that they had found a voice in decision making through management teams, half of that group felt that their management teams were either ineffective or existed in name only.

A study conducted in Michigan to identify the reasons for organizing bargaining units of school administrators showed, similarly, that the major reason cited by principals was erosion of administrative authority. Inadequate communication with the superintendent and the board was given next most frequently, and the third problem was role definition and responsibility under current conditions of conflict between teachers and management (Michigan Congress of School Administrator Associations, 1971). Commenting on this study, McNally noted that "a major conclusion of the study was that the key factor influencing the creation of formal administrative bargaining units was the superintendent. The degree of trust between him and the principals and other administrative officers in the school system, the degree to which he fostered their participation in school system decision-making, and the extent to which he nurtured openness and effectiveness of communication in the system, all helped to determine whether or not the administrative group resorted to formation of a formal bargaining unit" (McNally, 1973).

In 1978 a national Educational Leaders Consortium (ELC) was established that brought together ten national professional organizations to "encourage participative management through the administrative or leadership team concept'' ("Focus: Administrative Team," 1978). There is little question that this major consortium of professional organizations was calling for fundamental organizational change and not mere tinkering with traditional arrangements. As the opening sentence of the announcement of the consortium's formation put it, the intention is to "support . . . school organization patterns which encourage participative management."

To anyone even remotely aware of the literature in American educational administration in this century this small document was, indeed, a bold manifesto for practitioners.

EFFECTIVENESS OF TEAM ADMINISTRATION

Any assessment of effectiveness must be in terms of the goals that have been set in the first place. In general, team administration is initiated in local school districts for one of two reasons, or a combination of them:

1. *To blunt the trend toward the formation of collective bargaining units by administrators and, simultaneously, to solidify the ranks of management in the school district in the face of increasingly skillful and aggressive bargaining by teacher organizations.* There is some evidence, at this early stage, that the adoption of administrative team methods can be useful in achieving this goal. There is also evidence that teams that are not perceived by the team members as facilitating full participation in a meaningful way are not likely to achieve this goal. In other words, in school districts where superintendents begin to use the rhetoric of team but do not significantly change their methods of dealing with subordinates, it is unlikely that the principals and other middle managers will feel either less inclined to want to organize a bargaining unit or more cohesive as a total management group.

2. *To improve the functioning of the school district as an organization.* The goal here is a more positive one: to improve decision making, to encourage greater involvement and commitment in the whole school district enterprise, and to encourage more ownership of decisions and policies by middle management. While there is a large body of empirical research and practical experience from the social sciences to support the expectation that such an outcome is highly likely, it is still too early to have much data from local school districts in this country.

The State of the Art   Early in the history of the development of team administration it became evident that merely designating some key people as members of an administrative team was probably insufficient to achieve either of these goals. A study of the management team in one Michigan school district reported, for example, that the team existed in name only (Boles, 1975). Principals and assistant principals were convened at meetings, called team meetings, which exhibited few of the characteristics normally looked for in teams. Indeed, these team meetings often did not even have well-prepared agendas. Topics discussed were often only of interest to a few members and crucial issues such as goals, philosophy, and curriculum were rarely touched upon. Perhaps worse, the study of this team revealed that there was a great deal of confusion among team members as to what role expectations were and that they were not even in agreement as to what terms such as *policy* meant.

In a survey of school districts in Indiana, Duncan (1975) found that many meetings of so-called administrative teams closely resembled the pattern of traditional administrative cabinets, though they were now called teams. Frequently, this meant that the superintendent did most of the talking, controlled the agenda, and generally devoted most of the time informing and directing his subordinates. It did not take long, however, for it to become obvious that merely putting a new label on traditional practice was unlikely to achieve much of importance.

By 1978 it was becoming clear that in order to achieve the negative purpose of adopting the administrative team concept (i.e., to head off the alienation and unionization of middle management) it was necessary to accentuate the positive. In order to be effective, administrative teams have to function in new and more effective ways: with emphasis on team members participating *actively* in decision-making processes (not merely as passive recipients of information and instructions). As the executive director of Association of Supervisors and Curriculum Development (ASCD) put it, "the team approach to decision-making as 'the way of life' in administering . . . school districts . . . can help to avoid the trend toward unionization of 'middle management' and provide the kind of communication and coordination needed to assure decisions that are in the best interests of students" (Cawelti, 1978).

So, as the decades of the 1970s drew to a close, the catch-phrases in the "real" world of school boards, superintendents, and other school district administrators in America's school districts echoed the insights of the organizational theorists of a decade before. We are told by the president of the San Diego Board of Education that "It is our intention to continue the participative management concept of school district administration" ("Focus: Administrative Team," March 1978, p. 5). And the superintendent of Corpus Christi supports the notion, saying that "better decisions are made when those affected are involved in the decision-making process."

In a scant five years, from about 1973 to about 1978, school boards and superintendents in this country moved rapidly from a sense of defensiveness and isolation in the face of organized bargaining by teachers to a realization that there is more to the management of a school district than the board and the superintendent. The middle management group must support top management. And the only practical way to generate this support is to recognize and deal with the interdependence among the people involved in these various levels. This has focused a good deal of attention on "process": if we want people to function as team members, then we must recognize their worth, learn to communicate candidly with them, and find participative ways of working with them in deciding what to do.

But to a generation of school board members and district superintendents schooled in the military model of line-and-staff hierarchy, wherein policy and strategy decisions are made at the top and passed down the line of authority to be implemented, all of this new talk of "participative management" is a bit confusing and very difficult to work out in practice. Conversely, to a generation of middle managers, who have viewed their job as following orders and waiting for top brass to make up its mind, the new team approach demands new skills.

Enter at this point the "process" people who emphasize such things as trust development, involvement, shared management, team building, and team climate. In the more sophisticated school districts, at least, there is a very rapid and easily discernible trend toward recognizing the fact that the development of effective teams is not any more likely to occur by happenstance in school districts than it is on football fields or basketball courts. Members of administrative teams must develop new skills that will not only contribute to the development of the team but also its decision-making performance in the real world.

Participative Decision Making in Team Administration

A central—perhaps defining—concept of team administration is participative decision making. Duncan states it succinctly: "Team administration simply refers to genuine involvement—before the fact—of all levels of administration in goal-setting, decision-making, and problem-solving processes" (Duncan, 1974). Similarly, a state association of school principals said, "In place of the unilateral decisions which were made by the superintendent and passed down through the ranks to the level of final implementation, this new format would require a team approach to decision-making, providing an opportunity for all administrative and supervisory personnel to contribute . . . to the process . . . In return for this participation on the part of . . . principals, the superintendent must be willing to demonstrate his confidence in group processes; he must involve individuals so that they may feel a part of the decisions which are made . . . he must understand that this type of involvement is imperative if the principal is to consider himself a member of an administrative team" (Ohio Department of Elementary School Principals, 1971). Views such as these answer the question, "Why participative decision making?" from *one* perspective: that is, in this era of adversarial relationships in American public education, in order to maintain the support and effectiveness of middle management it is vital to include them in significant ways in the central decision-making processes of the district.

What price will school districts pay for this effort to develop the school district's management group into an effective, cohesive team? What, for example, will be the quality of the decisions from such a group? By turning to a group, are we not watering down the ability of qualified leaders to make the decisions that they are being paid to make? In short, is there a danger in team administration of trading off sound, organized, proven decision-making processes in the hope of getting higher esprit in the group and stronger loyalty?

PROBLEM SOLVING IN TEAM ADMINISTRATION

Answers to questions of this sort may be found by taking a closer look at the nature of group problem solving. Whenever administrative teams are discussed, for example, the desirability of developing trust relationships is inevitably mentioned. But, more exactly, what function does trust play in getting the best solutions to difficult problems in school districts? Why is it necessary to develop trusting relationships (open, collaborative, "leveling") in administrative teams?

Trust in Problem-Solving The level of trust between people affects the degree of defensiveness. People in groups that have a defensive climate have difficulty concentrating on messages, are inaccurate in assessing the motives and feelings of others in the group, and tend to distort messages. Intensive and persistent criticism increases mistrust and defensiveness and makes it difficult to recognize and accept good ideas. In general, defensiveness has been shown to have long-term negative effect on the ability of groups to solve problems effectively (Meadow, Parnes & Reese, 1969).

The reasons for this are relatively straightforward. As Zand (1972, p. 230) puts it,

One who does not trust others will conceal or distort relevant information, and avoid stating or will disguise facts, ideas, conclusions and feelings that he believes will increase his exposure to others, so that the information he provides will be low in accuracy, comprehensiveness, and timeliness; and therefore have low congruence with reality. He will also resist or deflect the attempts of others to exert influence. He will be suspicious of their views, and not receptive to their proposals of goals, their suggestions for reaching goals, and their definition of criteria and methods for evaluating progress. Although he rejects the influence of others, he will expect them to accept his views . . . and, further, when individuals encounter low-trust behavior initially they will hesitate to reveal information, reject influence, and evade control.

The level of trust between people is observable in the way they behave toward one another. If O has little trust of P, for example, he will disclose very little relevant or accurate information to P. Of course, P accurately senses this low level of trust and concludes that O is untrustworthy; P, therefore, is guarded in dealing with O and tells him very little that is helpful and, in fact, is suspicious of O's motives. O, in turn, senses that he was correct in not trusting P so he is confirmed in his original estimate that he should not be frank or become overly involved with him. What develops is a loop of interacting behaviors that continues to confirm and reinforce the mutual feelings of mistrust. To quote Zand (p. 233) again—

The interaction will continue around the loop, inducing O and P to behave with less and less trust until they arrive at an equilibrium level of low trust, each attempting to minimize his vulnerability and to maximize his control over the other. In the process the effectiveness of problem-solving will decrease. After interaction has continued, each will tend to hold more firmly to his entering beliefs. They will not have a reliable basis for accepting or sharing influence, and the mutual resistance to influence will arouse feelings of frustration in both. If they have a deadline, each will attempt to impose controls on the other. If P is O's organizational superior, he may command O's compliance, which will reinforce O's mistrust. Usually, by the middle of the meeting the level of trust will be lower than the initial level.

Thus, the participants are caught in a continually self-reinforcing downward spiral with trust getting lower and lower, defensiveness increasing, and—concomitantly—communication worsening and the ability to produce good solutions to problems declining. Generally, of course, this process stabilizes at some point and the group may continue to function for some time at a given level of effectiveness.

An administrative team formed for the purpose of generating greater mutual support and loyalty in the face of adversarial conditions should be the very antithesis of such a situation. Instead of norms of mistrust, suspicion, and alienation the administrative team seeks norms of trust, mutual support, and collaboration. Successful teams, therefore, devote considerable planned, conscious effort to developing new skills to help make the new norms realistically possible—to create a climate in the team that will lead not to a downward spiral of increasingly ineffective behavior but to an upward spiral of increasingly more effective norms (or climate) in the group.

In this vein, Schmuck (1974) points out that—

> Matters of size and structure are only skeletal beginning points. It will be the social psychological climate of the team that will undergird its success or failure. Some of the basic ingredients of a team's climate are group processes involving interpersonal expectations, influence, attraction, norms, and communication. Ideally, the climate of a management team will be one in which the members expect one another to be responsible and supportive; where the members share high amounts of potential influence—both with one another and with the formal leader; in which some attraction exists for the team as a whole and among members; where norms are supportive of collaborative problem-solving as well as for maximizing individual differences; wherein communication is open and featured by dialogue; and where the processes of working and developing as a group are considered relevant in themselves.

Thus, the very processes of building a team with the values and skills required to develop group climate that contributes to the high esprit that characterizes all effective teams virtually mandate emphasis on participative problem solving and decision making. But, will this emphasis yield better solutions to problems? Or will it, perhaps, lead to stronger team support for mediocre solutions to problems? Are we sacrificing strong leadership in the school district and, in the face of increasingly adversarial relationships with teachers, drifting toward "group think" and settling for the tyranny of the average of the group? Is the administrative team with its emphasis on participative decision making appropriate for an era that requires innovative responses to constantly changing circumstances? To deal with questions such as these, we need to take a look at the kinds of problems that must be dealt with.

A Contingency Approach
There is much discussion in educational administration circles today concerning the relative merits of participative decision making (sometimes still called "democratic") versus more traditional directive approaches in which decisions are made at the top and handed down the organizational line of authority to

be implemented by those in the lower ranks. Those who favor the latter tend to stress the apparent speed and efficiency of the more traditional approach as contrasted with the time-consuming and frequently fruitless committee meetings often associated with democratic procedures. The quality of decisions reached is a concern, too. Group think, conformity to mediocrity, and the stifling of individual initiative and creativity all lurk as likely consequences of moving from the practices of the past to the team approach.

Those favoring team administration often emphasize the apparent benefits of participative decision making. One of these benefits is the increased ownership that group members feel concerning decisions that they helped to make: the deeper commitment to make the decision work, born of one's own personal involvement in making the decision. This, the view goes, is more than an individual phenomenon. For as the administrators in the school district work together in an effort, ideally, to achieve consensus on important issues, the group develops a greater cohesiveness and esprit: it tends to become a team in the true sense. The outcome is likely not only to more fully utilize the knowledge and skills of the individuals in the group in working out high-quality solutions to problems, but to increase the focus and impact of the school district organization as the solution is applied in practice.

This issue very appropriately brings to the fore (1) increased concern for the psychological climate surrounding organizational decision making and (2) emphasis on developing such group process skills as the ability to give and receive information, deal productively with differences and conflict, and better utilize the abilities of the organization's greatest resource: its people. A danger in this new emphasis, however, is that we may conclude that participative decision making is the best approach to virtually every kind of problem.

While the rise of the administrative team in American public education offers a rare opportunity to capitalize on the positive aspects of participative decision making, we must recognize that it cannot be usefully applied to all kinds of problems. If administrators fail to discover early when participative decision making is appropriate and when it is not, it is likely that the new team approach may be needlessly associated with apparent failures and shortcomings as attempts are made to apply it in practice.

It is useful to examine the nature of the problems to see whether they, themselves, suggest helpful ways of dealing with this issue. For example, many problems have the following characteristics:

1. The elements of the problem are relatively unambiguous and clear cut.

2. The elements of the problem are readily separable from one another by objective means.
3. The solution to the problem requires a logical sequence of acts that may readily be performed by one person.
4. The problem itself is *discrete;* that is, its boundaries are relatively easy to discern.

Problems such as these are generally amenable to highest quality solutions in the most efficient manner by individuals who possess the necessary expert knowledge and skills to deal with them and who command a full view of the dimensions of the problem and the implications of various alternative actions.

Many problems appear to have quite different characteristics:

1. Not only is the problem itself complex, but the elements of the problem are themselves ambiguous, uncertain, and not readily quantifiable.
2. The elements of the problem are so dynamically interrelated that it is difficult to separate them on the basis of objective criteria; indeed, obtaining dependable objective measurements may, in itself, be difficult.
3. The solution to the problem requires the continued coordination and interaction of a number of people as they deal with the dynamic interrelationships of the elements and as the dimensions of the problem unfold.
4. The problem itself is *emergent:* that is, knowledge of its dimensions and boundaries cannot be fully known at the time of decision.

The highest quality solutions to problems of this kind are likely to come from a group of people who (a) are in the best position to possess between them the necessary knowledge to solve the problem and (b) who will be involved in implementing the decision after it is made.

A typical discrete problem in a school district is handling school supplies. The myriad problems involved in consolidated purchasing, warehousing, and distributing supplies to schools are relatively clear cut and can be ordered into a logical sequence by an expert. Indeed, as compared with the skilled business manager—with his intimate knowledge of the budget, contract law, purchasing procedures, and the vagaries of the school supply market—a group of school district administrators trying to deal with the problem of getting the right supplies at the right price to the right place on time could well be a matter of the blind leading the blind. Similarly, laying out school bus routes for maximum economy and efficiency is normally a discrete problem. The use of mathematical models and computer simulations, now relatively common in larger districts, virtually requires the use of experts who have the requisite technical skills and the techniques for grasping the full dimensions of the problem.

Policy issues, on the other hand, are very often emergent problems in public education. The matter of implementing competency-based education, for example, clearly meets the description of an emergent problem. Often the issue confronts school district administrators on the level of "How shall we implement the decision, which has been handed down to us?" rather than in terms of "Should we do it?"

As every educator knows, concepts of competency-based education involve many facets of the school enterprise in dynamic interrelationship, and certainly, the specialized knowledges of many individuals in the system must be brought to bear on the problem in highly coordinated fashion even to understand the problem. But making any decision to undertake such an endeavor as competency-based education will require commitment to the program by many people, continuous close collaboration, free flow of communication, and recognition that success depends upon an iterative process of decision making as the extent and implications of the problem unfold over time.

Many of the problems encountered in the course of day-to-day administrative practice are, such as this, emergent. Indeed, as education grows more complex, there appears to be less and less certitude that many important issues can be resolved by experts who pass their solutions on to others to implement. Appropriate solutions require free and open communication among a number of individuals who pool and share information. Close collaboration is necessary to weigh and evaluate information in the process of developing an informed judgment as to which of several alternatives might be best. Commitment to the implementation of the solution is essential in order to maintain the collaboration that is the basis of the iterative processes of decision making, which is crucial to the solution of emergent problems.

A STRUCTURALIST VIEW

Much of the rhetoric surrounding team administration—with its appropriate emphasis on process issues (such as participative decision making, collaboration, developing open and trusting climates)—tends to mask the fact that the move to team administration requires the adoption of new organizational structures. It specifically does not mean retaining our present organizational arrangements but only somehow doing a better job with them. More pointedly it does not mean retaining our present organization and laying on a veneer of "human relations" in the sense of allowing the middle management people to be better informed and to discuss relatively minor issues while key decisions on critical issues are made at the top and communicated downward to be carried out. Such an approach, which has not been unknown in education, is highly manipulative and almost certainly will defeat the essential purposes for having a team in the first place.

Consider the hypothetical situation described by Wright and Lipham (1976). Although it was a study of teacher participation in decision making at the school level, it raises an important issue relevant to administrative teams. They describe one school in which teachers and paraprofessionals were involved in making forty-five decisions in one month in the areas of student personnel, staff personnel, physical and financial resources, curriculum, and home-school-community relations. One could reasonably conclude that, in comparison to a second school in which teachers and paraprofessionals participated in only three decisions that month, there was a high degree of participation in the first school. But, first, consider the *kinds* of decisions in which they were involved.

In the second school (where teachers and paraprofessionals dealt with only three decisions that month), look at the power of the issues they confronted:

1. The choice of a new basal reading program to be adopted
2. The adoption of a program of cross-age grouping of pupils for instruction
3. Selection of a new school principal

Then consider, the *nature* of participation.

In the school with forty-five decisions during the month, participation by the staff consisted of expressing views and opinions to the school principal. However, in the school with only three (but crucial) decisions the teachers had two voting representatives on district-wide committees that had responsibility for making recommendations to the school district administration.

This simple case (hypothetical though it may be) points up a basic consideration in moving toward more participative management through teams: administrative structures must be developed that are specifically designed to facilitate participative involvement. In the case of the schools just discussed, the district-wide recommending committees are an example of a simple yet critical adaptation of the organization to the new approach to making decisions. Instead of filtering their views upward in the organization through the principal, then the director of elementary education, then perhaps the assistant superintendent for instruction, and finally the superintendent, these teachers were enabled to have a clear voice directly at the top.

Designing Organization Structures

The organizational structure found overwhelmingly in American school districts is characterized by the classical "line-and-staff" concepts. This is usually depicted in the ubiquitous organizational chart. To many people, this idea of organization virtually defines what organization is all about. But it may be worthwhile to take a moment to review some basic ideas, or assumptions, that underlie this concept of organizational design.

The basic function of *any* organizational structure is to assure administrators that people in the organization will behave in certain, specified, *predictable* ways. It would be a rare school district, indeed, where teachers were hired and then sent out to schools and simply told to teach. Rather, administrators create an organizational structure designed to assure top administration that teachers in the classrooms will behave in relatively predictable, definable, and desired ways. In school districts, this usually takes the form of a line organization. The idea is to have goals and intentions generated at the top of the organization and communicated downward to be implemented by the ranks below. In order to be sure that this is done as intended, each succeeding level of the organization supervises the level below: superintendents supervise assistant superintendents, who in turn supervise principals, and principals supervise teachers.

To supplement this hierarchical structure, administrators seek to increase control of the behavior of subordinates by creating rules, regulations, and standard operating procedures. Thus, programs are developed, and it is usual for teachers to be given curriculum guides, policy handbooks, copies of the rules, adopted textbooks, and other documents intended to assure that their behavior as teachers will more predictably conform to what the administrators of the system think is appropriate and productive.

Sooner or later, however, all organizations encounter unanticipated circumstances that the rules, programs, and standard operating procedures did not foresee. Ideally, classical line-and-staff provides a clearcut way of dealing with this: the problem is communicated up the line of authority to a level where a decision as to how to deal with the problem can be made. The new decision is then communicated down the line of authority to the lower ranks to be implemented; this often takes the form of revised regulations, modified procedures, supplementary operating instructions, new programs, and clarifications of the rules. Thus, the line-and-staff organization of the typical school district in America proceeds.

There are problems, of course. Everyone knows about some of them. There is the problem of communication being distorted on the way up the line of authority with the result that higher-echelon administrators often make decisions with an imperfect grasp of either the problem or the likely impact of the new decision. Often, even in rather small districts, the lines of up-and-down communication become overloaded and things bog down; when this situation becomes severe, a common response is to assign additional people to administrative duties. As often as not, of course, this creates even greater delays and clogs the communication channels even more. Unfortunately, as the organization confronts an increasingly uncertain environment—marked by change, new developments, unforseeable events—the demands on the decision making and control mechanisms of the traditional hierarchical line-and-staff organizational system become greater and its ability to respond flexibly and appropriately is reduced rather than increased.

When administrators design an organization such as this, they are acting on some clearly discernible assumptions. For example, one assumes that the task of top management is to set the organization's goals, decide how these goals are to be reached, and how to get the work done, and that the task of people in the lower echelons of the organization is to implement these decisions.

A different view of this holds that people who have the best information, and the greatest expertise, should be the ones who are directly involved in the critical decisions as to goals, programs, work methods, and so forth. As a practical matter, many school districts have for a long time sought to tap the skills and knowledge of its people in grappling with difficult decisions. But almost universally, such involvement has been on an informal basis and has rarely been a part of the official organizational system.

For example, when sixteen of the top-echelon administrators in the central office of a large city school system were interviewed, each was asked to describe the organizational structure of the system. Each unhesitatingly responded by accurately describing the "official" line-and-staff table of organization. But when asked to identify the organizational problems that were troubling them the most, *each one* of the administrators mentioned only problems of coordinating decision making between the line divisions. A typical problem, for example, was the coordination of programs, planning, and the work of in-school supervisors of the many reading programs in the district: the "regular" reading program and the numerous "special" reading programs that had been devised to deal with the educational needs of various populations in the school population.

Organizationally, the problem might not have been significant except that (for sound reasons) a number of the programs were housed in different line divisions. Since the organizational structure was designed to deal with problems up and down the lines of authority of the various divisions, there was difficulty in communicating and problem solving across these lines of authority. Of course, the problem *was* being dealt with and in a fashion rather typical of school districts: concerned people from various programs in the different divisions made it their business to establish informal contact with their counterparts about operational problems and did their best to informally deal with problems for which the district's official organizational structure made no provision. But the very fact that the ways of dealing with problems such as these *are* informal and, therefore, often sub rosa if not catch-as-catch-can is a constant course of uncertainty and organizational weakness.

If the administrative team concept is to become a part of the way of life in school districts in America, it will be necessary to legitimize it by incorporating teams into the organizational structures of the districts. Because the concerns of district-wide administrative teams cut across school levels and across traditional concepts of line authority, incorporating teams into the regular organizational structure can only be achieved by modifying the traditional hierarchical organization in basic ways. Early attempts to do this suggest that this may mean moving in the direction of matrix organization to link the schools as "operating departments" to the central staff in new, more functional ways than has traditionally been the case. Experience with organizational structure in school districts leaves little doubt that team administration has a dim future, indeed, if we focus our attention exclusively on the group process concerns that arise and fail to build teams into the mainstream of organizational structure.

REFERENCES

Ball, A. L., & Miller, E. W. The case for replacing your district's hierarchies with teams. *The American School Board Journal*, 1975, *162*, 34–36.

Boles, H. W. An administrative team? *Journal of Educational Administration*, 1975, *13*, 73–80.

The brewing—and, perhaps, still preventable—revolt of the school principals. *American School Board Journal*, January 1976, *163*, 25–27.

Cawelti, G. Administrative team concept can assure better focus on educational improvements. *ASCD News Exchange*, 1978, *20*, 1 and 12.

Duncan, R. The administrative team in Indiana: report of a survey. *Indiana School Boards Association Journal*, 1975, *21*, 17–19.

――――. Public Law 217 and the administrative team. *Indiana School Boards Association Journal*, 1974, *20*, 10.

Erickson, K., & Gmelch, W. *School management teams: their structure, function, and operation*. Arlington, Va: Educational Research Service, 1977.

Estes, N. *Can we make the administrative team concept come alive?* Paper presented at the AASA annual convention, March 20, 1973.

Focus: administrative team. *Educational Leaders Consortium*, March 1978, *1*, 1.

It's late, but there's still time to give your principals a real say in management. *American School Board Journal*, February 1976, *163*, 32–44.

McNally, Harold J. A matter of trust. The administrative team. *National Elementary Principal*, Nov.-Dec. 1973, *53*(1).

Meadow, A. S., Parnes, S. J., & Reese, H. Influence of brainstorming instructions and problem sequence on creative problem-solving tests. *Journal of Applied Psychology*, 1959, *43*, 413–416.

Michigan Congress of School Administrator Associations. *A survey of administrative bargaining units in Michigan public schools*. Ypsilanti, Mich.: Author, 1971.

Ohio Department of Elementary School Principals. *The administrative team*. 1971, pp. 2–3.

Schmuck, Richard A. *Development of management teamwork: a national overview*. 1974 (ERIC Document Reproduction Service No. ED 094 456).

Wright, Kenneth W., & Lipham, James M. Real and ideal decision structure and involvement in IGE schools. Technical Report No. 374. Report from the project on organization for instruction and administrative arrangements. Madison, Wisc.: Wisconsin Research and Development Center for Cognitive Learning, The University of Wisconsin, June 1976 (ED 126562) EA 008 503.

Zand, Dale E. Trust and managerial problem-solving. *Administrative Science Quarterly*, 1972, *17*, 229–239.

CHAPTER 17

Managing Organizational Conflicts: A Contingency Theory with a Collaborative Bias

C. BROOKLYN DERR

CONFLICTS ARE NORMAL, the natural consequences of human interaction in an organizational setting. They can occur for a myriad of overt or hidden reasons. For example, a teacher becomes upset because he or she feels a colleague is getting preferential treatment at a professional meeting: his or her internal stress interferes with the work process, setting up conflict problems within the organization.

Disruption within an organization can also be caused by external pressures that breed disagreement and tensions. Administrators fighting for the fiscal survival of a big-city school district as well as their own emotional and even physical survival can become so involved with life-and-death tasks that they neglect to give attention to the routine needs of those around them. Subordinates and colleagues, in turn, build up feelings of resentment and ill will.

Most disputes of the type illustrated above should not be resolved by more closely defining rules and regulations while, as a consequence, restricting open communications; they should be managed. Management techniques vary according to the situation.

Organizational theorists in the early and mid-1960s emphasized that there is no "best" way to design an organization's structure. They felt that an appropriate structure is contingent upon the variations in both task and environment, as well as the needs of individuals and groups within the organization (Lawrence & Lorsch, 1967; Burns & Stalker, 1961; Woodward, 1965; Thompson, 1967; Gabarro, 1974). Their studies have led to a body of literature called contingency theory. As Thomas and Bennis (1972, p. 20) put it—

> An effective paradigm incorporates what might be termed a "situational" or "contingency" framework, a point of view reflected in much of the current theoretical and empirical work in organizational theory. There is a primary emphasis upon diagnosis and the assumption that it is self-defeating to adopt a "universally" applicable set of principles and guidelines for effecting change or managing conflict.

It is proposed herein that the appropriate management technique depends upon the causes and preconditions of a conflict. A contingency theory of conflict management is based on this proposition.

Contingency theory comprises three major conflict management approaches: collaboration, bargaining, and power. When problems within an organization cannot be solved using normative or traditional approaches, the conflict manager designs a contingency strategy somewhere between the idealistic (normative) and realistic (one of the three conflict management approaches).

While all the approaches might be appropriate for a given situation, none is appropriate for every situation and one might, in the process of solving an immediate conflict, create additional problems for an organization. If in spite of conflicts there is a basic healthy mix within an organization of goals, environment, structure, and human and other resources, the conflict manager may find she or he can mix two or more of the approaches to solve a dilemma.

PREFERRED MODES OF CONFLICT MANAGEMENT

The *collaborative* approach assumes that people can surface their differences and work at them until mutually satisfactory solutions are found. This implies that people will be motivated to expend the time and energy for such problem solving. It exploits the possibilities of conflict as a creative force pushing parties toward mutual gains to which all are fully committed.

Bargaining assumes that neither party will emerge satisfied from the confrontation but that both, through negotiation, can get something they did not have at the start, or more of something they need, usually by giving up something of lesser importance. One party generally wins more than the other; through skillful trading he or she can wrest the maximum possible from the other side. Sometimes the tactics used are underhanded and create bad feelings. In the end, when an agreement is reached, it is usually enforced by a written contract with sanctions in case of noncompliance. In the event no agreement is reached, a third-party mediator may be employed to bind the sides to eventual arbitration.

Power strategy differs from the above approaches in that its emphasis is on self-interest. Whereas in collaboration and bargaining two sides come together to resolve their problems, when power is the dominant mode the actions are unilateral or in coalitions acting unilaterally. All of the power technicians' resources are unleashed against their opponent to win on a given issue or a long-range program, promising no internal commitment to joint decisions nor agreeing to external sanctions guaranteeing compliance.

Order of Preference Collaboration is the preferred strategy because it (1) promotes authentic interpersonal relations; (2) is a creative force for innovation and improvement; (3) enhances feedback and information flow, and (4) promotes openness, trust, risk taking, and integrity within an organization (see Schmuck et al., 1972; Kelley, 1970; Blake and Mouton, 1970; Litterer, 1966; Ewing, 1964).

Bargaining is the next preferred alternative. It at least brings the parties together and can bind them to joint decisions. It lays the substantive issues on the table where they can be better understood and acted upon. It demands interaction on the problem.

For organizational effectiveness, power strategy is the least desirable method of conflict management, although it may be preferred by the party with the potential for winning. Usually agressive and hostile feelings develop in a power struggle, shutting off communication and interaction. Gossip, rumors, and distortions tend to drive information underground so that there is little honest feedback and the parties cannot react intelligently or learn from the experience. Much sabotage and noncompliance result; people acting from self-interest often subvert the organization.

RELATIONSHIP BETWEEN THE THREE MODES

Collaboration The collaborative approach commonly used in organization development is fairly carefully defined in theory and method. The conflict manager (CM) first helps each party share its problems and disagreements with the other party and exchange information openly and willingly. Ideally, the adversaries then search for mutually satisfactory and workable solutions. Sometimes the process stagnates because the parties are too close to the issues to perceive creative options or underlying restraints prevent full exposure of the issues. The CM can then act as or bring in a third party to help clarify the issues, find commonalities, synchronize time and space, restructure the process to be more constructive, diagnose the restraining forces more objectively, summarize, and generally give needed support. He is, however, merely a facilitator and does not participate in making the decision or even become too involved in the substance of the problem (Walton, 1969).

Here the energy derived from conflict is viewed as creative tension generating energy for problem solving and innovation. For constructive confrontation to occur, a supportive climate (e.g., trust) must exist and the parties must be proficient at problem-solving activities or willing to use the skills of a facilitator.

Power   Except in authoritarian situations where employers rule by command, power stratagems are covert, the tactics undefined, in direct contrast to collaboration and bargaining where openness and definition of the problems are principal ingredients of resolution. People who play power games do so instinctively, using information strategically and revealing as little as possible to the opponent. Consequently, not much is known about the theoretical framework for using power (see Alinsky, 1946; French & Raven, 1960; Peabody 1971; McClelland, 1970; Crozier, 1964, p. 145). Obvious tactics that could enhance the power tactician's position in an organization are manipulating and hoarding scarce information; systematically engaging in acts of sabotage and noncompliance; forming and joining coalitions to serve a purpose; becoming withdrawn or autonomous in order to resist the influence of others; creating conditions of uncertainty for others and certainty for oneself; giving and collecting favors; co-opting; using force or threats of force. The basic idea of power play is to bias other people's perceptions of one's potential power and gain favorable outcomes for oneself, usually at the expense of others.

We know little about how these stratagems are effectively employed or the consequences, outcomes, ground rules, and limits of the approach. Power strategies are secretive and observable mainly in the form of results instead of processes. What we do know is that power tactics are extremely oriented toward serving one's self-interest and information is used most strategically and unilaterally. Thus, they are qualitatively different from bargaining and diametrically different from collaboration.

In the power approach the third party plays an ultimate role. When conflicts are not resolved in a manner satisfactory to the organizations' best interests, an authority person steps in and takes over. He is the final protector of the organization's interests and, as such, decides the limits of organizational tolerance for power struggles. Rather than helping people or groups work through their differences, he dictates the solutions. His method is direct and incisive: he dismisses people from the organization, legislates new rules, or restructures the hierarchy. Finally, he elicits external commitments ("do it or else") from the parties in dispute.

Bargaining As an approach to conflict management, bargaining contains elements of both collaboration and power. Like the collaborative process, it is systematic and in some of its forms allows for collaboration between negotiators, especially once power parity and trust have been established (see Walton & McKersie 1965; Stevens, 1963; Walton, 1969). Solutions reached through bargaining may fail to win strong endorsement from the disputants, but at least the manner is conciliatory and congruent with some overall organizational purposes.

The commitments are often guaranteed by legalistic sanctions. The difference between bargained and power-won resolutions is that in bargaining the disputants themselves make the agreements and set the sanctions and are committed to them. Power players tend to push the rules as far as they can, their sole limit being endangerment of their jobs. They have little to no commitment to anything except to not lose.

The third-party mediator in bargaining differs from his counterpart in collaboration in that he has the power of decision. But even in a bargaining session, the conscientious mediator will use the conciliatory procedures of the facilitator, encouraging parties to arrive at mutually acceptable solutions. He resorts to mandates and more active initiatives only if the two sides prove irreconcilable.

Bargaining has two facets similar to power strategies. First, the parties are encouraged to represent their self-interests. Unlike the power approach, however, bargainers put these interests on the agenda. Furthermore, they are prepared to compromise these interests for the overall good of the organization. Second, while information is used strategically, in bargaining it is eventually shared (although not always accurately) so that there can be a basis for negotiation. Parties divulge what they want or what they are prepared to relinquish in order to obtain information. They put priorities on their demands.

In other words, in pure power play the end justifies the means. In bargaining, self-interest is mitigated by the process of developing a long-term relationship. Thus, the parties consciously try to arrive at resolutions that will not engender later dissatisfaction. When they do not achieve their objectives to full measure, they assume they will meet again to negotiate further. The next time around, they are often prepared to "give" on a substantive issue in order to assure a more effective process or pay a debt of reciprocity. Power strategists, on the other hand, take all they can at any time and give as little as possible.

The gap between the collaborative and power approaches is great. Collaboration is benevolent and systematic; power is survival-oriented and intuitive. The former is optimistic, the latter often reactive, its purpose being to coexist with conflict rather than manage it. Bargaining can be viewed as a theoretical "connecting bridge" between the most salutary (collaboration) and the most destructive (power) uses of conflict-energy. When a conflict has been neutralized to the point of a standoff between a power tactician and the opposition, bargaining can be implemented effectively. This is possible because it borrows motivational factors from each of the extreme modes. Nearly every organization recognizes the need for internal harmony and cooperation. When cooperation is not the reality, bargaining can be used as an introductory method that may in time achieve an ongoing system of collaboration (see Walton & McKersie, 1965; Brown, 1972). However, Richard Walton's article (1970) demonstrates how the bargaining and collaborative approaches often work at cross-purposes.

The first item on the bargaining agenda is an agreement to release information heretofore private to both sides. Item by item, information is exchanged until a degree of power parity is reached. The conflict energy thereby released becomes a collaborative problem-solving resource.

Figure 17.1 illustrates the relationship between the three strategies. Note especially the distance between power and collaboration and the use of bargaining as a halfway strategy between the two.

FORMULATING A CONTINGENCY THEORY

The determination of when to use which approach—or which combination—awaits a diagnosis of the causes of the conflict and the presence or absence of certain preconditions. A rule of thumb in contingency theory is that the prescription is only made after a careful diagnosis of the problem. The CM has to determine whether the causes are personal, interpersonal, intergroup, environmental, or a combination thereof.

When individual stress influences an employee's work and relationships, it becomes an organizational conflict. Regardless of the origin of these personal tensions (they may, for example, result from marital

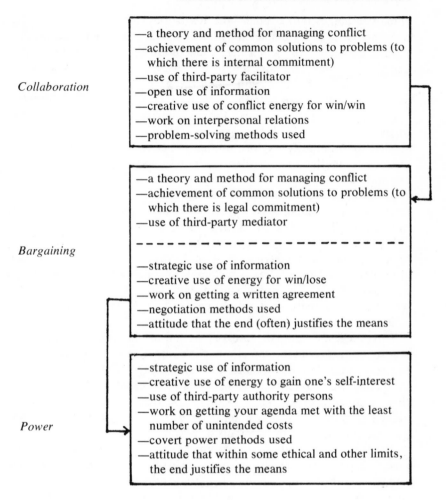

Collaboration

—a theory and method for managing conflict
—achievement of common solutions to problems (to which there is internal commitment)
—use of third-party facilitator
—open use of information
—creative use of conflict energy for win/win
—work on interpersonal relations
—problem-solving methods used

Bargaining

—a theory and method for managing conflict
—achievement of common solutions to problems (to which there is legal commitment)
—use of third-party mediator

—strategic use of information
—creative use of energy for win/lose
—work on getting a written agreement
—negotiation methods used
—attitude that the end (often) justifies the means

Power

—strategic use of information
—creative use of energy to gain one's self-interest
—use of third-party authority persons
—work on getting your agenda met with the least number of unintended costs
—covert power methods used
—attitude that within some ethical and other limits, the end justifies the means

Figure 17-1   Relationship between strategies

problems or psychological pathologies), the CM has only a few tools for dealing with the situation. He can, one-to-one with the employee, counsel and coach the employee to help him manage the problem. He can recommend personal therapy and hope that the problem will be resolved. He can, where possible, influence the organization to favor the individual (e.g. accommodate his values, adjust expectations of him). He can transfer or dismiss the person.

Individual issues become interpersonal conflicts when an unhappy employee comes into contact with his work group. Interpersonal disputes are more easily managed when the CM is able to act skillfully as a third-party facilitator; when the organization is willing to spend time and money on team building and problem-solving activities; when work roles are well structured; and when the parties can openly negotiate among themselves and with the system for their mutual self-interest.

Intergroup disputes increase the complexity of the conflicts in the organization but are still manageable. The groups must either be persuaded to voluntarily explore mutual benefits and solutions, or they must be committed to more formal negotiations and contracts. Another alternative is to design the units to interact as little as possible so that each is able to maximize its own self-interest. For organizational effectiveness, the collaborative approach is most preferred (see Blake, Mouton, & Sloma, 1965; Beckhard, 1967).

For some years, organizational theorists have been aware of the impact of the external environment on the organization. Indeed, human enterprises are labeled "open systems" to connote the permeability of their boundaries. The system must carry on a responsive exchange with its environment or it simply ceases to exist (see Katz & Kahn, 1966).

This suggests a fourth category—conflicts between organizations whose interests collide. Sometimes the competing systems are external to the organization, but sometimes they are internal subsystems acting as if they were external organizations (e.g. unions). In every case, these competing organizations want to take from the system scarce and valued resources, such as economic resources, legitimate authority, popular support, and the symbols of power.

Theories for resolving interorganizational and environmentally imposed disputes are at best primitive (McWhinney, 1972). Bargaining and power strategies are more likely to be effective than the collaborative approach in these situations. This is due to the lack of commonalities—separate authority structures, competition for scare resources, and distrust of a foreign entity—that obscures interests.

A form of environmental pressure that has lately gained in importance and under which the CM must use his most persuasive powers and, to a lesser extent, his bargaining tactics, is the profligation of revolutionary and adversary groups, which scrutinize and question not only the actions of the enterprise but sometimes its actual existence. Collaboration is not likely to be an effective strategy when confronting these revolutionary attitudes. As noted by Oppenheimer (1969, p. 68)—

> Any opposition must be total opposition, prepared for prison, exile, and hopefully, ultimate revolution . . . the symbol "compromise" enjoys a bad

reputation almost on a par with "opportunism." Compromisers are there-fore perceived as betrayers. When independence or liberation is achieved, the moderates are dealt with: objectively, they had sided with the enemy.

Most of these forces rely on public support for their attacks against the system. Thus, the more the radical organization can do to assure its public legitimacy, the better is is for the group. Figure 17.2 summarizes these systemic levels of organizational conflict.

Diagnosis of the causes of conflict includes assessing whether or not the conditions for using any one approach do, in fact, exist. Major requisites for each approach are listed below according to the author's judgment of what constitutes the most to the least important criterion. In collaboration, for example, the most important precondition is in-terdependence.

Collaboration Collaboration is best employed when a combina-tion of factors exists to assure the method some reasonable degree of success. These factors, in order of importance, are required inter-dependence, power parity, evident mutual interest, and organizational support.
Let us examine them separately.

PROBLEM		ALTERNATIVE	
	Collaboration	*Bargaining*	*Power*
Individual	counseling	negotiation	dismiss or transfer
	coaching	organizational accommodation	
Interpersonal	third party skill building time and support	negotiation	role design
Intergroup	collaborate	bargaining	structure for autonomy
Environment	adoption proactivity	bargaining	self-defense

Figure 17-2   Diagnostic contingencies

REQUIRED INTERDEPENDENCE. For collaboration to be successful, persons and groups in the enterprise must be dependent on each other in the accomplishment of organizational tasks. Some point out that the nature of the tasks depends on the product which, in turn, depends on environmental inputs and demands, making interdependence a function of external circumstances.

To surface and work through disagreements requires considerable commitment of time, energy, and emotions. It is doubtful that people will (or should) invest themselves in managing a dispute that is not compelling. People should be required to openly manage differences only when accomplishing the work is at stake.

POWER PARITY. Interdependence means more than acting our roles in order to accomplish a mutual task. It is also having a real and equal stake in the outcome and, thus, having few constraints in the collaborative relationship to interact frankly, even to deal with conflict when necessary. A kind of power parity must exist in which no party is one-sidedly dependent. Rather, they should feel free to interact and use all their resources to further the total organizational objectives. While the parties may recognize that they hold different rank, if they cannot put aside status and authority differences in order to work for the common objective, then by definition there cannot be true collaboration.

In many instances, power parity will directly vary with how compelling the task is. If the task is a short-term crisis of extremely important consequence to the organization, people will voluntarily work at full capacity, without being "hung up" about power relationships. At other times, it may be necessary to group peers if the task is to be accomplished. Perhaps dysfunctional authority relationships will have to be revised for productivity to occur.

EVIDENT MUTUAL INTEREST. In addition to a compelling organizational reason and sufficient parity for collaboration, the parties themselves must be motivated to resolve a conflict. The person or group must experience a felt need to work out the disagreement. Motivation often depends on whether mutual gains are self-evident.

Common goals, positive feelings, and benefits that could accrue from the process need to be elaborated. A facilitator, because he is not involved directly, may help uncover and clarify the incentives. But the relationship itself may have to be tested and trust built before such open management is possible.

ORGANIZATIONAL SUPPORT. When collaboration becomes appealing because interdependence, power parity, and evident mutual interest exist, then the fourth prerequisite comes into play. This is the extent of organizational support for such behavior.

If a complex organization has not stored up some energy beyond simply existing (homeostasis), it has no surplus energy for improvement programs. It will live on management-by-crisis, its goals restricted to survival. It must have excess energy to engage in conflict management programs.

If, however, the organization can be made to recognize that long-term survival depends on improvements, it will realize the importance of supporting such efforts. One way to avoid crisis management is to defuse incipient crises while they are still conflicts. The process of arriving at a creative solution generates energy for further innovation in the search for alternatives to organizational dilemmas. Moreover, when felt tensions are admitted, they may bring to light larger organizational problems. This feedback can lead to modifications and improved performance which, in turn, can lead to extra survival capital.

Considerable resources are needed to manage conflict using the collaborative strategy, including commitment of time, money, and energy. Collaboration must be system-wide—norms, rewards, and punishments of the enterprise should be adjusted to encourage the new behavior. Since most people are unaccustomed to open disagreement, particularly with superiors, assurance must be given that such behavior will not draw reprisals.

To confront one another and emerge with the problem resolved requires skills. Learning how to communicate, how to synchronize the process, when and how to use a third party, how to engage in effective problem solving, and how to keep the tension level moderate for optimal results all require skills that can be taught. Probably many organizations would initially view such openness as deviant. They would have to be convinced of the long-term benefits to be gained by training people and orienting the company to collaborative conflict management.

Bargaining Bargaining, which also requires working together to solve disputes, is best used when the requisites for collaboration are *not* present. Its compromising approach has significant disadvantages. It may result in neither party being satisfied. Half-a-loaf is not much better than none when information is released for strategic purposes rather than out of cooperation; information is withheld; bluffs and threats are made; strict adherence to existing oral or written agreements is insisted upon although they might be counterproductive to the organization; and sanctions are imposed for violations of old terms and conditions. Bargains made in wariness and resentment can, when the quasiagreement is signed and operative, sharpen into personal feuds and finally into all-out power struggle between factions. Inevitably these quasiagreements prove futile in solving emerging problems; outside the framework of the immediate bargain they foster mistrust and deleterious stratagems.

Another disadvantage is that the term of legalistic solutions (contracts) is often rigidly set, with a fixed date for the next round of negotiations. They are not adaptive or flexible nor do they provide opportunities for creative and proactive management. Finally, when "beating the other side" becomes more important than enhancing the organization's working atmosphere and modalities, the bargaining process only reinforces the erosion of the power struggle.

However, in deadlock or revolt, where productivity and survival are threatened, the power player who has overplayed his hand has two options: chancing imminent total takeover by a third party, in which event he loses all power and possibly his job; or opting to submit the issues to bargaining. Bargaining is only meaningful when the issues are limited to the substantive so that agreements can be reached that result in power parity. Once this balance is attained, the stage is set for dynamic conflict management that can move the parties toward a collaborative mode.

SUBSTANTIVE ISSUES. No matter how good the management procedure or how much the parties want to collaborate, they may stalemate over an issue. The problem may lie outside the control of either party: in a recession, for example, salaries must be held at a certain level or cut back; there may be a work procedure or safety measure about which both sides feel strongly while respecting the other position. In such a case, they agree to disagree because in good conscience they cannot abandon their own argument. They also concur in the search for some mutually acceptable solution.

It is possible to solve most organizational conflicts by finding creative new alternatives that help both parties. However, this is not always successful, even when there are good intentions on both sides. Bargaining is a method designed to help resolve substantive issues; when the parties are bogged down, it encourages a breakthrough by compromise. All other considerations—the relationship, the procedure, the climate, any related dimensions that distract from the substantive issue—are set aside. Bargaining forces a solution through binding arbitration, albeit a decision that may not be entirely satisfactory to either party.

GAINING POWER PARITY. Sometimes the required interdependence between individuals or factions is not great enough to make collaboration compelling or advisable. The climate, hierarchical relationships, and norms may not support such open problem-solving behavior: a person who confronts his boss with valid criticism may be punished later; information divulged might later be used against an employee. The individual(s) who feels he lacks equality and leverage in the relationship could test his influence with minor suggestions; if they are accepted graciously, it would indicate the other(s) is willing to work together without reprisals.

Bargaining, as indicated, is a method for winning power parity. Just getting into trading position assumes some equality; it implies that each party has something of value to offer or withhold from the other. The actual acts of trading and compromising highlight the felt or assumed strength of each party within the organization—the power of each is clearly defined by the information it reveals to the other, the concessions it makes, the punishment or penalties it can impose.

LACK OF ORGANIZATIONAL SUPPORT. Bargaining does not require developed conflict management machinery to function. That is, the organization does not have to possess the infrastructure of supportive climate, skill building, norms of openness, and confrontation and interpersonal trust that are essential to the collaborative process. (This machinery usually develops later, when the bargaining process has stabilized through achievement of power parity.) The process of one group marshalling its grievances and forcing another to a decision on its demands can be straightforward and easily begun if the grievances are backed by any degree of power. It is here that bargaining is most useful, when the conflict management machinery is not well developed but some coalition is possible around issues.

MOVING TOWARD COLLABORATION. It must be reiterated that bargaining is a bridge between the power and collaborative modes, a lever for moving a system toward collaboration. When the most powerful faction of a system is reluctant to collaborate (refusing to grant power parity, foster new norms), ironically a meaningful threat by the anti-power faction to unleash its own arsenal in a win-lose struggle often turns the situation around, cementing once and for all a parity relationship. Once there is equal recognition of rights and needs, and good faith exists between factions, and these as well as interpersonal dynamics have been tested and proven, conflict management machinery can be fully implemented.

In some industries and organizations where bargaining is the established method of settling differences, informal arbitration is being used rather than the hard "take and give" of formal bargaining sessions. The savings in time, energy, money, and emotions, reflected in the organizations's goal achievements, inspires both sides to set up conflict management machinery to handle not only issues already in conflict, but to seek out sources of potential conflict that can be collaboratively problem solved before they become dynamic issues. Some older union-management relationships, such as those in the steel industry, have established enough parity and trust that they engage in informal arbitration and pre-problem solving on a continuing basis. Here the bargaining mode is evolving into the collaborative mode.

Power Power is different from the other two strategies in that a mutually acceptable solution to a problem is not the intended or expected outcome. Rather, the power person(s) tries to exercise as much control over others (for the good of themselves or the organization) as possible.

Before we list the preconditions, let us examine kinds of power dynamics in an organization.

Formal authority (referred to earlier as third party authority) is the dimension of power effective to the extent that it is legitimate and accepted; it is backed by sanctions for noncompliance. Scholars since Barnard (1938) have raised questions about the effectiveness of authority in controlling others. Crozier (1964, pp. 180–190) points out that it is difficult ever to legislate behavior closely enough to limit the individual's descretion about compliance.

Informal influence refers to one's personal leadership style, expertise, ability to manipulate and persuade, or access to informal sources for coercion (blackmail, physical force, outside-the-organization normative pressures). Not everyone in formal authority has influence, but some authorities are able to use their offices to acquire influence. This is a powerful combination.

Autonomy, the third dimension to the power triangle, is the ability to resist formal authority and informal influence in favor of one's own self-interest. One influences others by exercising complete control over self or "being his own man."

Using a power strategy may be most appropriate when the conditions listed below are present.

UNDER CONDITIONS OF LEGITIMATE AUTHORITY. When an authority is accepted by subordinates as having a right to exercise control, power strategy may be appropriate in the management of conflict. For example, this model may work for certain religious organizations, where authority is inspired, or for the military, where authorities may jail or dismiss someone for not following orders. Authorities so endowed, especially where they also have influence, could redesign the rules for managing conflicts, command individuals to suppress their views, and coerce parties into collaboration. These persons can design strategies without much attention to compliance.

UNDER CONDITIONS OF AUTONOMY.   Just as rarely, a person may be quite autonomous within an organization. Some university professors, scientists, or other professionals may fit this category. Few people can command or influence them with any consequence, and they may resist those who do to preserve their independence. However, if they try to influence others, they are bound to lose some autonomy because, by so doing, they extend rather than retreat.

TO COPE WITH CRISIS OR ROUTINE.   When the organization environment is stable, an authority structure and procedures and norms can become routine—via rules and job descriptions, for example. This can lead to excessive control with employees using power tactics to make themselves heard by heavy-handed bosses or to subvert noxious practices.

Where turbulance threatens the very survival of an organization, administrators may manage by crisis. In crisis, authorities tend to assume emergency powers. They may react aggressively and even oppressively toward others because they themselves are threatened. Subordinates will probably decide between assenting to emergency power for the good of all concerned or using power tactics to actively resist. If management-by-crisis becomes the predominant style, power struggles will almost certainly ensue.

EXTERNAL THREATS.   When some external force seeks to destroy for whatever reason, it is best to combat the aggressor using power tactics. Some organizations lack the incentive for or are philosophically opposed to collaboration, although they may bargain if there is something to exchange. In most such cases, detente will be struck or a balance of power.

A DESIRE OR NEED TO USE POWER.   Power is an alternative when it becomes clear that winning is imminent. A person may choose not to bargain or collaborate if he is clearly in a position to get his way.

Some people have personality traits, nonorganizational interests, and psychological needs that are best served by power strategy. They may crave independence, dislike interaction, and fear supervision, preferring autonomy or withdrawal. They may need to compensate for childhood experiences by sabotaging, gossiping, and subverting those in authority. They might have strong needs to be "somebody" and influence others. Thus, they might be more comfortable in a power setting. Some might simply be more skilled at politics and manipulation than at bargaining and collaboration, so they choose what they do best.

It may seem imperative to "win" on a certain issue for a number of perfectly sound reasons, some of them to the organization's benefit. The use of raw power is costly in the long run, however; others easily coalesce to combat it, and it may alienate important supporters. While immediately successful, it can have unfortunate residual effects.

IDEOLOGICAL ORIENTATIONS. The newspapers are full of accounts of government employees who leak information to the press. This, and the values of the youth movement, are of great concern to many top executives in recruiting, for many employees would be loyal to their own moral code in case of a discrepancy between organizational practices and personal values.

Workers may become convinced that an enterprise or parts of it are corrupt or socially irresponsible. They may seek to destroy it from within or join causes designed to overthrow the organization. Others may simply refuse to participate if they believe a course of action or policy is "wrong."

NO PERCEIVED ALTERNATIVES. When a participant feels desperate, he may turn to power tactics for survival. In many organizational settings there simply do not exist the underlying trust, sincere intent, organizational support, power parity or interdependence to use the collaborative mode. Bargaining is not possible because the right issue and the right conditions are not present. Thus power is the only viable alternative.

Research tells us that if a person or group—the poor in the ghetto, low-level participants in a bureaucracy—is desperate to be heard or is extremely threatened, she or he is more likely to be aggressive and hostile (see Deutsch, 1960; Milburn, 1961; Hall & Mansfield, 1971). Where there is little to lose, people might opt for extreme forms of power strategy. Thus, desperation forces persons to use this mode—and often, use it destructively.

CONCLUSIONS AND IMPLICATIONS

For managers, settling disputes is central to improving the organization. When a CM studies the power dynamics in the enterprise, he can often discover some basic motivators of human behavior. In regard to power strategy and to some extent bargaining, diagnosing the nature of the interaction is analogous to getting at the heart of the conflict.

Unfortunately, many organization developers champion collaboration to such an extent—even when it doesn't "fit" the situation—that they have ignored the organizational realities of power and bargaining. The contingency theory articulated here takes a strong normative position but attempts to match it to reality. By making better diagnoses and beginning where the disputants are, developers will find they can really work through the conflict in a manner that is realistic yet improvement oriented.

The author made two conflict management efforts that illustrate this fit. The first was an attempt to get people in a power-oriented, big-city school bureaucracy to collaborate because, according to our understanding at the time, it was the "best" way to manage differences. The technology was powerful and compelling, and several people surfaced their disagreements openly in order to set the stage for problem solving. The information they readily shared was later used aginst them (Derr, 1970).

In the second instance, an attempt to help an elementary school faculty become more collaborative by using a bargaining intervention proved to be successful. Power parity was established between grade unit teams, and once this was accomplished, teachers were better able to manage their conflicts through problem solving (see Derr, "Surfacing and Managing Organizational Power, 1972).

Theorists are becoming more realistic about the appropriateness of several conflict management strategies. For example, National Training Laboratories, long proponents of collaborative values, now supports laboratory education for power. All three approaches are perceived by members of the enterprise as viable alternatives in a particular organizational setting. The strategies should be acknowledged and used appropriately and with awareness (*California Management Review*, Winter 1979; Derr, "Managing Organizational Conflict: A Place for Collaboration, Bargaining and Power Approaches," 1972)

Furthermore, it is now assumed that all types of organizational conflicts occur naturally. Many will promote creative tensions that lead to system improvement. Even some power strategies will serve the individual and possibly the organization in a variety of ways without disrupting the organization itself. Only disputes that are proving dysfunctional should set conflict management machinery in motion.

The importance of an accurate diagnosis of the situation cannot be overemphasized. A manager is not ready to intervene until he has determined the nature of the dispute and the major contingencies and is able to formulate a contingency theory. A key to effective conflict management is to appropriately use one of the three strategies to move the conflict from where it stands to a position more "healthy" for the organization.

The literature is full of examples of inappropriate interventions: consultants who push the organization into collaboration without the necessary preconditions and without bargaining as a transition step; the executive who advocates collaboration but does not support it, provide the conditions for it, or understand when and where to use it.

The Figure 17.3 step-model might prove useful to diagnosis and arriving at an operative contingency theory.

The conflict manager diagnoses and then attempts to use the most preferred strategy. If the necessary conditions are not present in combination to assure success, he retreats in order to build them. For example, he may lead out with a bargaining strategy and then be compelled to employ power tactics in order to provide the preconditions for successful bargaining. During the power sessions, he reevaluates the existing conditions and then tries to move the situation to the highest, most responsive order of intervention in the interest of the organization, which might very well be the bargaining mode. He is behaving realistically, and once he has settled the existing crisis, he has the normative situation as a guide to help manage persons and factions toward a more collaborative state—that is, if he can create the precon-

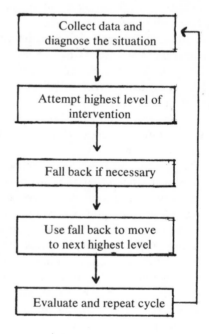

Figure 17-3 Intervention model

ditions that make this possible. He opts for the collaborative state whenever feasible. Yet collaboration may, in fact, be very difficult to attain because of its difficult preconditions.

In short, the manager must consider collaboration, bargaining, and power, all three, as possible strategies for effective conflict management.

REFERENCES

Aldrich, Howard. Organizational boundaries and interorganizational conflict. *Human Relations*, August 1971, *24*(4).

Alinsky, Saul. *Reveille for radicals*. Preston Wilcox, 1946.

Barnard, Chester A. *The functions of the executive*. Cambridge: Harvard, 1938.

Beckhard, Richard. The confrontation meeting. *Harvard Business Review*, 1967, *45*(2), 149–153.

Blake, Robert R., & Mouton, Jane S. The fifth achievement. *Journal of Applied Behavioral Science*, 1970, *6*(4), 413–426.

Blake, Robert R., Mouton, Jane S., & Sloma, Richard L. The union-management intergroup laboratory: strategy for resolving intergroup conflict. *Journal of Applied Behavioral Science*, 1965, *1*(2), 167–179.

Brown, Robert L. Arbitration: an alternative system for handling contract-related disputes. *Administrative Science Quarterly*, June 1972, *17*(2), 254–264.

Burns, Tom, & Stalker, G. M. *The management of innovation*. London: Tavistock Publications, 1961.

Conflict management. *California Management Review*, special edition, Winter 1979.

Crozier, Michel. *The bureacratic phenomenon*. Chicago: University of Chicago Press, 1964.

Derr, C. Brooklyn. Managing organizational conflict: a place for collaboration, bargaining and power approaches. *OD Practioner*, 1972, *4*(2).

———. Organization development in one large urban school system. *Education and Urban Society*, 1970, *2*(4).

———. Surfacing and managing organizational power. *OD Practioner*, 1972, *4*(2).

Deutsch, Martin. Productive and destructive conflict. *Journal of Social Issues*, January 1969, *25*(1), 7–42.

Ewing, David W. Tension can be an asset. *Harvard Business Review*, September/October 1964, *42*(5).

French, J. R. P., Jr., & Raven, B. The bases of social power. In D. Cartright & A. Zander (Eds.), *Group dynamics*. New York: Harper & Row, 1960, pp. 607–623.

Gabarro, John J. Diagnosing organization-environment 'fit'—implications for organization development. *Education and Urban Society*, February 1974.

Hall, Douglas T., & Mansfield, Roger. Organizational and individual response to external stress. *Administrative Science Quarterly*, 1971, *14*(4).

Katz, Daniel, & Kahn, Robert L. *The social psychology of organizations*. New York: Wiley, 1966, Chapters 2 and 3.

Kelley, Joe. Make conflict work for you. *Harvard Business Review*, July/ August 1970, *48*(4), 103–113.

Lawrence, Paul R., & Lorsch, Jay W. *Organization and environment*. Cambridge: Harvard Business School, Division of Research, 1967.

Litterer, Joseph A. Conflict in organization: a re-examination. *Academy of Management Journal*, September 1966, *9*(3), 178–186.

Litwak, Eugene, & Hylton, Lydia F. Interorganizational analysis. A hypothesis on coordination agencies. *Administrative Science Quarterly*, March 1962, *6*.

McClelland, David C. The two faces of power. *Journal of International Affairs*, 1970, *24*(1).

McWhinney, Will. Open systems and traditional hierarchies (Working Paper). UCLA Graduate School of Management and Institute for Developmental Organization, September 1972.

Milburn, Thomas W. The concept of deterrence: some logical and psychological considerations. *Journal of Social Issues*, 1961, *17*(3).

Oppenheimer, Martin. *The urban guerilla*. Chicago: Quadrangle, 1969.

Peabody, George L. Power, Alinsky and other thoughts. In Harvey A. Hornstein et al. (Eds.), *Social intervention*. New York: The Free Press, 1971, pp. 521–533.

Schmuck, Richard A. et al. *Handbook of organizational development in schools*. Palo Alto, Calif.: National Press Books, 1972.

Stevens, Carl M. *Strategy and collective bargaining negotiation*. New York: McGraw-Hill, 1963.

Thomas, John M., & Bennis, Warren G. *Management of change and conflict*. Baltimore: Penguin Books, 1972.

Thompson, James D. *Organizations in action*. New York: McGraw-Hill, 1967.

Walton, Richard. How to choose between strategies of conflict and collaboration. In Robert T. Golembiewsku & Arthur Blumber (Eds.), *Sensitivity training and the laboratory approach*. Itasca, Ill.: Peacock, 1970.

————. Legal-justice, power-bargaining and social science intervention (Working Paper no. 194. Krannert Graduate School of Industrial Administration, Purdue University, 1969).

————. Interorganizational decision making and identity conflict. *Special Technical Report* #2, The Harvard Business School Division of Research, 1969.

————. *Third party consultation*. Reading, Mass.: Addison-Wesley, 1969.

————. & McKersie, Robert B. *A behavioral theory of labor negotiations*. New York: McGraw-Hill, 1965.

Woodward, Joanne. *Industrial organization: theory and practice*. London: Oxford University Press, 1965. ˙

CHAPTER 18

Conflict and Change Strategies: The Agony of Choice

JAMES A. CONWAY

THE EDUCATIONAL MANAGER of the eighties will be expected, more than ever, to exercise supreme skills of choice and management. The future described by Toffler (1970) is already fact. The educational enterprises of the fifties built their foundations upon the expansive environment where the problems were glorious ones of growth; then, with unparalleled rapidity, education experienced the savage discord of the sixties when the tremors in the educational bulwarks signaled a foreboding decade. Out of that past has emerged the period of decline of the seventies. From the monochromatic past where the variables were simple, one-on-one, and controllable, there emerged at a logarithmic pace a phantasmagorical complexity. The conflicts of the sixties have spawned and mutated to make conflict a way of life for the present. Power groups, tax revolts, budget defeats, and demands for basics from the school community intertwine with vandalism, violence, and the physical molestation of teachers and staff within the "little red schoolhouse." This fabric of conflict encompasses intrasystem events such as negotiations, militancy, boycotts, and the counterresponses of contract management.

Each of these forms of conflict indicate that we are in a new era for management where the complexities of managing the organization are

When one works in the same department as the editor the frequency of interaction is bound to be significant. I want to acknowledge the very helpful critiques of my colleague Mike Milstein in the development of this chapter.

convincing more and more administrators to leave their positions for early retirement or other employment. The manager in this wave of education needs multimethods and Machievellian skills coupled with a source book of strategies for handling conflict. These source books are available as catalogs of change strategies with excellent coverage in such reviews of literature as Havelock (1970, 1971), Owens (1973), or Gaynor (1975); and more recently, in a review of *Factors Influencing School Change* (Sikorski et al., 1976) that involved over four hundred sources as well as in a book by Zaltman, Florio, and Sikorsky (1977) devoted entirely to a presentation of models, strategies, and tactics for educational change. But catalogs of sources *alone* are not the answer for the manager of tomorrow; rather the need is for a kind of road map that shows the *linkages* between the states of conflict and the change strategies that are most likely to have an impact on those states.

The purpose of this chapter is to sketch a rough map that will assist the school administrator in reducing the agony of selecting appropriate strategies for coping with conflict and to help the reader to know *when* to respond and *how* to respond. We will begin the map with some general considerations that lead to alternative choices for action, then move to examine certain causes for conflicts together with a range of strategies for coping with conflict. At all times the perspective that will be maintained will be to provide tomorrow's administrators with a scheme for contemplating the probable future of managing change and conflict.

INITIAL CONSIDERATIONS FOR CHOICE

As the leader of an organization faces an emerging problem or conflict, he or she needs to consider the nature of the conflict and decide what position to take. There are four possibilities from which to choose: (1) ignore the conflict till it passes; (2) tolerate the conflict and help the organization cope with it; (3) decrease the conflict and its effects; or (4) increase the intensity of the conflict. But are these real choices? If so, when would they be applied? We will try to answer these questions by describing the sequence of decisions that an administrator may need to consider in facing an emerging conflict. This sequence is pictured in figure 18.1 as a "decision tree." The tree begins with the assumption that conflict has already emerged in the organization so that the first question that the administrator faces is to decide if the impending conflict is functional (branch one) or dysfunctional (branch two) to the organization. To clarify we will move down the two main branches and examine them through examples.

Branch One: Functional Conflicts   Functional conflict occurs as a part of development or growth in a living system. To prevent

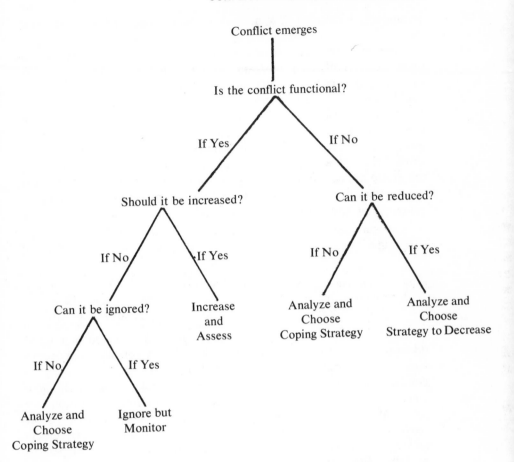

Figure 18-1   A decision tree for conflict response

the conflict may retard or at least slow down the growth process. Conflict may also be functional when it is used to unfreeze the system so that another event may occur more easily, thus creating a climate for change. We will use these two examples to clarify the choices on this branch of the decision tree.

GROUP DEVELOPMENT EXAMPLE.   Tuckman (1965) has indicated that groups tend to move through four periods as a natural course of development. The first is a period of *testing and dependence* wherein the members seek to establish acceptable behaviors; the second is *intragroup conflict* where an emotional undercurrent predominates; the third is a stage of *group cohesion* as norms for openness and feedback materialize; and the fourth period is *functional role-relatedness* characterized by minimal strains of an emotional nature. The four stages are commonly referred to as "forming, storming, norming, and performing."

If the administrator has seen a group developing over time so that there are currently signs of strain, and if it would appear that increasing the intragroup conflict would not be beneficial (although at times it could be so), then he or she may need to decide whether to ignore the strain or to assist the group in moving through the conflict. If the conflict period appears to be one that is short lived, then the administrator may decide to ignore the problem and give the group time to work it through as it moves to form new norms. On the other hand, if the group appears to be gyrating out of balance, then an active intervention may be needed so as to help the group to cope with the conflict.

CHANGE CLIMATE EXAMPLE. In a discussion of the processes of change and innovation, Zaltman, Florio and Sikorski (1977, p. 58) indicate that—

> Conflict *inevitably* arises during both the initiation and implementation phases. During the former, conflicts generally revolve around deciding which innovation to accept. During the latter, they are generally concerned with choosing processes for implementation. (emphasis added)

Thus, if the administrator should find a group stalemated or bogged down in trivia, it may be prudent to stimulate a period of conflict to unfreeze the group (Robbins, 1974). The tactic may be to increase conflict already present or even to create a situation for conflict to emerge. But if the conflict is associated with the implementation of a new curriculum and the period of strain seems to be relatively short term, then the best action may be to ignore the conflicts but to remain aware of the developments in case a latter intervention may be needed to reduce the system stress.

ORGANIZATION GROWTH EXAMPLE. As groups grow and develop with time so too do organizations. Greiner (1972) has identified five distinguishable stages of development that most organizations pass through, with each period of growth lasting from four to twelve years. For each stage Greiner postulates an associated crisis that gives the impetus for movement to the next level of growth. The five stages and associated crises are—

1. The initial period of growth is characterized as "creativity" with the crisis developing in the area of leadership.
2. The next stage is one of sustained growth characterized as a period of "direction"; here the crisis that emerges is a press for autonomy.
3. The third state sees "delegation" as the typical behavior leading to a crisis of "control."

4. Movement through the "control" revolution brings on a period of "coordination" that eventually leads to a crisis labeled as "red tape."
5. The last stage is seen as one of "collaboration" where the focus is on team actions and temporary structures; the crisis that moves the organization to the next growth plateau has not yet been identified.

For each of the passages there is an extended period of crisis, which can be characterized as a functional period of conflict. However, the *extended duration of time* for the crisis is too long to ignore. The administrator must develop strategies with the organization that will facilitate the movement to the next level. The problem then becomes one of determining appropriate strategies for coping with the extended state of conflict.

Branch Two: Dysfunctional Conflicts   While it is comforting to think of some conflict as being helpful or even necessary, more frequently than not they are found to be contrary to group life or dysfunctional. Such conflict erodes trust and confidence and forces the organization to divert energy from goal accomplishment as maintenance activities take on primacy. On this branch of the decision tree the goal is to reduce the conflict or at least reduce the effect that it has on the organization. Again some examples may clarify the flow.

ECONOMIC DECLINE EXAMPLE.   If the environment for the organization should suffer an economic decline that erodes financial support, then the organization is likely to experience demands for savings that get translated into program and personnel cuts. Assuming that the regressive economy is widespread it would be beyond the control of the school system to exercise any direct and significant effects that might correct the economic plight. When the source of the conflicts originates outside of the organization, then the possibility for direct actions to counter the forces may be diminished. The system would rather expend more of its energies on developing strategies for coping with the threats.

TEACHER EVALUATION EXAMPLE.   One role for the principals of schools is to help teachers improve instruction and another is to evaluate for purposes of retention and the awarding of tenure. The two expectations for the principal are in direct opposition; that is, one expectation is for helping while the second is for evaluating with possible threat to personal security. The conflicting role expectations can result in interpersonal conflicts between principal and staff. Are such conflicts within the power of the administrator to reduce? It would seem that if they have originated within the organization, then they would be amenable to change. Even if the expectations for the conflicting role behaviors for the principal stem from the local board of education, the likelihood of taking action to counter or change those expectations may be possible, given that the internal school forces have been unified to bring pressure for change.

The end points of the decision tree in figure 18.1 call for the administrator to analyze the conflict situation and to select a strategy or strategies to decrease the conflict or at least sustain the organization as it copes with the threats. It is here that the administrator needs assistance in determining which strategies if any would be most beneficial in accomplishing the desired ends. This calls for a framework that will link the sources of conflict with appropriate strategies for managing the conflict. It is just such a mapping that we will develop in the remaining pages of this chapter.

A FRAMEWORK FOR CHOOSING STRATEGIES FOR CONFLICT MANAGEMENT

A framework requires dimensions so that strategies can be logically placed. From the examples we viewed above it would appear that one dimension might be concerned with whether or not the conflicts are short of long in *duration*, since this factor was important in deciding whether or not it was necessary to intervene in a conflict deemed functional to the organization. A second dimension might deal with the *origin* of the conflict; that is, whether it was outside of the control of the administrator or if it were of internal origin and thus within the area of administrator control.

We have found that these dimensions are consistent with a framework that Kilmann and Thomas (1978) have presented. Their reviews of the conflict literature led them to construct a table with two key dimensions as sources of conflict behavior. For one dimension the conflicts are seen as resulting from either *forces* or *events*,* concepts that include the *duration* of the conflicts. For the second dimension they consider whether the source is from *within* or from *outside* the person, group or organization, which coincides with our need to know the *origin* of the conflict. For each dimension there is an artificially created dichotomy which, when combined (see figure 18.2), results in four quadrants. The artificial nature of the dichotomies must be emphasized, for it is unlikely that conflict erupts solely as a result of *an*

---

*Kilmann and Thomas use the terms *process* and *structure* rather than forces and events; however, since their terms may have other meanings in the organization and intervention literature we have adopted the terms *events* for their process and *forces* for their structure.

event or force or *only* from within or outside the subject. Rather both dimensions are more likely continuums. The first dimension, which we have labeled the "duration dimension," covers those sources of conflict that result from single, short-lived, isolated events on through to complex, long-termed, interrelated forces. The second dimension, which we label "origin dimension," covers those sources coming from within and/or from outside of the subjects. The two dimensions are described more fully below.

Duration Dimension: Sources from Events or Forces

On the *events* side of the continuum the assumption is that conflict behavior results from a single event or discrete episode, while the

Duration Dimension

Conflict Behaviors from Events and Forces

	EVENTS	to	FORCES
OUTSIDE	Quadrant I Conflicts emerging from *Outside Events*		Quadrant II Conflicts emerging from *Outside Forces*
WITHIN	Quadrant III Conflicts emerging from *Events Within* the Individual Group or Organization		Quadrant IV Conflicts emerging from *Forces Within* the Individual Group or Organization

ORIGIN DIMENSION
Sources Coming from Within or from Outside

Figure 18-2   A framework of sources of conflict with basic dimensions and quadrants identified

---

The framework is loosely patterned after the Kilmann and Thomas (1978) "Attributional Framework."

forces end emphasizes the continuity of occurrences as complex forces that act on the subjects over some extended period of time. As examples of the discrete events Kilmann and Thomas (1978, p. 61) list verbal threats, acts of physical aggression, and an exchange of evaluative remarks. Any one of these *events* could result in conflict, depending upon how the event is received and interpreted by the receiver. Thus, for example, if an individual does not consider a threat of "loss of pay" as believable or serious, then no conflict behavior is likely to emerge. When the threat is credible, however, then there is likely to be high anxiety with the possibility of a counterthreat and the conflict incident is in full action.

On the *forces* side of the continuum the examples are conflicts of interest, or of norms, beliefs, attitudes, or values. The behavior here is explained by the complex forces as they ebb and flow in constant interaction with the subject. No single event gives rise to the behaviors but rather the complexity of interactions playing on the subject is the basic stimulus.

Origin Dimensions: Sources from Within or from Outside
This dimension is concerned with where the events or forces are coming from—that is, Are they coming from *within* the person, the group or the organization; or are they coming from some *outside* source such as the community or the central office or a legislative agency? When this dimension is combined with the other to form four quadrants, the basic structure of the map is formed.

As we move on now to fill in the map we will refer to each of the quadrants, present an analysis and examples of the conflicts that the quadrant includes, and then list a sample of intervention strategies that seem relevant to altering the conflicts. The reader should note, however, that the strategies that will be listed are those that *appear logically related*. The history of evaluation of intervention strategies has not provided us with the assurance that a particular approach will always work or only achieve success under particular conditions. That kind of systematic testing will be a welcome addition to the literature of change.

Quadrant I: Conflicts from Outside Events
This perspective highlights the events that act on individuals, groups, or the school from sources outside of the basic organization. From the isolated incidents or episodes there is a response or set of responses that are best characterized as conflict behaviors. Thus, in almost a stimulus-response manner the conflicts emerge in reaction to such events as

withholding of rewards, for example, being passed over for a merit increase or a school board holding back discretionary funds from the school; *exercising sanctions* as with a reprimand for missing a meeting, a letter to the local paper citing the poor behavior and/or conditions in the building, or court-ordered penalties for failing to comply with a law; *threats from an opponent* such as a promise to veto a provision developed by the student council or an expressed or implied threat from central office to retrench a program with implied loss of personnel; and *negative evaluations* whether of persons or departments as with an outsider's evaluation of a teacher or an agency evaluation of a school for reregistering their certification.

CHANGE STRATEGIES: FROM AWARENESS TO INTERACTION INTERVENTION The strategies that could be applied to conflict emerging from an isolated episode from outside must necessarily include a range of choices. Since the stimulus is outside of the organization at times it will be out of the sphere of influence of any of the organization leaders. In such cases the approach is not to influence a change in the source but rather to cope with the event. Frequently a threat from the outside can bring about a cohesive counterthrust from the members of the organization, *if* they are aware of the threat and its implications. Therefore, it would seem that those sources from outside that are *not* amenable to change might best be tolerated and even countered by providing an open and widely disseminated examination of the external threat, sanction, or negative evaluation. If, on the other hand, the source of the behavior *is* open to influence and change then a different course of action might follow.

The concern in this quadrant is less on the message or substance of the threat-sanction-evaluation, and more on the processes employed for conveying the message. Therefore, the intervention should be of a nature to focus on the interactions as processes. Some strategies or tactics that would likely have a direct effect on changing interactions would include:

Third-Party Interventions. Walton (1969, p. 23) describes this intervention strategy where an outside agent facilitates the interaction:

> The third party performed a diagnostic function during and after the confrontation. He listened to each of the disputants discuss his views and feelings, and sharpened what he understood to be an issue, to which the participants responded in ways which tended to confirm or disprove that this was the underlying issue. An effort was made to state these issues in ways which made each person's position understandable, legitimate, and acceptable.

Consultant Feedback. Observations of committee interactions are shared with and by group members (Schmuck, et al., 1977, p. 212). Behaviors of the parties are described and clarified and the communication between parties is aided through paraphrasing and similar tactics. The focus is not on *what* has been said so much as it is on *how* it has been stated. The purpose is to clarify and to increase understanding and awareness.

Organization Confrontation. Beckhard (1969) has described an approach to deal with stress where the purpose is to mobilize the personnel in a relatively short period of time toward an action plan of their devising. The approach requires a minimum of one day and is "most appropriate where the top group is relatively cohesive but there is a gap between the top and the rest of the organization" (p. 38). Essentially this strategy accepts the threat as a given and sets mutually acceptable goals for withstanding or decreasing the effects.

Interorganization Confrontation and Bargaining. On occasion a group or organization may muster sufficient power to confront another organization and enter into negotiations to reduce the conflicts. The act of coming together to confront the outside threat can be a catalyst for developing organization cohesion. The unified front may now serve to stimulate the outside agency to reconsider its threat, or at least to negotiate with the others for an equitable solution.

Quadrant II: Conflict from Outside Forces The causes of

conflict behavior in this state are found in a recurrent flow of forces from the environment that are seen as enhancing, restricting, or forcing behavior-responses. For teachers, the examples might include the felt conflicts that emerge from *overly prescriptive policy* as with regulations prohibiting field trips or specifying participation in essay contests that detract from lessons more than they enhance learning; conflicts associated *with discongruent expectations* from the environment as with pressures from parents, citizens, church leaders, and students. Admission committees may feel constrained by organization ratios at the same time as they sense concerns for equal rights or other social demands. Still other examples come from *real or imagined differences* for opportunities to govern and be governed; or the *incongruities* that emerge as demands for innovation as expressed by officials, parents, and society at the same time as citizens vote down budgets, pass propositions for tax cuts, and legislatures and governors demand new economies. In general, where external conditions are the primary sources of conflict, the felt pressures typically are multiple, unequal, and relatively enduring over time.

CHANGE STRATEGY: FROM POLICY CHANGE TO STRUCTURE MODIFICATION. Since the sources of conflict are a multiplicity of complex forces from outside of the organization, we cannot expect to use those interventions geared to altering a single event or a simple set of events as in the previous quadrant. Here we are looking for more permanent changes to counter the flow of pressures. Zaltman, Florio, and Sikorski (1977, p. 74) identify certain *power strategies* as potentially useful for countering conflict at the organization level: "Some power tactics used in education include passing bills or laws to force change; withholding funding; having change directions come from legitimate leaders; providing material rewards; and offering prestige or satisfaction." However, the possibility of exercising much influence on external pressures that arise from the community or higher is quite small. At best it is necessary to recognize the community influence in policy formulation and to capitalize on that pressure. A recognition of impending community forces in the form of demands and expectations by using a systematic program for community analysis (Conway, Jennings, and Milstein, 1972) might serve as an anticipation strategy ultimately leading to more open policy formulation processes.

At a more general level the basic approach to countering conflicts in this quadrant is to employ a modification in *structure* rather than process. Structural changes are relatively permanent modifications in the system that can resist the continual flow of forces, whereas processes are more transient unless continuously monitored and reinforced. Some potentially viable structural interventions might include:

A System Engineering Strategy. A program whereby the entire system or a major subsystem employs a formal and systematic plan for altering its ongoing procedures. An example of this strategy might be the implementation of a Program Planning and Budgeting System (PPBS). System engineering implies that the entire system is analyzed for making structural, mechanical, and procedural modifications. Certain subsections of a system engineering strategy could also be useful for conflict control, as in the next example.

Management Information System. An increased access to information might increase the openness of the system and reduce the constraints from external pressures. The management information system is typically a combined human-technical storage and retrieval system for that information that is needed for recurring decisions.

An Accountability System. If the system can generate data to clarify work objectives and also provide indicators of accomplishment of the objectives, then the system may be better able to reduce the pressures of divergent expectations from the environment. A management-by-objectives (MBO) system is one possibility for addressing pressures of this nature.

Structural Redesign. Modifications in the authority relationships and the decision-making mechanisms of the organization could produce significant changes in the form of clarified internal responsibilities and higher commitments to organizational goals. For example, movement from a traditional line-staff authority pattern to a more collaborative structure, as with Likert's (1967) linking pin concept, would be a formal alteration in the decision-making system that could reduce the felt constraints of groups and individuals in the organization.

Quadrant III: Conflicts from Internal Events

This quadrant looks to the events or sequence of events that occur with the individual, group or organization as the primary source of conflict. At the individual level the conflict behaviors are caused by perceptions, ideas, or emotions as with a personal decision-making process that breaks down in crises situations. At the group or school level the conflicts are more social and psychological in nature and include the interpersonal behaviors that occur during group decision making, abuses of process, or procedure as with selective listening, stereotypic thinking, unstated assumptions, or making use of parliamentary procedure to ward off an issue rather than discussing the issue itself. Other examples of conflict in this quadrant might be the use of force in a group as when coalitions form to block an item without regard to content, forcing a win-lose position; violent outbursts as emotions are touched, or the use of silence as an avoidance technique not only for individuals but for groups or even the entire organization. Thus, a school might choose, through its leaders, to anger a board member by simply ignoring an order. The individuals, committees, departments, and the organization become their own worst enemies as they adopt behaviors that alienate some or escalate conflicts among others.

CHANGE STRATEGY: CONSCIOUSNESS RAISING. Kilmann and Thomas (1978) supply the term *consciousness raising* as capturing the essence of this category of interventions. The underlying assumption is that the individual and/or group decision makers are rational, responsible, and capable of modifying their behaviors toward more constructive ends. Given that assumption the intent for the change strategy is to aid the parties involved by providing them with opportunities to ''see'' their typical behavior responses. The range of change strategies within this category include:

Transactional Analysis　(Goldhaber & Goldhaber, 1976). A system for enabling the individual to gain awareness of self in the everyday transactions with others. Increased awareness is expected to reduce dysfunctional behaviors.

Guided Self-Analysis　(Parson, 1971). An approach to behavior change by helping the individual view typical role transactions of herself or himself on videotape and then, using an ethnographic observation schedule, to focus upon self-selected behaviors for modification.

Process/Behavior Feedback.　Through the use of simulations or games that magnify the typical responses and behaviors that individuals employ in groups, the group can provide insights to its members as to their facilitating or impeding behaviors.

Simulations for Role/Style Analysis.　The University Council for Educational Administration has a series of ''in-basket'' simulations of the principal and central office personnel as they function in urban, suburban, or rural school systems. The simulations provide an opportunity for understanding roles and role expectations, examining an individual's style for decision making and its effects on others, or developing simple awareness of the processes for decision making and the likely consequences of actions.

Survey Feedback　(Schmuck et al., 1977). Based upon questionnaires and observations of the typical processes in a healthy organization, data would be presented to the organizational members for their edification. If they can validate the information through reference to incidents or examples within the organizational life, then they may also generate action plans to modify the behaviors.

Quadrant IV: Conflict from Internal Forces　The sources for conflict behaviors in this quadrant are not simply the result of procedural misperceptions nor processes that are avoided or improperly applied, but rather they emerge from deep-rooted prejudices,

value differences, and mismatched philosophic positions within the organization. Examples would include racial differences of teachers as they deal with one another in committees; conflicts that emerge as a result of clashes over status differences and the expectations for preferential treatment associated with status; creating teaching teams with divergent belief system orientations with consequent decreases in morale and probably enduring conflicts (Ables and Conway, 1973). At the departmental level there are strains that result from incompatible philosophies of teaching or discipline between chairpersons and their department members; at the school level examples include "contract management" as well as those leader behaviors that alienate or demoralize participants. An example of this would be a principal with a "Theory X" based style of leadership working in a school where the majority of staff are operating under "Theory Y" beliefs about life (McGregor, 1960).

CHANGE STRATEGY: FROM SOCIAL PSYCHOLOGICAL THROUGH TECHNICAL. Altering deep-rooted attitudinal positions may require any of a range of strategies from those associated with "reeducative approaches" (Chin and Benne, 1969) to the more technical and rational system changes implied by such terms as *selection* and *training*. The emphasis in this perspective, as it was also for Quadrant II, is on creating countervailing conditions that will bring about relatively lasting changes in the behaviors of individuals, groups, and the organization.

The more enduring changes of a social psychological nature would include:

Laboratory Strategies (Golembiewski and Blumberg, 1973). Most familiar are the group therapy approaches such as sensitivity training or T groups, but also included would be the more current group approaches to behavior change such as assertiveness training. Essential to all of these approaches is the removing of the participants from the work environment to the laboratory or retreat.

Participation Strategies. Characteristic of this category of attitude change are the classic experiments of Kurt Lewin during the period of the late forties. He applied a concept of participation and group decision making to the problem of changing the attitudes of housewives toward serving sweetbreads to their families. The same concept was the fundamental premise for the Coch and French (1948) experiments. They applied the "participation in decision-making" variable to the problem of changes in worker job descriptions and concluded that it was a useful approach for overcoming resistance to change.

Controlled Confrontation. This is an approach that captures some of the social psychological as well as structural change. It is best typified by a technique such as "imaging" (Schmuck, et al., 1977). Here the groups in conflict are brought together to share their respective favorable and unfavorabe images of one another; they clarify the images and then decide which of their behaviors that contribute to the images they may want to change. The outcomes of the exercise may be attitudinal shifts but may also result in physical changes in the system.

Retraining. If new expectations for performance evolve, either from an exercise such as imaging or from the more technical restructuring described below, then in-service type training may be useful. Here the focus is on learning new skills for the position as well as new content. Thus, for teachers this may include learning diagnostic skills and reading strategies, or it may be new content such as learning the metric system so that it can be taught to students.

At a technical-structural level the change strategies would probably entail modifications in work relationships, policy shifts as well as system modifications. Typical of this approach might be:

Personnel Changes. By changing the types of persons in the work environment we could expect a shift in the interpersonal relationships as well as in the mix of departmental philosophies and values. Thus, changes in recruitment and promotion criteria would bring in new persons or raise to positions of power persons with different perspectives from those presently in the organization. So too with reconstituting teaching teams, committees or even departments where a reorganization might reduce or increase differences in values, attitudes, and beliefs and consequently alter the group performance.

System Changes. These would be of the nature described earlier as strategies to use when conflict is rooted in forces outside of the organization (Quadrant II). The adoption of technical systems such as a management-by-objectives or a program planning system would necessarily unfreeze the organization lines, foster a period of deliberate conflict during the implementation of the system change, and possible have a relatively enduring effect on personnel behaviors.

Organization Support Strategies. As the organization is moving through a change in structure there is need for retraining in the processes for maintaining human relationships or for constructing new relations. Included here would be programs for building work teams, for setting or reaffirming goals, for improving meetings and resolving problems, that is the process skills that sustain a healthy organization.

SOME CONCLUDING CONSIDERATIONS

The basic framework of the map is now complete, but that does not mean that it is a complete mapping. The association of conflicts and strategies is more suggestive than saturated. The administrator of school organizations in the climate of conflict will need to test strategies, devise approaches yet unthought of, and expand the map to include the details that can only come from the real world of experience. Nevertheless, it should have sufficient detail to start the administrator on the way to creating a climate within the school where growth and change can continue in positive directions.

But the framework also highlights another factor that leaders of schools might need to consider. As complexity increases so that conflicts emerge from a number of sources, from both within the organization as well as from the environment, from isolated events as well as combinations of forces, then the types of strategies that seem appropriate become equally complex to initiate and control. It is difficult to assume that one person will have the skills and knowledge to employ all of the strategies that have been suggested, to build team relations, devise and institute management and information systems, to retrain others, or to conduct laboratory groups. In fact the classifications of strategies that were highlighted included some that could and should be operated from the position of administrator as well as some which require an outsider as intervenor. Implicit in this is that the manager of the future cannot be a *sole* agent for conflict resolution but rather needs to combine personal strengths and skills with an awareness of personal limitations and the courage to call upon outsiders for assistance. The management of the school seems more and more to be a team operation with the leader less a director and more a broker, that is, an individual who can diagnose a situation and bring to bear the best persons or teams to correct the concerns. The intent of this chapter has been to help that leader reduce the agonies of choosing appropriate strategies and increase the likelihood of organizational success in coping with conflict, with change, and with the future.

REFERENCES

Ables, Jack, & Conway, James A. Leader-team belief system congruence and relationships to morale within teaching teams. *Educational Administration Quarterly*, Spring 1973, pp. 22–33.

Beckhard, Richard. *Organization development: Strategies and models.* Reading, Mass.: Addison-Wesley, 1969.

Chin, Robert, & Benne, Kenneth D. General strategies for effecting changes in human systems. In Warren G. Bennis, Kenneth D. Benne, & Robert Chin (Eds.), *The planning of change* (2nd Ed.). New York: Holt, Rinehart and Winston, 1969.

Coch, Lester, & French, John R. P. Overcoming resistance to change. *Human Relations*, 1948, *1*, 512–532.

Conway, James A., Jennings, Robert E., & Milstein, Mike M. *Understanding communities.* Englewood Cliffs, N.J.: Prentice-Hall, 1972.

Gaynor, Alan K. *The study of change in educational organizations: A review of literature.* Paper read at UCEA-Ohio State University Career Development Seminar. Columbus, Ohio, 1975.

Goldhaber, Gerald M., & Goldhaber, Marglynn B. *Transactional analysis: Principles and applications.* Boston: Allyn and Bacon, 1976.

Golembiewski, Robert T., & Blumberg, Arthur (Eds.). *Sensitivity training and the laboratory approach: Readings about concepts and applications* (2nd ed.). Itasca, Ill.: Peacock, 1973.

Greiner, Larry E. Evolution and revolution as organizations grow. *Harvard Business Review*, July-August 1972, pp. 37–46.

Havelock, Ronald G. *A guide to innovation in education.* Ann Arbor, Mich.: Institute for Social Research, 1970.

————. *Planning for innovation.* Ann Arbor, Mich.: Institute for Social Research, 1971.

Kilmann, Ralph H., & Thomas, Kenneth W. Four perspectives on conflict management: an attributional framework for organizing descriptive and normative theory. *Academy of Management Review*, January 1978, pp. 59–68.

Likert, Rensis. *The human organization.* New York: McGraw-Hill, 1967.

McGregor, Douglas. *The human side of enterprise.* New York: McGraw-Hill, 1960.

Owens, Robert G. *Conceptual models for research and practice in the administration of change.* Paper read at the American Educational Research Association Conference, 1973.

Parsons, Theodore W. *Guided self analysis systems for professional development series*; "Teachers for Inquiry Schedule A, Questioning Strategies." Berkeley, Calif., 1971.

Robbins, Stephen P. *Managing organizational conflict: a nontraditional approach.* Englewood Cliffs, N.J.: Prentice-Hall, 1974.

Schmuck, Richard A. et al. *The second handbook of organization development in schools.* Palo Alto, Calif.: Mayfield Publishing Co., 1977.

Sikorski, Linda A., Turnbull, Brenda J., Thorn, Lorraine I., & Bell, Samuel R. *Factors influencing school change*. Far West Laboratory for Educational Research and Development, 1976.

Toefler, Alvin. *Future shock*. New York: Random House, 1970.

Tuckman, B. W. Developmental sequence in small groups. *Psychological Bulletin*, 1965, *63*, 384–399.

Walton, Richard E. *Interpersonal peacemaking: Confrontations and third-party consultation*. Reading, Mass.: Addison-Wesley, 1969.

Zaltman, Gerald, Florio, David, & Sikorski, Linda. *Dynamic educational change*. New York: Free Press, 1977.

Index

DATE DUE